FARES, PLEASE!

A POPULAR HISTORY OF TROLLEYS, HORSE-CARS, STREET-CARS, BUSES, ELEVATEDS, AND SUBWAYS

By

JOHN ANDERSON MILLER

Author of

"Master Builders of Sixty Centuries"

DOVER PUBLICATIONS, INC.

NEW YORK

International Standard Book Number: 0-486-20671-8
Library of Congress Catalog Card Number: 60-51682

Manufactured in the United States of America
Dover Publications, Inc.
180 Varick Street
New York, N. Y. 10014

DEDICATION

Sometimes it happens that the personality of a single individual makes a deep impression on the course of events—beyond what might normally be expected. This is true of James H. McGraw in connection with the development of the urban transportation industry. He was never an inventor or promoter, but as a keen observer, thinker, and publisher, he became over a period of more than fifty years a guide, counselor, and friend to countless men engaged in the active operation of the business. In recognition of the constructive influence he has thus exerted, from the days of horse-cars to those of streamliners, this book on the history of city transportation is dedicated to James H. McGraw.

PREFACE TO DOVER EDITION

At the time the first edition of this book was published (1941), the local transportation industry in the United States was carrying about thirteen billion passengers a year. This was a considerably smaller number than had been carried ten years earlier. Improvements in vehicles and changes in type of service were meeting with only limited success in competition with the private automobile. But World War II completely changed this situation. When the operation of private automobiles was sharply curtailed by tire shortages and gasoline rationing, people turned to the public transportation systems in hordes. By 1945, the number of passengers carried had reached the amazing total of more than twenty-three billion—nearly double the prewar figure.

This tremendous increase in patronage was by no means a bonanza for the local transportation companies. In most instances they were hard pressed to find enough rolling stock to handle the business. New equipment was almost impossible to procure. Operating costs rose rapidly. Despite all difficulties, however, public transportation carried out its task with an impressive degree of efficiency. This performance, beyond doubt, stands out as the high-point of the industry's entire history.

After the end of the war, riding soon began to taper off as tires, gasoline, and automobiles again became plentiful. In some places, the business fell below the point where it was financially possible to maintain it. In many others, particularly in the larger centers of population, the need for the service remained great, but the cost of providing it presented grave problems.

Many modifications were made in the industry's operations to meet changing public needs. New developments included construction of rapid-transit lines on private rights of way on the surface and underground, conversion of unprofitable suburban railroad lines into rapid-transit lines and the establishment of parking lots adjacent to outlying rapid-transit stations to encourage people to make their trips partly by private auto and partly by public conveyance.

To discuss adequately the various postwar developments would require a major addition to this book. A few pictures have been added to illustrate what has taken place in some cities, but the book remains essentially the story of the first century of the industry's history. It was in many ways a colorful and exciting period.

JOHN A. MILLER

Schenectady, New York
June, 1960

PREFACE

One hundred and ten years ago a young New Yorker got a new job; he was hired by Abraham Brower to ride on the rear step of the latter's Broadway Omnibus and with a polite "Fares, please!" collect the twelve and a half cents that was charged for a ride for any distance between Bond Street and the Battery. A few months later the same cry echoed on the Bowery where John Mason had started the New York & Harlem Railroad, the world's first street-railway line.

As the years passed the scene changed. Hoop-skirts were followed by bustles and then by leg-of-mutton sleeves. Men's luxurious beards disappeared and the handle-bar mustache came into vogue. Later, they too disappeared. Horse-cars were replaced by cable-cars and these in turn by electric cars, motor-buses and trolley-buses, but still the cry of "Fares, please!" rings up and down the aisles of transit vehicles throughout the land.

Americans—the world's greatest users of private automobiles—are also the world's greatest users of transit service. Every man, woman, and child of the urban population of the United States uses transit service 265 times a year on the average. Altogether they take more than 13 billion rides annually. No other product or service is bought with such frequency.

Since it started its career with horse-drawn omnibuses the transit industry has made use of a wide variety of vehicles. Older types have been replaced by newer types, until today the industry finds itself operating a combination of streamlined electric street-cars, motor-buses, trolley-buses, subways, and elevated railways.

The story of this remarkable development is full of romance and interest. It is colored by the presence of many vivid personalities. It is punctuated by bitter struggles and successful achievements under great difficulty. Never has this story been told in its entirety—only scattered glimpses have been given here and there. The purpose of this book is to present the complete picture of city transit from the time of the first horse-drawn omnibus down to the present day.

In the collection of the information for this story of public passenger transportation in cities, the author was fortunate in having the assistance of many men connected with the transit industry, both operators and manufacturers in the United States and Canada. Grateful acknowledgement is made of the assistance they have given. In particular the author wishes to acknowledge the valuable help given by:

J. H. Hanna, chairman, Capital Transit Company, Washington, D. C.; H. E. Johnston, president, New Jersey Chapter, National Railway Historical Society; H. E. Meade, vice president, New Orleans Public Service, Inc.; H. F. Peck, assistant supervisor public relations, Chicago Surface Lines; D. N. Phillips, publicity manager, Philadelphia Transportation Company; H. E. Potter, assistant superintendent of transportation, Union Street Railway, New Bedford, Mass.; H. S. Robertson, president, Denver Tramway; H. S. Simpson, research engineer, American Transit Association; H. W. Tate, assistant manager, Toronto Transportation Commission; R. S. Tompkins, director of information, Baltimore Transit Company; E. A. West, general manager, Denver & Rio Grande Western Railroad; A. H. Wood, commercial manager, Kansas City Public Service Company; A. R. Williams, vice president, United Electric Railways, Providence, R. I.; W. E. Wyckoff, vice president, New Jersey Chapter, National Railway Historical Society; and Houghton Mifflin Co., publishers of "Over the Teacups" by Oliver Wendell Holmes.

JOHN A. MILLER

CONTENTS

ILLUSTRATIONS

PLATES

The Horse-Drawn Omnibus

First local transportation in Paris
George Shillibeer's three-horse omnibus
Early New York omnibus
Pedestrian bridge at Broadway and Fulton Street
The heyday of the horse-drawn omnibus
Early type of double decker in London
London omnibus changing horses

The Horse-Car

Traffic congestion in Chicago, 1865
Double-deck omnibus converted into a horse-car
Car house at Belleville, New Jersey
Mules furnish the power in Richmond, Virginia
Mule-cars in Atlanta, Georgia
Canal Street, New Orleans, in the 1880's
Elaborate decorations brighten the horse-car's exterior
Plush-upholstered seats and a straw-covered floor
Main Street, Rochester, New York, in 1878
Getting ready for the morning rush hour at Philadelphia
Machine-driven horse clippers
Advertising in Rutland, Vermont, horse-cars
Two methods of snow removal
The Great Epizootic of 1878
"The Improved Street-Railway Carriage"

The Cable-Car

The Early Electric Railway

The Elevated Railway

THE SUBWAY

THE HEYDAY OF THE TROLLEY

THE TROLLEY-BUS

THE STREAMLINER

FARES, PLEASE!

1

TRANSPORTATION FOR ALL

The Story of the Horse-Drawn Omnibus

Everybody walked to work in New York in 1825 unless he was rich enough to own or hire a carriage. Although the city had at that time nearly two hundred thousand inhabitants it had no local passenger transportation service of any kind. Occasional stage-coaches ran to Boston, Albany, and Philadelphia. Suburban points, such as Greenwich Village, Yorkville, and Harlem were served by a more frequent stage-coach service. A single ferry line crossed the East River to Brooklyn, then a village of about fifteen thousand people. But vehicles operated for the purpose of picking up and setting down passengers within the city limits were entirely absent. This lack of local transportation service is not very surprising. It was in keeping with the fact that New York had no running water, no gas lights and no paid police, or fire departments in those days. But the city was expanding and distances were becoming greater.

Abraham Brower was the first person to recognize a real business opportunity in this lack of transportation. After cogitating on the matter he went to the coach-making firm of Wade & Leverich in 1827 and commissioned them to build him a vehicle with seats for twelve people. The body was a modification of that used for the stage-coaches of the times. It had open sides and was divided into two sections, each with one forward-facing seat for three persons and one backward-facing seat for the same number. Passengers got on and off by means of steps at the side. Appropriately enough, the vehicle was known as the "Accommodation." Brower operated it up

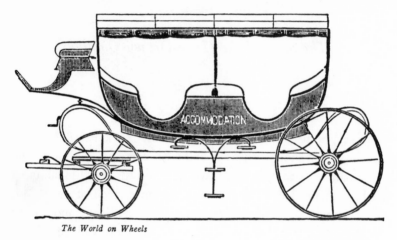

The World on Wheels

Abraham Brower's "Accommodation," first introduced in 1827

and down Broadway as far as Bleecker Street at a flat fare of one shilling a head regardless of the distance traveled. If the weather was bad, or a lady remained aboard when the northern terminus was reached, the driver would continue a reasonable distance farther to make convenient delivery of his passenger.

Two years later Brower expanded his service by adding a second vehicle, built by the same firm. This was designed quite differently. The seats ran lengthwise of the body and the door was at the rear, with an iron stairway to the ground. Placing the door at the rear was a definite break with stage-coach tradition. This vehicle was called the "Sociable" because the passengers were all together in a single compartment.

During the latter part of the same year Ephraim Dodge started a local passenger transportation service by operating a hack on a regular schedule between Boston and South Boston at a fare of twelve and one-half cents. Nowhere else in the United States did there appear to be any great interest in local service.

The World on Wheels

The "Sociable," put in service in 1829

London and Paris had been ahead of New York and Boston with respect to urban transportation. Back in 1819 a line of diligences had been established in Paris to carry passengers at five sous apiece. This type of vehicle did not prove altogether satisfactory and, in 1825, George Shillibeer was commissioned to build some coaches of an improved design. He was a Britisher who had served as a midshipman in the Royal Navy and then gone into business as a coach-builder at Paris.

Almost from the start the new type vehicle was known as an *omnibus*. This name was the contribution of another navy man, a retired French officer named Baudry, who ran a coach between Nantes and some baths he owned in the neighboring town of Richebourg. At first he called his vehicle simply the "Richebourg Baths Coach." Then, one day when he was passing a store kept by a man named Omnes, he noticed a sign over the doorway reading "Omnes Omnibus," or "Omnes for all." This so tickled Baudry's fancy that he immediately renamed his vehicle "l'Omnibus," and the word was soon adopted by the operators of other local coaches.

Shillibeer was greatly impressed with the usefulness of the service rendered by the omnibuses in Paris, so he decided to sell his coach-building business there and start a similar service in London. And in July, 1829, amid the jeers and howls of the hackney coachmen, the first omnibus began running from Paddington Green to the Bank of England. The vehicle itself was a clumsy affair, drawn by three horses. Seats were provided for eighteen passengers. The fare was a shilling for a through journey, with a half-way fare of sixpence. Public approval of the new service was instantaneous. Soon there were twelve omnibuses in service. Shillibeer's success attracted the attention of others and many new proprietors entered the business.

A law existed at this time which made the picking up and setting down of passengers in the city streets illegal, and the driver of the omnibus was liable to summary arrest by the police. So frequent were these arrests that some of the drivers actually chained themselves to their seats to prevent their being taken into custody. In 1832, however, the Stage Carriage Act was passed, recognizing the new form of service, but requiring the drivers and conductors to take out licenses. Thus was established the principle of public regulation at the very beginning of the business of providing local transportation service.

George Shillibeer, himself, never made much money out

of his omnibus business. In 1834 he sold his line in the city of London and started a suburban service to Greenwich. This was an unfortunate move, for the advent of the Greenwich Railway, the first in London, gave him unexpected competition. Before long his horses and omnibuses were seized for unpaid taxes. Shillibeer then set himself up as an undertaker and continued in that business until his death. His contribution to the advancement of local transportation went unrecognized for a long time, but in 1929, the centennial of the establishment of his first line, the bus men of London erected a memorial to him in the church at Chigwell, Essex, where he was buried.

One fine day in the spring of 1831 the good people of New York were startled by the appearance of a new kind of coach on Broadway. It was a big, lumbering vehicle with the word "Omnibus" painted on the side panels. Abraham Brower had borrowed George Shillibeer's idea and was following up his "Accommodation" and "Sociable" with the newest thing in transportation equipment.

John Stephenson, who had recently established a coach-making business, designed and built New York's first omnibus. Like its predecessor, the "Sociable," it had seats running lengthwise of the body and an entrance at the rear. The driver sat on a raised seat projecting from the front of the body. A small boy standing on the steps at the rear collected the fares, twelve and one-half cents for the run from the Battery to Bond Street. By 1835 there were more than a hundred of these omnibuses running up and down the streets of New York. They were elaborately decorated and named after such celebrities as George Washington, Lady Washington, Benjamin Franklin, DeWitt Clinton, Lady Clinton, and others.

The practice of having a boy collect fares was soon given up and the money was deposited in a box beside the driver's seat. Change up to the amount of two dollars was supposed to be furnished by the driver on request. This was passed back to the passenger in an envelope through a small hole in the roof. Not all drivers, unfortunately, were careful that the change in the envelope was correct. A passenger who was short-changed might storm and rage, but there was not much he could do about it, as it was practically impossible to talk

The World on Wheels

New York's first omnibus, built by John Stephenson in 1831

to the driver through the hole in the roof. Usually the victim's predicament aroused more amusement than sympathy among the other passengers—a fact well known to the drivers, who took advantage of it and ignored all but the most vigorous protests.

Since the driver could not see into the interior of the omnibus, it was necessary to have a special arrangement to signal him when to start and stop. This was done by means of a strap running from the rear door to the driver's leg. A pull on the strap indicated that the door was being opened by some one who wanted to get off or on. A slack strip indicated that the door was closed.

Most of these omnibuses were individually owned and

operated. Rivalry was keen. Each driver imagined himself to be a fancy whip. No one except a veteran could really handle one of these "Broadway beauties" properly. He alone knew how close to graze a lamp-post or how quick to cut in front of a rival driver. He alone could tell by the pressure of the strap whether it was a pretty girl who wanted to get off and should be allowed to dismount near the sidewalk, or a mere male who could just as well get off in the middle of the street.

In winter no attempt was made to clear the streets of snow, which frequently remained for weeks at a time. Then huge sleighs drawn by four, six, or even eight, horses, replaced the omnibuses. These public sleighs provided a popular and inexpensive form of winter sport for the citizens, who gleefully hurled snowballs at the helpless passengers, but that did not seem to detract seriously from the pleasure of the ride.

Reckless driving of the omnibuses was a common fault. The situation got so bad the newspapers directed heavy broadsides against it.

The character of the omnibus drivers [said one account], has become brutal and dangerous in the highest degree. They race up and down Broadway and through Chatham Street with the utmost fury. Broadway especially, between the Park and Wall Street, is almost daily the scene of some outrage in which the lives of citizens riding in light vehicles are put in imminent hazard. Not content with running down everything that comes in their way, they turn out of their course to break down other carriages. Yesterday a gentleman driving down Broadway, and keeping near the west side, was run down by an omnibus going up, the street being perfectly clear at the time, the omnibus leaving full twice its width of empty space on the right of its track. At the same spot a hackney-coach was crushed between two of them the day before. It is but a few days since we published the account of a physician being run down near the same spot, his gig ruined, and his horse nearly so, and his own life placed in the most imminent hazard. A ferocious spirit appears to have taken possession of the drivers, which defies law and delights in destruction. It is indispensable that a decisive police should be held on these men, or the consequences of their conduct will result in acts which will shock the whole city.

Not long afterward the comment was made that "the Broadway stage 'Alice Gray' was driving up the street at the rate of about nine miles an hour, when the axle-tree broke and down tumbled the driver, bringing his own same self with him to the ground. What a pity it did not break his ―― nose."

Philadelphia had omnibus service almost as early as New York. The first line was started on December 18, 1831. This effort to provide a regular and cheap method of conveyance within the city was announced in a newspaper advertisement to the effect that:

Joseph Boxall, having been requested by several gentlemen to run an hourly stage-coach for the accommodation of the inhabitants of Chestnut Street, to run from the lower part of the city, begs to inform the citizens generally that he has provided a superior new coach, harness, and good horses for that purpose. Comfort, warmth, and neatness have in every respect been carefully studied. This conveyance will start from Schuylkill, 7th & Chestnut Streets every morning (Sundays excepted) at 8:30 o'clock and every hour until 4:30 in the afternoon down Chestnut Street to the Merchant's Coffee House in 2nd Street and return from the coffee house at 9:00 and every hour until 5:00 in the evening. This accommodation will be conducted and driven solely by the proprietor, who hopes to merit patronage and support. Fare each way 10¢, or tickets may be had of the proprietor at 12 for $1.00.

The Boxall hourly stage-coach, known as "Boxall's Accommodation," proved profitable, and on July 1, 1833, an additional omnibus line was inaugurated between the Navy Yard and Kensington. This line also flourished and additional routes were soon established. Before long a regular omnibus service was running on all the principal streets of the Quaker City.

For a quarter of a century these vehicles were the only regular means of local travel. Adequate accommodations were provided within the business district, but it was difficult to secure any means of transportation for the sections immediately surrounding it. Colonel Alexander McClure, long editor of the Philadelphia *Times*, wrote that he frequently visited Willington, the home of Edward Gratz—a beautiful country place, rich with fruits and foliage, on Broad Street north of Master—and that it was usually necessary for him to walk there because no form of transportation was available in that section of the city in those days.

The necessity for more service and of a different kind became so pressing that street-railways, which were being constructed in other cities, began to be seriously discussed for Philadelphia. In 1854 a charter was granted to the Philadelphia & Delaware Railroad Company to construct a steam-railroad from Kensington to Easton. Failing to carry out this project, the promoters conceived the idea of utilizing the Philadelphia end of their project as a horse railway. On January 21, 1858, this route, the first in the city of Philadelphia, began operation with fifteen cars.

Boston had omnibus service in 1835 but conservative Baltimore did not follow suit until 1844. When service was started it was received with great enthusiasm. The editor of the Baltimore *Sun* remarked in his issue of May 1:

We are pleased to perceive than an Omnibus Company has been formed at last in Baltimore, which bids fair to be permanent and to afford all those facilities to our citizens which have long been considered of absolute necessity in other communities.

Two of the omnibuses have just arrived and commenced running yesterday. They are quite handsome affairs, well fitted up, richly decorated, drawn by good horses and we believe driven by careful drivers. Another will be here in a few days, and four more as soon as they are finished.

The route established is from the corner of Franklin and Eutaw Streets to Baltimore Street, thence to Gay down Gay to Pratt and from thence to Market Street—Fells Point, which will be continued unless the public demand some slight deviation.

In other cities, in addition to the general convenience, they have tended greatly to enhance the value of property in the outskirts of the City, enabling persons to reside at a distance from their places of business in more healthy locations, without the loss of time and fatigue of walking.

Any white person could ride as far as he liked for six cents. Baltimorians looked on the service as a great institution. The promoters of the line were Messrs. James Mitchell, Coleman Bailey and William Robertson. They operated it for fifteen years and then sold out to the Baltimore City Passenger Railway Company which introduced horse-cars in 1859.

London and Paris, which were ahead of American cities in starting omnibus service, were ahead also in putting the service on a business-like basis. This, however, did not take place immediately, but only after the passage of a good many years.

In London, with the departure of George Shillibeer from the scene, the omnibus service began to deteriorate. The original, well-appointed, three-horse vehicles were replaced by cheaper, two-horse vehicles, far less comfortably appointed. The polite, neatly uniformed drivers gave way to rough individual owner-drivers, wearing pretty much what they pleased, and acting as they pleased. The service became as unreliable as it was uncomfortable. The climax was reached in 1851, the year when the famous Crystal Palace was built in Hyde Park for the Great Exhibition. More than six million people visited this remarkable show and the London Omnibus operators reaped a rich harvest, augmented to no small extent by a general practice of raising fares and overcharging passengers. This game was great fun for the bus men while it lasted, but it brought down on their heads a storm of wrath, and a vociferous demand for a general reform of the whole omnibus service.

In Paris the local transportation problem was being handled much better than in London. This prompted a group of English businessmen to open negotiations with the company operating omnibuses in Paris with a view to establishing a similarly well-run service in London. But, before anything definite was done, there came the outbreak of the Crimean War, and the matter was dropped for the time being.

Early in 1856, however, the London omnibus proprietors were startled to learn of the formation of the Compagnie Générale des Omnibus de Londres, a part French and part English organization. Loud howls immediately went up from the bus men. The public, to which they had been so indifferent, was now asked to defend them against this "foreign competition." But the excitement proved to be premature. The new company was not planning competition. Rather, it was planning to buy out the existing owners at a fair price, and employ them as company drivers if they so desired. Within a year it had bought more than 600 of the 800 odd omnibuses then operating in London.

A new spirit was soon in evidence. Hundreds of the old vehicles were scrapped and replaced by new ones. Fares were lowered and uniforms again made their appearance on drivers and conductors. A year later the company changed its name to London General Omnibus Company. Expansion continued steadily, until, in 1905, the L.G.O., as it was familiarly called, owned some 17,000 horses and operated more than 1,400 omnibuses.

Never during this entire period did the L.G.O. enjoy a complete monopoly, though the number of its competitors gradually diminished. Most picturesque of these competitors was Thomas Tilling. He had started on a shoe-string before the formation of any big company and gradually built up a substantial business. Frequent efforts were made to get him to sell out to the L.G.O., but he steadfastly refused to do it. In 1905, the peak year of omnibus service, he had a stable of some 7,000 horses and was operating around 500 vehicles.

In the United States a development took place almost

simultaneously with the introduction of omnibus service that drove a nail in the coffin of that kind of local transportation. This was the establishment of street-railway service by the New York & Harlem Railroad in November, 1832, as described more fully in the next chapter. Steel wheels rolling on steel rails had so many advantages over wooden wheels rolling on cobble-stones that their ultimate triumph was inevitable. But a long time elapsed before any more street-railways were built and the omnibus business continued to enjoy prosperity for another generation. In 1855, for example, there were 593 omnibuses in operation on twenty-seven routes in the City of New York.

The building of the first street-railway had more disastrous results for John Stephenson than it did for the omnibus operators. He built the first cars for the New York & Harlem and became so enthusiastic over the possibilities in this field that he enlarged his plant to provide facilities for the manufacture of railway cars. Since no more street-railways were built for many years, the business depression of 1837 found him in financial difficulties. He settled with his creditors for fifty cents on the dollar and returned to building omnibuses and wagons. Within seven years he had paid his remaining indebtedness, in some instances by building vehicles for people to whom he owed money. John Malt, a creditor to whom Stephenson presented a four-horse truck instead of cash, was so impressed that he had the truck parade up and down Broadway carrying a sign, "This is the way one bankrupt pays his debts; his name is Honest John Stephenson."

During the 1850's street-railway operation took on new life in New York. Lines were built on Third, Sixth, and Eighth avenues in addition to the original line on Fourth Avenue. John Stephenson resumed car building and became the world's leading manufacturer of these vehicles. A few years later cars were run on Broadway north of Fourteenth

Local transportation was first operated in Paris with vehicles not unlike the long-distance stage-coach.

George Shillibeer's three-horse omnibus, which began operation in London in 1829, had seats for eighteen passengers.

Early New York omnibuses were gaily colored with flowers and coaching scenes painted on the sides.

Pedestrian bridge built at Broadway and Fulton Street, New York, in 1867, permitted persons on foot to cross without danger from vehicular traffic.

In the heyday of the horse-drawn omnibus these vehicles could be
seen going up and down Broadway about fifteen seconds apart in
each direction.

Early type of double decker in London had a stairway at the front.

London omnibus changing horses at Swiss Cottage, 1901.

Street. Below that point, however, the horse-drawn omnibus continued as the only form of public transportation.

In those days lower Broadway was so crowded with omnibus traffic that a person on foot could cross the street only at the risk of life and limb. Jacob Sharp, therefore, proposed the building of a street-railway to take the place of the omnibuses. To prove the need for this improvement he made a count at Chambers Street which showed 3,035 omnibuses passing that point northbound in thirteen hours and 3,162 southbound. That meant about four a minute, or one every fifteen seconds in each direction. The service, however, was far from satisfactory. Said the New York *Herald* of October 2, 1864:

Modern martyrdom may be succinctly defined as riding in a New York omnibus. The discomforts, inconveniences, and annoyances of a trip on one of these vehicles are almost intolerable. From the beginning to the end of the journey a constant quarrel is progressing. The driver quarrels with the passengers, and the passengers quarrel with the driver. There are quarrels about getting out and quarrels about getting in. There are quarrels about change and quarrels about the ticket swindle. The driver swears at the passengers and the passengers harangue the driver through the strap hole—a position in which even Demosthenes could not be eloquent. Respectable clergymen in white chokers are obliged to listen to loud oaths. Ladies are disgusted, frightened, and insulted. Children are alarmed and lift up their voices and weep. Indignant gentlemen rise to remonstrate with the irate Jehu and are suddenly bumped back into their seats, twice as indignant as before, besides being involved in supplementary quarrels with those other passengers upon whose corns they have accidentally trodden. Thus the omnibus rolls along a perfect Bedlam on wheels.

Jacob Sharp was not the only seeker for a street-railway franchise on lower Broadway. The New York & Harlem Railroad tried to get its charter amended so that it could buy out the omnibus lines and lay tracks there. A good many property owners favored this idea and got up a petition to the state legislature endorsing the company's plea. Among the signers were D. Appleton & Company and Lord & Taylor. But there was opposition, too. A. T. Stewart, one of the most

famous merchants of the day, fought the street-railway idea
with all his might. The opposition triumphed when the legislature refused to give its approval.

In an effort to protect pedestrians from being run down by
the horde of omnibuses, a foot-bridge was built across Broadway at Fulton Street in 1867. This was a graceful and attractive structure, but it did not meet with much popular favor.
A year after it was built it was torn down.

Eventually Jacob Sharp won his fight to operate cars on
lower Broadway. The franchise was granted in 1884. Despite
the obvious fact that the omnibuses had long outlived their
usefulness, the aldermen who voted for the franchise were
the target of violent criticism. Hugh Grant, then a member
of the aldermanic body, succeeded in disassociating himself
from this troublesome franchise fight. A little later the citizens
rewarded him by making him mayor and bestowing on him
the sobriquet of "Honest Hugh." Soliloquizing on the proposed change, the New York *Tribune* said:

In a few weeks the Broadway 'Bus will be but a memory. At the
edict of Jacob Sharp it will have faded into the limbo of the past,
and have become a subject for the folk-lore of the future. Yet this
imminent change need not evoke gloomy thoughts. The Broadway
'Bus, to say sooth, can well be spared. In fact, it could have been
spared some time ago; and there are those who go so far as to
maintain that its room would have been better than its company at
any moment since its first introduction. For it must be acknowledged
that the Broadway 'Bus is not a Thing of Beauty. It combines more
ugliness and discomfort than were ever crowded together in one
vehicle. During all the years it has lumbered and rumbled down
Broadway it has elicited the liveliest expressions of amazement from
strangers within our gates—amazement, for the most part, that so
progressive and inventive a people should tolerate a mode of conveyance as far behind the age as an old mail-coach is behind a Pull-
man drawing-room car. Of all kinds of public conveyances ever
devised it is the most clumsy and inconvenient.

The passenger is almost sure to knock his head both getting in
and out, and if he does not also tread on the feet of his fellow-
sufferers on both occasions he and they may congratulate themselves.
The arrangements for shooting passengers out into the mud suddenly

are unsurpassed, unless it be by the facilities for compelling them to plunge wildly forward toward the horses when they enter. The Broadway 'Bus is cold in winter and stuffy in summer. It has a perennially frowsy smell; a flavor of remote antiquity; of the strange period when people used straight, hard-seated, high-backed chairs, and otherwise mortified the flesh in their domestic arrangements. Its exterior always suggested the idea that the inventor of the machine had designs for a circus band-wagon floating through his powerful mind when he conceived this chaste and unique creation, and that these reminiscences were fused with hazy glimpses of the decorations of a dime museum. But he repressed these vagrant fancies, and confined the working of his artistic imagination rigidly to the ornamentation of the external panels. No hint of comfort or convenience was permitted to interfere with the grim realism of the vehicle as a whole. The Broadway 'Bus may be said to have typified the awkward period of the Republic's adolescence when it was thought necessary to advertise our democracy in all ways and when somehow the admission of any concession to public convenience was thought to savor of bloated aristocracy.

Once the street-cars began running, opposition vanished and public opinion became virtually unanimous in their favor. The wonder was, indeed, why some people had opposed them with such vigor and determination. This opposition was, according to the Brooklyn *Eagle*, "a curious commentary on the short-sightedness of a class who have gained a reputation for conspicuous shrewdness—the merchants of the metropolis."

Only on Fifth Avenue did the horse-drawn omnibuses continue to operate. There they reigned supreme until the introduction of motor-buses in 1905. Then it took but three years to prove that the horse no longer had a place in furnishing motive-power for vehicles used in local transportation service.

In 1908 the last of the Fifth Avenue Coach Company's horses were sold at auction and the ancient omnibus was no more.

2

OMNIBUS ON RAILS

The Story of the Horse-Car

Top-hatted gentlemen and satin-clad ladies of New York's best society crowded the sidewalks of the Bowery on a frosty morning in the late fall of 1832. Mayor Walter Bowne and the City Council were there in full regalia. Every window of the neat brick houses along the street was filled with eager faces. Over all hung an air of excited expectancy. This was the day when John Mason, president of the Chemical Bank, had promised to demonstrate his remarkable new idea—a novel kind of railway with coaches mounted on iron wheels drawn by horses over iron rails laid in the center of the street. Such a thing had never been heard of before. Most New Yorkers looked upon the experiment with grave suspicion, but everyone wanted to see the demonstration.

Like many another new development, the first street-railway was the accidental off-shoot of an entirely different idea. Railroading was then the topic of the day. The new locomotive, DeWitt Clinton, had just hauled three car-loads of frightened passengers at the sensational speed of fifteen miles an hour over the Mohawk & Hudson Railroad between Albany and Schenectady. Cynics scoffed at this crazy method of transportation, but some people believed it might have worth-while possibilities.

Among the believers was John Mason, wealthy merchant, banker, and prominent citizen of the country's metropolis. Before long, he thought, the iron horse would come knocking at the gates of the city. So he and a group of associates organized the "New York and Harlaem Railroad Company"

Pioneer street-car, the "John Mason," built in 1832

to provide a city terminus for the railroad which they expected would soon be built from Albany down to the banks of the Harlem River.

The charter granted by the state legislature permitted the company to construct " a single or double railroad or way" between Twenty-third Street and the Harlem River on any route which the Common Council of the City of New York should approve. After long argument the route selected was along Fourth Avenue, and the Mayor signed the ordinance on December 22, 1831, little realizing that his action would profoundly influence the future development of every large city in the world.

John Mason's enthusiasm was shared by a number of other men of wealth. Within an hour of the opening of the subscription books of the new company, the required capital of

$350,000 was fully subscribed. The company had scarcely been organized, however, when a brand new idea was conceived. The district through which the original route ran was a sparsely settled region inhabited by farmers and the residents of a few country houses, but the district below Twenty-third Street was closely built up. Why not extend the line farther down into the city and furnish local transportation service similar to that being given by the omnibuses? Permission was sought and obtained to continue the route down Fourth Avenue and the Bowery as far as Walker Street.

Construction was started at once on a one-mile stretch of double track between Prince and Fourteenth streets. The rails were simply flat strips which were fastened to blocks of stone imbedded in the ground. John Stephenson, builder of omnibuses, was commissioned to construct two cars. Their general design was not unlike that of the ordinary stage-coach, though somewhat larger, there being seats for a total of thirty passengers. Each vehicle was divided into three separate compartments, and each compartment had an entrance door of its own. Interiors were upholstered in fine cloth and exteriors embellished with gorgeous painting. John Stephenson thought so well of the design that he had it patented, the grant being signed by President Andrew Jackson.

By early November, 1832, the line was ready for operation, and the whole town turned out to see the show. On the opening day John Mason made a speech which was received with great cheering although a contemporary remarks in his diary that "Mr. Mason can make money better than he can make a speech."

Amid the shouts of the eager spectators the horses trotted off in handsome style pulling the two cars at breath-taking speed. After them followed a flock of carriages and horsemen. The first car, filled with city officials, was in charge of "Lank" Odell, a veteran stage-coach driver. Closely following was the second car filled with company officials. This was in charge of a local hackman, hired for the occasion.

At this point in the proceedings, Vice-President John Lozier, operating head of the road, decided to make a demonstration of the safety of the new form of transportation. The plan was for him to stand at the corner of Bond Street and give the drivers a signal, at which they would bring their cars to a quick stop. With the cars approaching at a fast trot Lozier raised his arm and gave the signal. The veteran "Lank" Odell, driving the first car, performed admirably and brought his vehicle to a quick halt, but the local hackman driving the second car forgot to apply the brake and tried to stop by simply pulling on the reins and shouting "Whoa!" The horses did their best to arrest the progress of the rapidly moving vehicle, but its momentum was too great for them to accomplish it without the mechanical aid of the brake, and the tongue crashed into the rear of the leading car in the first street-railway accident on record.

The distinguished guests were somewhat shaken by the collision and a little frightened. The spectators lining the curb were vastly amused, and Mr. Lozier was much embarrassed. No one was hurt, however, and the ceremonies, including a big dinner at City Hall, proceeded. When they were all over, everyone agreed that the trial trip had been a grand success. "This event," said the Mayor, "will go down in the history of our country as the greatest achievement of man." Even the newspapers were impressed. "Those who made violent objections to laying down these tracks and fancied a thousand dangers to the passing traveler," according to the New York Courier & Inquirer, "now look at the work with pleasure and surprise." The completion of the road, the paper added, "will make Harlem a suburb of New York."

Within a year another mile of track had been added to the system, and by 1834 the length of the route had grown to four miles. Cars were operated on a fifteen-minute headway, and the fare was twelve and one-half cents. Additional cars were built and the street-railway began to give serious competition to the omnibuses which had been, up to then, the main reliance of people wishing to travel about the city.

Scarcely had John Mason's street-railway begun operation in New York when the City Council of New Orleans authorized a similar undertaking in that city. This was a line to run from Canal Street to the little suburb of Carrollton, four and one-half miles to the west. Carrollton, like New Orleans, was on the banks of the Mississippi, the river describing a huge crescent between the two. Its great attraction was an elegant resort hotel topped by an observatory from which the winding course of the river could be viewed for many miles. Commenting on the hotel's attractions the New Orleans *Bee* could find no criticism to make except the absence of bowling alleys and shooting galleries.

Once again the impatience of the promoters caused a change from the original plans. Some months before the New Orleans & Carrollton line was completed it was decided to commence local operation on a branch line on Magazine Street. On December 9, 1834, a contract was signed with George Baumgard to furnish, "two horses and a driver for the Magazine Street railway car at $4.50 a day." This arrangement did not prove entirely satisfactory and on April 3, 1835, it is reported that, "the contract with the driver ended on April 1, and the company's own horses are now used and a man engaged to take in the money and the revenue has considerably increased." It was said, however, that this did not imply any reflection on the old driver.

For some reason the blessings of the street-railway were not quickly recognized elsewhere. No more were built until the early 1850's when additional lines were started in Brooklyn and New York. Then Boston took up the idea. Construction of a line from Bowdoin Square to Harvard Square in Cambridge was undertaken in 1855. To finance this venture the Cambridge Horse Railroad Company undertook to sell $43,000 of securities, part of which were bonds, and part common stocks. With true New England caution the security buyers showed a strong preference for the bonds, and the company found itself able to sell only $6,000 worth of stock. Nevertheless the necessary money was finally raised, and the contractor started to work.

Meanwhile, another company, the Metropolitan Railway, was striving with might and main to achieve the distinction of being the first to operate in Boston. Track construction presented no great problem. The question was where to get cars. The Metropolitan implored the car-builder to hurry the construction of its vehicles. To beat its rival the Cambridge Railroad sent its representatives to New York to buy second-hand cars. This trick won the victory. When the first street-cars in New England began running on the Cambridge Railroad on March 26, 1856, they carried on their sides the painted legend "Car to Greenwood Cemetery," the destination in Brooklyn to which the cars had previously been operated.

In the beginning the Cambridge company decided to assure its popularity by letting everyone ride free. This was a great idea. Within a week it was carrying more than two thousand passengers a day, and the public was loud in its praise of the wonderful new institution. There came a time, however, when the conductors started to collect fares from the passengers, and the outcries were dreadful. The more conservative citizens simply wanted the company's franchise revoked; those of violent temper wanted the officials to be hanged on Boston Common.

Two years later the street-railway idea spread to Philadelphia. Its advocates insisted that the building of street-railways would be the greatest thing that ever happened to the city, but opponents shook their heads in doubt. Some claimed that it was unfair to the horses, hard-worked enough when pulling omnibuses over the cobblestone pavements, to ask them to pull the heavier rail-cars which carried more people. To this the proponents of the railway replied that its great advantage was that it employed the principle of iron wheels on smooth iron rails, thereby making the work of the horses easier, as well as providing a smoother, more comfortable ride for the passengers.

Other objectors tried to prevent street-railway construction by getting a court injunction on the ground that it would be a public nuisance. In answer the Judge declared that while a street-railway "may occasion loss or inconvenience, and may depreciate the value of property and render its enjoyment incommodious and almost impossible, yet this is a *dammum absque injuria*," or, in other words, the plaintiff was "damaged without injury" in a legal sense. The injunction was therefore refused.

Though opposed to the idea of street-railways, the Philadelphia *Sunday Dispatch* seems to have recognized them as an inevitable step in the progress of civilization. "It is perhaps scarcely worth while," said this paper, "to allude to the fact that in New York City they kill one person each week on city railroads and mangle three or four on an average in the same space of time. Human life is really of little value nowadays."

At Baltimore the public was unanimously opposed to the new form of transportation. The cars, people believed, would interfere with traffic, carriages would be upset driving across the tracks, and people would be killed by the dreadful juggernauts. As in Philadelphia they sought to prevent construction by getting a legal injunction.

This move failed and the laying of tracks began. Opposition then took a new form. At a certain curve, the track came close to the curb in front of a drug-store kept by a man named

Moore. Declaring that the company was encroaching on his property, he planted an armchair in the street and sat defiantly in the path of the construction gang. Crowds gathered and cheered the brave man. When he had to go inside the store to wait on customers or eat, his wife relieved him in the armchair. In the end the company paid Moore three hundred dollars, and he withdrew his opposition.

Once a street-railway began operation, public opinion usually changed. The horse-car was faster than the omnibus. It carried more people, and it ran more quietly. In 1859, Cincinnati, Pittsburgh, and Chicago joined the ranks of cities having street-railway service. Others followed in short order.

The idea was spreading abroad, too. Paris began horse-car operation in 1853. Birkenhead had the first passenger-carrying tramway in England in 1860 and London was not far behind. An American, George Francis Train was the builder of the first lines in both of these places.

By this time the design of the horse-car had undergone a great change from that of the first two cars built by John Stephenson for the New York & Harlem line. Instead of having three separate compartments with seats running across the car, the interior was now a single compartment with seats running lengthwise on both sides of a center aisle. These seats —upholstered in figured plush—would accommodate from twenty-four to thirty passengers, depending on the length of the car. Doors connected the car interior with platforms at front and rear, one for the driver and one for the conductor. The car roof extended over these platforms, and they were provided with low metal dashboards, but otherwise they were entirely open, assuring the car crew of plenty of fresh air in all weather. Some of the smaller cars had no rear platform, but only a step from the rear door to the ground. They were called "bob-tails."

Passengers inside the car did not have the benefit of the same plentiful supply of fresh air as did the driver and conductor. Opening of the doors admitted gusts of air from time to time but the main reliance for ventilation was an arrangement whereby the center part of the roof was a few inches higher than the outer part with a row of small ventilating windows between the two. How many of these windows

Perforated veneer seats were sometimes used in early street-cars

should be open was a question that provoked endless argument.

Oil lamps illuminated the car interior at night. These lamps were often rather smoky, a characteristic which aggravated the ventilating problem. All in all, it must be admitted that the atmosphere inside the early horse-cars not infrequently left a good deal to be desired.

Two tons was the weight of the ordinary horse-car, and the passengers weighed another two tons, making a total loaded weight of about four tons. Many companies used two horses per car, although Alexander Easton, in his *Practical Treatise on Street or Horse-Power Railways*, published in 1859, characterized this as "a waste of motive power arising either from a miscalculation of the horses' power, inferiority of stock, or defectiveness in the wheels or track."

John Stephenson, ripe with the experience of many years of car building, was of the same opinion.

The best statistics and sources of information accessible to us [he said in the *Street Railway Journal*], show that in the United States and Canada there are about 428 tramways, of which Canada has about a dozen. Of these 428 roads, 279 are operated with small (bob-tail) cars, and 149 are operated with large (conductor) cars. A reference to our order book for the year 1882 showed that two-thirds of our orders were for small cars. The small system is a boon to the public because: (1) Tramways accommodate the public when otherwise they could not exist; (2) The accommodation is better, because usually three small cars are used successfully when the effort to sustain two has proved a failure; (3) Economy of time equal to fifteen to twenty per cent, because the small cars make fewer stoppages, and being lighter, are stopped and put in motion more quickly; and (4) Merciful to horses. Two horses seldom start in unison. In the bob-tail car the one horse easily does the work, with better footing in the track.

The chief objection urged by the public against the use of the bob-tail car was the trouble of depositing the fare in a box at the forward end of the car. By the invention of a fare conveyor this difficulty was obviated if the passenger was provided with the exact change or ticket. He or she could then place the amount of the fare in the conveyor with as little trouble as to hand it to a conductor. The conveyor consisted of metal tubes fastened to each side of the car, extending from the rear end into a fare box at the front end of the vehicle. The top of the tube contained an opening its entire length. As the tube was inclined from the rear to the front, a piece of money or a ticket of vulcanized rubber, or any hard material, would roll forward into the fare box.

Before this invention came into use the passenger had either to walk to the forward end of the car and deposit the fare in the box, or ask fellow passengers to pass it forward, frequently to their inconvenience and annoyance. It was more or less difficult, especially for ladies, to maintain an equilibrium. Frequently some tender corn was tramped upon in the effort, resulting in curses, not loud, but deep. Moreover, while the passenger was taking his fare to the box some one else would

Bob-tailed street-car with platform at one end only

frequently take his seat. All this was eliminated by the invention of the conveyor.

The same faithful animals which furnished the motive-power for the horse-cars also furnished most of the stopping power. Their efforts, however, were supplemented to some extent by a system of brakes which the driver applied by means of a great, goose-necked handle on a vertical staff attached to the dash-board. Watching the winding and unwinding of this handle was one of the most entertaining features of riding on the horse-cars, and was rivaled only by the fun of listening to the clanging of the bells—the little bell by which the conductor signaled to the driver when to start or stop, and the big bell by which the driver warned pedestrians and other vehicles out of the way of his prancing steeds.

There were about as many different track designs in the early horse-car days as there were operating companies. Some features, however, were common to nearly all of them. The rails, as we have said, were mostly flat strips of wrought-iron, and were laid in short lengths on wooden stringers resting on cross-ties spaced about five feet apart. It was not until after the introduction of the steel rail of much greater depth and strength that the stringers were eliminated and the rails laid directly on the cross-ties.

At one time there was an idea that the head of the rail should be on the inside and the flange of the wheel on the outside. This arrangement was the direct opposite of steam-railroad practice, but its advocates contended that it was more satisfactory for the other vehicles using the streets. How far apart the rails should be placed was the subject of endless discussion—the argument finally being won by the proponents of the four-foot eight and one-half-inch gage. The best shape for the rail was another matter of controversy, but this was never settled until after the horse-car had passed out of the transportation picture.

The problem of establishing street-railways was simple compared with the problem of operating them after they were built. The most serious of the operating problems centered in the horse himself. Some of the larger street-railways had a thousand or more of them. A good animal for this kind of work cost about one hundred and twenty-five dollars. This was less than the cost of a car, which averaged around seven hundred and fifty dollars, but it was necessary to have several shifts of horses for each car, so that the total investment in animals was unusually greater than that in equipment. As a matter of fact, an early report of the American Street Railway Association states that about forty per cent of the entire investment of the average company was in horses and stables.

Street-railway managers had definite ideas about the kind of horses they wanted. "I am convinced," said one, "that nothing will average equal to the roan, so far as you can get it, from the strawberry roan to the steel roan. A dark gray is good, and there is nothing better than a dark dun with a black stripe down the back, and black legs. Dark grays are also good; what is known as a flea-bitten gray, with little specks all over him is generally very good. If you can avoid it never get a horse with a white hoof." Other conclusions the managers came to were that the best age for a street-railway horse was not less than five years or more than nine; horses subject to fits were undesirable; and flat feet were a serious drawback. Certain authorities favored small Canadian horses as being more hardy and sure-footed. When each new horse was delivered to the stable of the operating company, it was allowed to rest for one day, and then given a pint of linseed oil to prevent constipation after its trip from farm to city.

Thought was given to stabling the horses. Aside from any question of humane feeling, it was bad business to have damp, dark, and dirty stables. Most horses worked only four to six hours a day, so the greater part of their lives was spent in the stable. But the work was hard and the animals deserved commodious quarters. A committee which made a careful study of the care of horses recommended that the width of the stall should be not less than four feet and the length not less than nine feet. Partitions between the stalls should be at least four feet high. Ventilation and drainage were matters of great importance. The floor of the stall was given a pitch toward the gutter of about one and one-half inches in the nine-foot length. Stabling the horses head to head was not recommended, as it tended to spread infectious diseases by breathing. Cast-iron food boxes were found to be best and it was said, too, that confining the feed to hay and oats increased the use-

Traffic congestion at State and Washington Streets, Chicago, in 1865.

Double-deck omnibus which was converted into a horse-car for
operation in New Orleans in 1861.

Car house at Belleville, New Jersey, about 1882.

Traffic congestion was no problem in Richmond, Virginia, in the
days when mules furnished the power for street-railway operation.

Atlanta, rising from its ashes after the end of the Civil War, used
mule-cars for city transportation.

Canal Street, New Orleans, in the 1880's, had four tracks to accommodate the many mule-cars then in operation.

Elaborate decorations brightened the exteriors of the horse-cars in the 1880's.

Seats upholstered in figured plush, oil lamps, and a straw-covered floor were the mode for the car interior.

Main Street, Rochester, New York, in 1878 when all public transportation service was given by one-horse street-cars.

Getting ready for the morning rush hour at Philadelphia.

Machine-driven horse clippers were an early labor-saving device.

Howard Johnston photo

Horse-cars in Rutland, Vermont, carried advertising signs on the roof in the 1890's.

Two methods of snow removal—a two-horse scraper and a twelve-horse sweeper at Toronto.

When horses were laid low by the great epizootic in 1872, men pulled the cars by hand.

"The Improved Street-Railway Carriage" patented by George Francis Train was introduced in London in the 1860's.

ful life of the horse considerably over what might be expected if corn was on his daily menu.

What kind of a shoe was best for a horse engaged in street-railway work was the subject of lively debate. At one of the meetings of the American Street Railway Association, Mr. Brayton of Providence, Rhode Island, suggested that no shoes at all should be used. "When the horse was created," he said, "didn't he work without shoes?" To this W. H. Hazzard of the Brooklyn City Railroad replied, "So did man, but could you pull a car barefooted on coblestones?" Everybody agreed that many good horses were ruined by unskilful shoeing. Whether the shoe should be made to fit the foot or the foot to fit the shoe was a question not so easily answered. Then, too, there was disagreement as to whether the shoe should be fitted hot or cold. Patent horseshoes of various sorts were constantly being offered to the operating companies.

Another headache for the early street-railway operators was the manure problem. Eventually the manure was sold, often for a very tidy sum. In a single year, for example, the Third Avenue Railroad in New York realized $13,750 from the sale of manure. The crux of the problem was how to store it pending its final sale and removal. Keeping it in a cellar under the stable was not considered good practice. Outdoor storage, on the other hand, was likely to evoke loud protests from the neighbors. The company managements tried their best to convince people that the presence of a manure pile, far from being a danger, was actually a benefit to public health. No completely satisfactory solution of this problem was found as long as the horse-cars remained in operation.

Some companies preferred mules to horses. A survey by the *Street Railway Journal* disclosed that two mules could be fed for the cost of one horse, and that they could do one-third more work. They could stand the cold as well as the horse, and could stand the heat better. One drawback, however, was that a mule had practically no resale value when he got too old to pull a car, whereas a horse could be sold for about three-fourths of the original cost.

Winter brought its troubles for the street-railway manager. Snow removal developed into an exceedingly knotty problem. Nobody had ever thought of removing snow from the public streets until the horse-car came along. Then it had to be done so that the wheels would stay on the rails. This, however, interfered with sleighing. In Boston, the Mayor and Aldermen solved the problem by forbidding the street-railway companies to clear the tracks at all so long as sleighing was good. The companies could operate passenger sleighs, they said, and charge the same fare as on the cars, but the snow had to remain on the tracks until it melted away of its own accord. Some companies attempted to clear their tracks by melting the snow away with salt. Objection was made to this on the ground that it worked on the same principle as an ice-cream freezer; lowering the temperature of the air sharply, and endangering the health of people on the streets.

Winter weather also brought with it the problem of car heating. One company tried the experiment of placing box furnaces under the car floor with pipes to convey the heat into the car body. This plan might have been all right if it had not had an alarming tendency to set the car on fire. Other companies put heaters on the front platforms of their cars, and distributed the heat inside through registers. Sometimes it was difficult to discover what the public really wanted in the way of car heating. President Hazzard of the Brooklyn company said at one time concerning heating, "The people want it so we must give it to them, whether it is detrimental to health or not." Soon afterwards his customers appeared to have changed their minds, for in 1882, Mr. Hazzard took the heaters out of his cars. In great indignation a patron of the road offered to take up a collection to put the heaters back if the company was too poor to do it. "Keep the money," said Mr. Hazzard, "and buy yourself an overcoat."

Not the least of the problems of the early street-railways was to make sure that the company's treasury received fares from all of the passengers carried. After careful consideration, the following rule was adopted as a model for street-railways throughout the state of New York:

Conductors should never go inside the cars or to the front without first counting the number of passengers on the rear platform; and if more are there on his return he should call out, "Fares, if you please," without addressing anyone in particular.

To discourage cluttering up the cars conductors were directed to collect a fare

for every trunk, box, basket, or package placed in the cars, too large to be held by the owner.

Keeping of accounts was not very scientific in the days of the early horse-car lines, and it is difficult to tell how profitable the lines were. Apparently they were able to pay a fair return on the investment, but were never gold mines. Mr. Easton in his *Practical Treatise on Street or Horse Power Railways*, showed that a group of eight companies, four in New York and four in Boston, were earning about nine per cent on the money spent to organize, build, and equip them. Earnings would have been higher, he pointed out, if large sums had not been expended in the purchase of "imaginary omnibus rights."

The actual cost of operating a horse-car seems to have been a little more than twenty cents per mile traveled, or not much different from the cost of operating a modern motor-bus. Wages, in horse-car days, were only a fraction of what they are now, but cars often had crews of two men and speeds were seldom better than five miles an hour, so that a good deal of labor cost went into every mile traveled by the car.

Wide differences existed in the margin of profit earned by the various companies. On the Sixth Avenue Railroad in New York, and on the Brooklyn City Railroad, it cost only three and three-quarter cents to carry each passenger, whereas the fare was five cents. In contrast to this it cost the Third Avenue Railroad four and one-half cents and the Metropolitan Railway of Boston four and seven-eighths cents to carry each passenger. Even so, both of these roads were able to show nice profits at the end of the year.

Hard times came to the street-railways during the Civil War. General business declined and fewer people patronized the service. Then the Federal Government began seizing the horses to pull artillery and to serve as cavalry mounts. Perhaps the horses welcomed this change from the monotony of their daily lives, but it was hard on the operating companies. Conditions improved after the war, but a near disaster hit the industry in the fall of 1872, when the great epizootic—a kind of influenza among horses—broke out in Philadelphia, New York, Baltimore, and other cities. So many horses died that a number of companies were compelled to suspend service entirely. In some places the idle drivers and conductors formed groups to pull the cars by hand. A few companies tried to restore service by using oxen to haul the cars, but they frequently proved obstreperous, and their feet were too tender to stand the constant pounding on the hard pavements.

The 1880's were the great years of the horse-car business. Hon. Moody Merrill, president of the Highland Street Railway of Boston, proudly told the first convention of the American Street Railway Association there were more than 100,000 horses and mules engaged in pulling 18,000 street-cars on 3,000 miles of track in cities all over the United States. The omnibus had been lifted from cobblestone pavements and placed on steel rails to a far greater extent than anyone had dreamed of when John Mason started his first experiment.

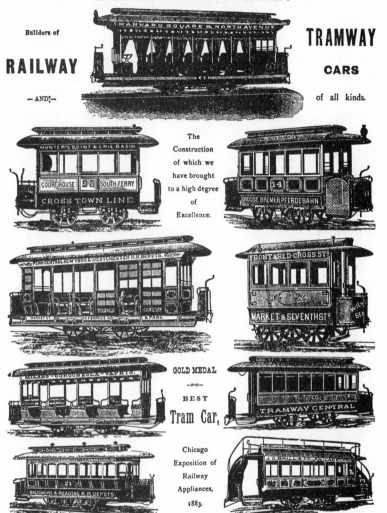

Street-car styles of the 1880's

Cities had expanded and their suburbs had been brought closer by this new and better means of transportation. But it was, to some degree, the pride that goes before a fall. Two serious competitors of the horse railway had arisen. One was the cable railway and the other was the electric railway. The end of the horse-car era was in sight. The decade of the 1890's was to witness a steady decline in the importance of animal traction. By the end of the century it was little more than a memory. One line kept running on Bleecker Street, New York, until July 26, 1917, but it had long ceased to be of any importance as a means of transportation. During its last year it collected less than thirty cents a day from the passengers it carried. With its passing came the end of a type of transportation that had faithfully served the needs of three generations of city dwellers.

3

HORSES GET A REST

The Story of the Cable-Car

The Chinese had a phrase for it: "No pullee, no pushee, allee samee go." This apt comment was not originally inspired by the gasoline automobile, as might be supposed, but by the cable-car which made its appearance on the streets of San Francisco in the 1870's.

The city by the Golden Gate was booming in those days. It had emerged from its wild and lawless infancy and had become a rich and progressive community. Every one was excited about the new Palace Hotel, destined to be, for its time, the biggest and most expensive hostelry in the world. Every one had money and wanted to spend it.

Horse-cars had long been a familiar sight in the streets of the city. How highly they were regarded is shown by a contemporary newspaper comment that: "It is hardly too much to say that the modern horse-car is among the most indispensable conditions of metropolitan growth. In these days of *fashionable effeminacy* and *flabby feebleness*, which never walks when it can possibly ride, the horse-car virtually fixes the ultimate limits of suburban growth."

Andrew S. Hallidie, a manufacturer of wire rope, was the

inventor of the cable railway. He had noted the "flabby feebleness" of the citizens of the city, at least in so far as they preferred riding to walking. He had also noticed that the nags pulling the horse-cars had a pretty tough time of it on hills. Some of San Francisco's hills, in fact, were so steep that horse-cars did not even try to go up them. Hallidie knew that for some time the coal-cars had been hauled by cable on the English colliery railways, and, he thought, "Why not do this job the same way?" His plan was to have a stationary steam-engine operate an endless wire rope on rollers in a conduit below the pavement. A gripping clamp on the car, extending downward through a slot in the pavement, would take hold or let go of the moving cable at the will of a "gripman." Brakes, similar to those on horse-cars, would be provided on the vehicle to bring it to a stop after the grip on the cable had been released.

This was a brand new idea in city transportation, but Hallidie got permission to try it, and Clay Street hill was selected for the experiment. At one place the hill rose three hundred feet in half a mile, a grade of more than twelve per cent. Besides Hallidie, the promoters included, among others, Henry L. Davis, sheriff of the city and county of San Francisco.

The chill gray dawn of August 1, 1873, saw a small group of people gathered on the brow of Clay Street hill to witness the daring demonstration of Andrew Hallidie's invention. One good look down the steep slope into the cold waters of the bay convinced the appointed "gripman" that he had not been cut out for the rôle of hero—or martyr. He resigned then and there. Hallidie promptly rose to the occasion. Taking the grip himself, he ran the car down the hill and brought it up again.

The *Daily Bulletin* was highly enthusiastic over the experiment. According to its report:

At five o'clock this morning the first car on the Clay Street Railroad was sent down the hill and back again by means of the wire rope. It was a platform car, or dummy, loaded with men and boys. No difficulty was experienced in stopping it at any point desired. The success of the experiment was greater than the projectors anticipated. This evening between five and six o'clock a passeger car will be attached to the dummy and put on the road, but regular travel will not be attempted at present.

Cable grip-car and trailer on Clay Street, San Francisco, in 1873

Hallidie had, in fact, been a little hurried toward the end of the construction period, and the trial trip was made on August 1 only because a car had to be run from one end to the other of the line on that day in order to comply with the terms of the charter. All went so well, however, that regular service was soon started.

San Francisco's "big four" lived on the top of fashionable Nob Hill in those days: the quiet dreamer, Leland Stanford; the energetic builder, Charles Crocker; the long-headed lawyer, Mark Hopkins; and the shrewd financier, Collis P. Huntington. After having built the Central Pacific Railroad, and obtained a virtual monopoly on railroading in California, they

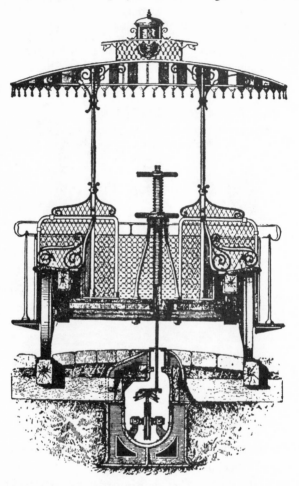

Andrew Hallidie's arrangement of conduit, cable, and grip

became interested in the business of providing local transportation.

On June 14, 1876, a franchise was granted to the "big four" for a cable line on California Street. Henry Root, the engineer, estimated the cost of building the road at $350,000. On hearing this estimate Mark Hopkins said emphatically that it was too much money ever to get back in five-cent fares. Governor Stanford, however, paid no attention to Hopkins' pessimism and went right ahead with the construction of the line. Before long the cars were scurrying up and down between the top of Nob Hill and the Embarcadero. Property values doubled

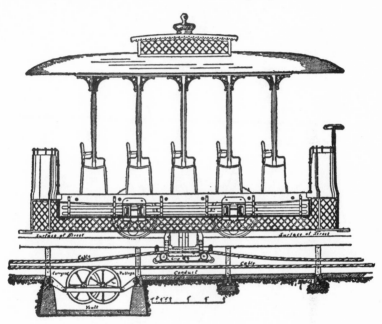

Relation of cable, carrying sheaves, and grip

overnight—the beginning of a real-estate boom that lasted for years.

The track o_ the first cable line consisted of two horse-car rails supported by cast-iron yokes five feet apart, connected to each other by wooden stringers and boards, forming a conduit twelve inches deep, in which the cable ran, supported on rollers at every third yoke. The yokes curved in to partially close the top of the tube and carried two steel bars parallel to the rails, forming a three-quarter-inch slot through which passed the "grip." Later cable roads did not differ materially from this original design.

At the power-station the cables ran over two fifteen-foot wheels on which they made several turns. After running over these drive wheels and before returning to the conduit, each

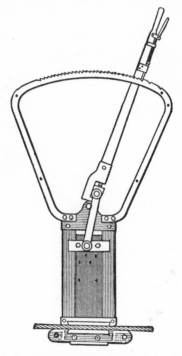

Typical grip used in cable-car operation

cable passed over a large pulley on a movable carriage which ran on a track about one hundred feet long. The carriage was fastened to a heavy counter-weight, and served to take up or let out the slack in the cable, which varied with the number of cars taking power at one time.

The steel cables used for these railways were of one and one-half to one and three-quarter-inch diameter, usually made with six strands of nineteen wires each, with a hemp core to give greater flexibility. The gripping mechanism, a vital part of the system, consisted of grooved steel bars pressed together by means of levers, operated by the "gripman" in the car above.

San Francisco was the first city in the world to have a cable railway, but it was Chicago that gave this form of transportation its greatest impetus. The far-flung system of the Chicago City Railway, which commenced operation in 1882, was the sensation of the day. Horse-car managers from all over the country came to inspect it and went home to tell what they had seen.

At first there was violent opposition to the plan of building cable railways in Chicago. A flood of protests came from State Street property-owners who said their business would be ruined. Aldermen objected because they thought the horse-car drivers would rise in revolt against the innovation. Others took up the cry that cable-car operation would "throw a lot of men out of work." It was also feared that cars running at the terrific rate of speed which was forecast, would kill and maim hundreds of people and frighten the wits out of the horses on the street.

Vociferous though the opposition was, the company found a supporter in Mayor Carter H. Harrison. After an enabling ordinance had passed the City Council, which it did with far less opposition than had been predicted, Mayor Harrison quickly signed it.

Innumerable difficulties hampered the construction efforts. The greater part of the work was done during the fall and winter months when rain and snow made conditions extremely difficult. Then, too, some sections of State Street had never been brought to grade. North of Twelfth Street, a fill to a depth of three feet was necessary. South of that point a foot and a half had to be removed. Another difficulty was encountered in attempting to "find bottom." Originally the site of the city had been a swamp, so it was not surprising that the workmen excavating for the cable line encountered some bogs which were found to be deeper than they anticipated. Load after load of stone was thrown into sloughs of this kind, seemingly without accomplishing any result in the direction of filling them.

In the construction of the first four miles of double track, 1,500 men and 200 teams were employed for over four

HENRY KOENKER

North Chicago Street Railroad Co.

———

Admit Bearer and Ladies,

TO OPENING OF THE CABLE LINE.

Mar. 26. 1888.

Chicago Pictorial Society

Invitation to attend the opening of cable-car service in Chicago

months; more than 10 million pounds of iron and steel were used; 50,000 wagon-loads of stone, sand, and gravel; 44,000 barrels of cement, and 300,000 feet of timber. The cost of that first stretch was $100,000 per mile of single track—big money in those days. Later construction was done for somewhat less.

The first section of the cable railway, from Madison Street to Twenty-first Street, was completed early in 1882. Its opening was a great event and brought out one of the city's largest crowds. The company sent invitations to the mayor, the aldermen, and many prominent citizens to attend the ceremony. People packed both sides of the street and waited for hours to see the first car go by.

Promptly at 2 P.M. on January 22 the start was made. While bands played and 300,000 spectators cheered, a train of ten trail-cars drawn by a single grip-car made the run from Madison Street to Twenty-first Street. Some two hundred feet in advance of this train a solitary grip-car went ahead as a pilot. According to the Chicago *Tribune:*

> The cars were covered with flags and banners, and in spite of the general prediction that they would jump off the track, it was agreed universally that they were the airiest and most graceful vehicles of the sort ever seen in Chicago or anywhere else.

According to an enthusiastic member of the crowd which rode the first train:

> The enterprise which had for months been the sole thought of the company, and which had provoked the criticism of every citizen, was at last proved to be a brilliant success. Thousands of people witnessed the trial trip and applauded the work. It was pronounced at the time the most gigantic undertaking ever attempted by any street-railway company. So it was, and it marked an era of wonderful improvement in the construction and operation of street-railways in Chicago.

The successful start of the State Street line gave encouragement to the building of similar lines in other parts of the city. By March, 1894, there were eighty-six miles of cable tracks and 469 grip-cars in the city. Roughly speaking, the ratio of trail-cars to grip-cars was two to one, for the average cable train consisted of one grip-car and two trailers. The total number of trailers, however, was more nearly four times as large as the number of grip-cars, for there were trailers of both the open and closed type. The open cars made their first appearance with spring weather and reigned supreme until the chill winds of winter forced their abdication in favor of the warmer, closed type of trailer.

Grip-cars ranged from twelve to thirty-three feet in length, with four or eight wheels. The smaller type cost approximately $1,000 each. A thirty-three foot, eight-wheel grip-car cost about $2,000. Seating capacities of the cars varied from twenty to thirty-eight. The speed ranged from six to eight miles an hour in business districts and twelve to fourteen miles an hour in residential districts.

The Chicago City Railway's favorite type of grip-car was a single-truck vehicle sixteen feet long, six feet wide, and ten feet high, with reversible seats for twenty passengers

H. H. Windsor, secretary of the company, said:

The wheels of this car, as of all cable-cars operated by this company, are guarded with wooden fenders coming to a point at each end of the car, the lower edge being lined with strips of rubber. These fenders are suspended from the running gear so as to barely clear the street surface, rendering it impossible for anyone to get beneath the wheels. The determined attempt of an insane lady, who one night threw herself directly across the track of a cable train approaching at full speed and only a few feet distant, was frustrated and the would-be victim pushed uninjured to one side.

Strong headlights, thirteen inches in diameter, are carried on the front platform of the grip-cars at night, and illuminate the track for a long distance. These bright lights do not frighten horses, nor does the rapid moving of the cable-cars. When the cable system was proposed the objection was raised by some that the absence of animals in connection with the rapid motion of the cars would cause great annoyance, by the horses in the street becoming frightened. Nothing could have been farther from the truth or fact, for horses do not seem to notice the change, and pay no more attention to a cable train than to the cars drawn by horses.

The cost of trailers ranged from around $850 for the open type to about $1,250 for the closed type. The latter were from twenty-two to thirty-two feet over all with seating capacities varying from forty to fifty. The open cars were, in general, slightly longer and had a greater average seating capacity. Closed trailers were heated by stoves, and gas lights furnished illumination at night.

Eleven power-plants in various parts of the city supplied

Waiting for the grip-car at the foot of Clay Street Hill, San Francisco. Andrew Hallidie sits in the front seat wearing a stovepipe hat.

The Market Street Railway continues to operate cable-cars on the original Clay Street route.

"Riding on the grip"—an early three-car cable railway train
in Chicago.

Grip-car and trailer operated on the Madison Street line at Chicago.

Three-car cable train at Washington, D. C., with passengers hanging on by their eyelashes, shows how these lines handled heavy traffic.

Open grip-car, with seats running lengthwise, and closed trailer at Seattle in 1888.

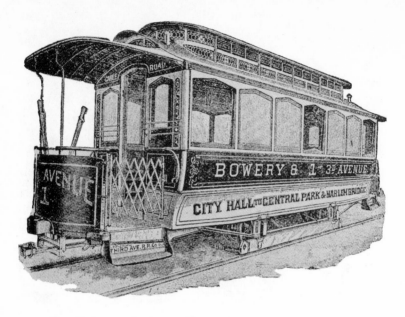

New York type of grip-car with operating levers on the platform.

Massive and intricate machinery in a cable-railway power station.

power for the cable trains. Huge steam-engines drove the wheels over which the cables passed. The wire itself was of one and five-sixteenths inch diameter and was supposed to have a life of 60,000 miles. For a time every night the operation was stopped so that the cable could be inspected for incipient breaks.

Among the advantages of the cable system, according to Mr. Windsor, was its contribution to cleanliness and health. "The value," he pointed out, "of removing from a street the voidings of two or three thousand horses is a matter not to be lightly estimated in point of health; while the constant clatter of hoofs on the pavement is supplanted by the quiet gliding of a train, scarcely audible from the sidewalk."

Another advantage was

its immediate and lasting effect upon the value of real estate. Within six months after the conversion of this company's lines from horse to cable power, property along those lines rose in value from 30 to 100 per cent, and on adjoining and contiguous streets in amounts proportionate to its distance from the cable lines. So well established is this fact, that the mere announcement that this company was considering the construction of a cable line on any street in the city, would be sufficient to put values up at once. One of Chicago's earliest, most successful and best-known financiers said, "Only let me know six weeks in advance where the City Railway intend building a cable line, and I will make an independent fortune every time." The enhanced value of property in the South Division of Chicago due wholly to the construction and operation of cable lines will not fall short of $15,000,000.

The cable-cars proved their prowess in winter. They were excellent snow fighters. On more than one occasion when all the steam railroads entering the city of Chicago were tied up for hours by a heavy snowfall, the cable-cars were running as usual and their tracks afforded the only path of travel for pedestrians and teams. It is said, in fact, that the City Railway never lost a single trip from snow, frost, or ice upon the track.

Compared with the horse-cars the cable-cars were very

economical. The Kansas City Cable Company had net earnings of 30 per cent for the first year of operation. In Chicago,
according to Charles B. Homes, superintendent of the City
Railway, "Twenty-five cents a mile for horses—half of that
for cable-cars—of course interest on a heavy investment but
big profits after that."

The investment was, indeed, heavy. The cost of cable construction in San Francisco with a tube thirty inches deep is
said to have been about $50,000 per mile of double track.
These figures were greatly exceeded in later construction. In
Washington, in the 1890's track construction cost about
$125,000 for each mile of double track line, the cables $3,500,
cars about $30,000, power-station equipment $25,000, or a
total of $183,500 per mile of double track, exclusive of land,
buildings, and general expense.

Cable-car operation was no child's play. The machinery
required to keep miles of cable running smoothly over the
rollers under the pavement was vast and complicated. The
proper operation of the grip was extremely difficult. A "gripman" had to be of strong physique, well trained and careful
to follow instructions. He needed plenty of muscle and skill
to manipulate his grip lever so that the car would not start
too suddenly. This was particularly true when the cable was
new and had not worn to a smooth surface. He had to know
his line. There were many places, such as crossings and
switches, where the cable had to be released and grasped again
at exactly the right time. As the life of the cable was adversely
affected by sharp horizontal bends, the designers, wherever
possible, passed it over large grooved wheels, ten to twelve
feet in diameter, instead of many smaller pulleys, to carry it
around curves. When this was done the cable had to be released and picked up again at the proper place, the car being
carried by its momentum in the interval. This was accomplished by having the car approach the curve at maximum

speed, keeping the grip attached up to the last possible moment, and then coasting around the curve.

If anything got in the way of the car as it was coasting, the gripman had a choice of two alternatives. He could either let the car knock the obstacle out of the way, or he could stop the car in the dead area on the curve. If he followed the latter course it then became necessary for all the passengers to get off and help push the car around until the cable could again be engaged. The number of accidents resulting from this method of negotiating curves was considerable, and inspired the name "Dead Man's Curve" for at least one location on almost every cable road.

Sometimes a loose strand of the cable would become wrapped around the grip of a car so that the grip would not release. Then the car just kept on going. The spectacle of a car dashing unchecked along the street at a speed of eleven or twelve miles an hour was awe-inspiring. The car could be halted only when the conductor jumped to the pavement, found one of the infrequent telephones of those days, and called the power-station to stop the cable. Episodes of this sort were rare, of course, as very careful attention was paid to the condition of the cable.

This attention required skilled men. Each cable was run slowly through an inspection pit in the power-stations every night. The engines were stopped and repairs made when needed. Sometimes individual wires in the strands would break and be bent back by the cable sliding through the grips. One of the cardinal sins for a "gripman" was to open his grip while going down hill because the car, running faster than the cable, would bend forward these broken wires and cause serious trouble. When the cable was badly damaged, a delay of two or three hours while repairs were being made was not unusual.

Small boys sometimes added to the headaches of the cable-railway management by hitching their express wagons to the cable. This was done by tying a rope to the handle of the wagon, finding a spot where the cable passed over a roller, and allowing the rope to dangle down through the slot until it became wrapped around the cable as the latter came into contact with the roller. Then off would go the express wagon and the boys would have an exciting ride until they met a policeman. If the policeman appeared suddenly and unexpect-

Splicing the cable after a break

edly the boys jumped off and disappeared, leaving the wagon to travel down the street by itself. If there was time enough the boys would cut the rope free from the wagon and escape with the latter intact. Cutting the rope was a more satisfactory procedure so far as the boys were concerned, but was not so good from the standpoint of the railway company. When the rope was cut and left wrapped around the cable, the man on duty at the power-house had to shut down operation and untangle the rope when that part of the cable approached the machinery.

Philadelphia joined the ranks of cities with cable railways in the early part of 1883 and other cities soon followed, among

them being New York, St. Louis, Oakland, Denver, Washington, Kansas City, Cleveland, Providence, Seattle, and Baltimore.

In New York, as in Chicago, heated argument raged over
the desirability of installing cable railways. A certain Lawson
N. Fuller appeared before the Cable Railway Commissioners
in the spring of 1885 to urge the granting of a franchise for a
line on Broadway. In this he claimed to be representing a
large number of uptown property owners.

The elevated roads were built [he said], notwithstanding the many
and strenuous objections urged at the time. Now they carry in a year
500,000,000 passengers—so many, in fact, that people are huddled
together like sheep in a cattle train, and often are obliged to stand
during the entire trip. We were told that the value of property along
the route would be destroyed, yet it has increased more than $150,-
000,000. The first rides I took in public conveyances in this city were
in the Knickerbocker stages. I had to hold on to a strap and stand up
all the way down town, and I have been holding on to a strap ever
since. The city is constantly and rapidly growing, and the facilities
for travel are wholly inadequate. I have counted eighty passengers
in one car going from the Astor House to 155th Street. The lawyers
appearing here in opposition to the proposed cable road are nearly
all employed by the horse railroads. The grant of a surface road in
Broadway should compel the company to carry passengers from one
end of the island to the other for five cents, and give transfers to
all parts of the city. The Sharp people want the franchise for a road
in Broadway, and only propose to carry passengers to Fifty-ninth
Street.

Some of the cable systems in other cities were almost as
extensive as that of Chicago. For example, St. Louis had some
fifty-five miles of cable railway; Denver had forty-four miles.
The cable power-house at Denver was especially notable because it operated a greater length of cable than any other
single power-house in the country. Six cables ran from it,
aggregating nearly thirty-four miles. One individual cable was
seven miles long. By 1890 there were about 500 miles of cable-
railway track in the United States and some 5,000 cars. Altogether these lines carried about 400 million passengers a

year. The scope of cable operations increased somewhat in the years immediately following and then began to decline as electricity came to the fore. At no time, however, were there cable systems in more than fifteen or sixteen cities in the United States. Some cable lines were built in other countries, but in the main, the cable-operated street-railway was an American institution.

A considerable part of the cable construction in Kansas City, New York, and Washington was done by Edmund Saxton, a contractor specializing in that work. He was an unusual man, cultured, capable, and honest, an eccentric old bachelor who did his work thoroughly and economically. Many stories are told of him. He was a great student, and had a booklet of four-place logarithms which he always carried in his pocket. This he could use as quickly as a modern engineer uses a slide rule. He would order seven suits of clothes from the same piece of goods and seven pairs of shoes exactly alike, a separate one for each day in the week. Once he gave a party to some of his friends at his tool yard. When the guests arrived he showed them an impromptu rifle range he had prepared, with a number of 22-caliber rifles. On a high board fence were hung a number of cheap watches. He told his guests that anyone who could hit a watch could have it. The watches were his sole recovery from an investment in a watch factory. His eccentricities furnished much amusement for his friends, but it no way lessened their admiration for the quality of his work which was generally recognized as being exceptionally high.

To have cable-railway lines was a real asset to a city in the 1880's. As one Kansas City newspaper expressed it, "The value of their services in the development, expansion and upbuilding of the city is universally recognized. They attract the admiring attention of visitors and sojourners. They are the pride of the citizens."

Riding on the cable-cars was popular with the public. A contemporary comment was:

The swiftly moving cars enable the tired worker to reach his home in one-half the time formerly consumed by the fastest horse-cars. In the morning the business man finds it very convenient to be able to linger at the breakfast table from a quarter to half an hour longer than before, and still by means of the cable reach his office on time. Its unlimited power and tireless energy make possible the operation of cars of generous size affording ample seating capacity and better light and ventilation. On every warm summer evening the open cars are crowded with people riding solely to enjoy the cool and refreshing breeze always created by their rapid motion.

The wealthy owner of the finest equipage is glad to let his handsome horses rest in their stalls while he indulges in the pleasures of a "ride on the grip." The choice seats especially sought for by the ladies are the front seats of the grip-car, for which there is always a bold but good-natured scramble. Sedate dames, dignified and fat old gentlemen, society belles and spruce young men all join in the rush for these favored locations. In the morning these same seats are in equal demand for nurses taking the children out for their usual morning airing, until such a load would often lead a stranger to believe that some kind soul had chartered the train for an orphan asylum.

A morning ride on a cable-car is as pleasant and invigorating as can be imagined, and when the warm winds of summer have given place to snow and cold, there are still a large number who religiously occupy their favored seats on the grip-car and, well wrapped, take a health-giving constitutional on their way to business every morning.

Cable railways were well adapted to handling "swamping loads" on special occasions as they had vast resources of power. At Washington, D. C., the Washington & Georgetown Railroad underwent a severe test of its capabilities less than a month after operation began. This happened when the Grand Army of the Republic held a convention there in August, 1892. On one day during this convention the railway carried 170,000 passengers, nearly four times the number on an ordinary day. The high mark set at that time was not attained again until ten years later when the Grand Army came back to Washington for another convention. By that time, however, the cable lines had been electrified.

This electrification was the outcome of a bad fire which completely destroyed the company's principal power-station on the night of September 30, 1897. Three cables were operated from this station, one running to the Navy Yard, about nine miles long, and two other shorter ones. Beginning just before midnight the fire completely gutted the six-story building in which the cable machinery was located and destroyed the company's general offices and car-repair shops as well as the power-plant. The cars, of course, were left stranded all along the fifteen miles of track operated from this plant.

Heroic measures were adopted to meet the situation. There was only one possible way to maintain service. That was to borrow animals and operate with horse power. Railway executives spent the entire night begging and borrowing horses, mules, and harnesses enough to pull the vehicles. Practically every Washington business which employed any considerable number of horses turned over its stock to the railway for the time being. Wiffle trees were hurriedly chained to the small iron bumpers with which the cars were equipped. But at six o'clock the following morning the first car pulled out on its regular schedule. While the ruins of the power-station were still smoking the directors of the company met and decided to electrify the lines.

Similar decisions were being made in other cities. Philadelphia had abandoned cable operation in 1895. So had Providence. Baltimore changed to electricity the same year as Washington. In St. Louis there was practically no cable operation after 1900. An investment of more than six million dollars had been made in the cable plant, of which about three million dollars was net loss when operation ceased. By 1902 the mileage of the cable railways in the country had dropped to half of what it was in 1890. By 1940 only one city continued to use Andrew Hallidie's invention. Appropriately enough it was San Francisco, where cable-cars were still bobbing up and down Clay Street, California Street and four other steep hills, just as they had in the 1870's.

One of the last cable lines to be abandoned was that on State Street, Chicago, which had started so auspiciously in 1882. On July 22, 1906, the Chicago *Tribune* stated:

State Street bade an unregretful farewell to the last cable train of the Chicago City Railway in the dark and early hours of the morning when good people were asleep. . . . Groaning and wobbling, as one decrepit and one having earned a long rest, the final cable train rattled and bumped around the loop for its last performance at 1:35 A.M. The train consisted of a battered grip-car and a twenty-year old trailer. Just behind it came the first State Street trolley-car, forerunner of a faster means of transportation.

4

CARS RUN BY LIGHTNING

The Story of the Early Electric Car

Pigs and cows held the greatest interest for nearly everyone attending the Toronto Agricultural Fair in the summer of 1885. They were a farming people. But James A. Gaboury's interest was elsewhere. His eye spied a car running back and forth on a short piece of railway track without any visible means of propulsion other than a small wire overhead; after spotting this car he had no interest in anything else.

"What have you got here?" he asked the young man who was collecting five cents a ride for trips on this railway.

"It's an electric car," the young man answered, "but I don't know anything about it except how to run it. The inventor is uptown at the hotel."

Now this Mr. Gaboury was an engineer and promoter who had been active in building street-railways in a number of cities in the southern part of the United States. These lines were operated by mule-power, as was customary in the South in those days, but Gaboury realized that animal traction had many limitations as a means of providing transportation service. He had heard about various experiments with electricity, but none of them had seemed to amount to much.

He was excited by the thought that the inventor of what appeared to be a practical means of electric propulsion was in town, and went straight up to the hotel to look for him. There he found Charles J. Van Depoele, a Belgian sculptor who had come over to the United States some years before and had since been experimenting with the use of electricity in various ways. Gaboury started to question him about the railway at the fair grounds.

"Can you haul people as cheaply with electricity as I can haul them with mules?" he asked.

"Much cheaper," Van Depoele replied.

"Then why haven't you put your electric cars in American cities, if they are so practical?"

"I have hawked the idea over the whole Middle West," said Van Depoele. "I have given demonstrations in several cities, but I can't get the financial backers of the street-car systems interested in the idea. They have all turned me down, and I've been forced to give demonstrations at exhibitions and fairs to earn enough money to get along."

"I'm the man you have been looking for, then," exclaimed Gaboury. "I own the controlling interest in the street-car system at Montgomery, Alabama, and I'll finance a trial of your idea there."

Van Depoele and Gaboury talked until long after midnight. Before the discussion ended it had been decided that Van Depoele should follow Gaboury to Montgomery as quickly as possible and work out a plan for electrifying the Capital City Street Railway.

When word of this scheme reached the minority stockholders of the railway some of them raised a howl about the "fool way" Gaboury was proposing to spend the company's money. He paid no attention to them, however, and went right ahead with the project. On November 2, 1885, the company asked the City Council for permission to operate its cars by electricity. Some delay followed, but the permission was granted early in January, 1886.

Construction work proceeded rapidly. By the end of March the system was practically complete, so Gaboury and Van Depoele made a trial trip in secret one night between 12 and 1 A.M. Everything went well. The car moved smoothly and quickly over the moonlit track. Trial trips continued for the next several weeks, always at night when most people were asleep, lest some slight mishap should undermine public confidence in the new venture.

Finally the company was ready to start regular service. On April 15, 1886, the Montgomery *Advertiser* announced:

> The Capital City Street Railway Company had the two new cars out and running by the electric motor system last night. One of the cars had never run before, but both went like a charm and made the round trip without a hitch or bobble.
>
> The electric street railway in Montgomery is a success. Both the cars on the Court Street line will be operated by the motor system today, beginning at ten o'clock this morning. Heretofore, no attempt has been made to run the cars on the "Lightning Route" in the daytime, as the running was only to test the system. Some unexpected delay has been met in getting the new machinery in working order. The company ordered a steel roller chain, and an iron chain was sent them. It gave way and the steel chain was ordered again, but did not come promptly on account of the flood and high water. But everything is now in running order, and the electric system will prove a great success in spite of all doubting.

The cars used for electric operation were essentially the same as those previously used for animal traction. Each had a single motor mounted on the front platform. Power was transmitted to the wheels by a steel chain. At first the electrical energy for the motor was obtained through a small two-wheel carriage, called a "monkey," running on an electrified overhead wire and connected to the car by a flexible cable. The wheels of the overhead carriage were arranged somewhat like a pair of pulleys in tandem. Endless trouble resulted from this arrangement, especially at turnouts where cars passed each other, as no satisfactory means could be devised to permit the "monkeys" to pass. Instead, the flexible cables had to be detached from the cars and the "monkeys" exchanged. In doing this the motormen often received severe shocks. Finally an arrangement was worked out whereby a pole extending upward from the roof of the car pressed a rolling contact against the underside of the wire.

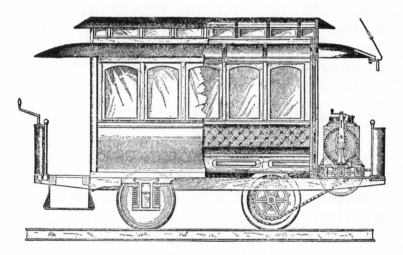

Platform-mounted motor with chain drive to axle

So successful was the Court Street line that electrification was gradually extended until the system had eighteen cars running on fifteen miles of track. Montgomery thus became the first place in the world to have a city-wide system of electric transportation, since none of the lines placed in operation in other cities up to that time had attempted to give a complete service.

Following the electrification, Montgomery experienced a great boom in general business. Real estate increased in value so rapidly "as to astonish the old natives who predicted the failure of the attempt to run the mule cars by lightning."

The success of the Capital City Street Railway at Montgomery was the outgrowth of a long period of experimentation. As far back as 1835, Thomas Davenport, a blacksmith of Brandon, Vermont, had operated a little car on a circular track by electrical energy obtained from batteries. A few years later at Edinburgh, Scotland, Robert Davidson designed an electric locomotive that is reported to have attained a speed of four miles an hour, about as fast as a person can walk. In 1847, Moses G. Farmer operated some small cars electrically at Dover, New Hampshire. In both of these instances the electrical energy was obtained from batteries. There was, in fact, no other reliable source of electrical energy in those days. But the cost of batteries was very high, while their operating efficiency was quite low, and these experiments produced no immediate, practical results. They serve to show, however, that electricity was beginning to assert itself as a factor in transportation even while the steam locomotive was still in its infancy.

Professor Charles G. Page, an official of the United States Patent Office, was another who tried to run an electric railway on battery power. In this way he managed, in 1851, to propel a small car over the track of the Baltimore & Ohio Railroad near Washington, D. C., at a speed of nineteen miles an hour. This was no small achievement in its way. Human beings had been accustomed for centuries to speeds of not more than six miles an hour in vehicles drawn by horses. The early steam locomotives did not exceed fifteen miles an hour. So here was an electric car setting a new pace. The destination of Professor Page on this trip was the famous dueling ground at Bladensburg, Maryland. That may have had an evil influence on his experiment, for when he got there he found that his batteries had almost destroyed themselves during the journey.

Between 1860 and 1870 experiments were made to produce electricity by some better means than batteries, but they were not very successful. Moses Farmer managed in 1867 to operate a small railway car on power generated by a crude dynamo. Then, in 1873, it was discovered that an electric motor could be made to generate electricity if rotated by mechanical means.

On the heels of the discovery came a new series of attempts to utilize electricity to drive a railway car. Dr. Werner Siemens built a short electric railway line that was one of the sensations of the Industrial Exposition at Berlin, Germany, in 1879. Later he built another, at Lichterfelde, that furnished regular commercial service, and then a somewhat longer line between Portrush and Bushmills in Northern Ireland.

Thomas A. Edison was among the first Americans to become interested in this new form of transportation, though his interest was primarily in the electrification of steam railroads. There was nothing wrong electrically with the railway he built at Menlo Park, New Jersey, in 1880. In fact, the locomotive ran so fast the passengers were nearly scared out of their wits. Soon after this Edison lost interest in electric railways and gave his attention principally to electric lighting.

By this time it was clear that electricity could be harnessed successfully as a motive-power for railway cars. What practical use to make of such an arrangement was another question. The longest distance over which electrical current could be transmitted was not yet very great, and it seemed likely that the largest field of usefulness of the electric railway would be in city transportation where no part of the line would be more than a few miles away from the power-generating station.

Most street-railway men, however, looked with suspicion on all attempts to employ electricity as a means of providing local transportation service. Horse-cars had proved themselves able to do a satisfactory and efficient job. There might be a field for the cable-car under special circumstances, they thought, but a majority of them were agreed that "no self-propelled car could meet the conditions to be found on American tramways."

"If you want to pull a car," said one of them, "you must put something in front to pull it."

At the same time there were some men of vision in the business, too. They recognized the difficulties, but thought they could be overcome. "I see in the recent subjugation of the subtle and hitherto illusive force of electricity to the needs of man," said President H. H. Littell at the American Street Railway Convention in 1883, "boundless possibilities for the world's three greatest requisites of advancement, heat, light, and motion."

Of all the problems faced by the early electric-railway builders the most troublesome was that of conveying electric current from the dynamo in the power-house to the motors of cars moving along the track. The easiest solution of this problem was the use of an electrified third-rail from which the cars could obtain power through a sliding contact of some sort. That was all right where the track was on private right-of-way, but it was no good in city streets where a charged third-rail might electrocute men and animals.

A dozen other solutions were put forward by an equal number of inventors before a really satisfactory plan was developed. To say how much each inventor contributed to the final solution would be impossible. Fights over alleged infringements of patents were frequent. Differences between the device of one man and that of another sometimes hinged on highly technical points.

Among the inventors who were active during this period were Edward M. Bentley and Walter H. Knight, who electrified the East Cleveland Street Railway in 1884, using a third rail in an underground conduit to supply current to the cars. This was the first commercial electric railway in the

Dr. Werner Siemens' electric railway at the Berlin Industrial
Exposition in 1878.

Electric locomotives drawing power from a third rail were used to
pull horse-cars on a line opened between Baltimore and Hampden
in 1885.

Charles Van Depoele's electric railway at the Toronto Exposition
in 1885.

Montgomery, Alabama, in 1886, was the first place in the world to
have a city-wide system of electric transportation.

Meriden, Connecticut, had an electric railway using a two-wire overhead from which was suspended a little carriage to furnish current to the car.

Franklin Street Hill, Richmond, Virginia, where a critical test was
made of Sprague's new electric-railway system.

Some of the twenty-two cars which Frank Sprague assembled in the outskirts of Richmond to demonstrate the feasibility of starting a large group at one time.

Start of electric-railway service at Asheville, North Carolina, in 1889.

Atlanta, Georgia, operated its first electric cars in 1890 amid such
pastoral surroundings as this.

Crowds attending Chicago Day at the World's Fair in 1893 imposed
a severe test on the city's new electric railway.

Early electric cars had open platforms which assured plenty of fresh air for the crew.

Cars of a slightly later period had platform windows to give the motorman some protection from wind and rain.

W. E. Wyckoff photo

Double-deck, open trail-car operated at Altoona, Pennsylvania, in 1893.

"Take the trolley to the park" was the slogan of many electric railways in the early 1900's.

United States, and was viewed with awe by everyone who saw it.

Said the Cleveland *Herald* when cars commenced to make regular runs:

It was amusing to watch the passengers who boarded the car. Some took the invention as a matter of course, while others, especially the ladies, evinced great curiosity. . . . An unexpected drawback is

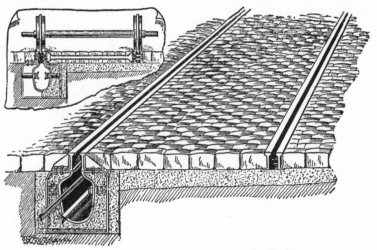

Early underground conduit system in Budapest

the fact that half the horses that pass the car are frightened by it. There is nothing unusual in the appearance of the car. . . . But even old plugs were frightened; and one passenger opined that the horses, jealous of loss of business, had combined to express their disapproval of the invention.

The East Cleveland line was successful after a fashion, but its operation was discontinued at the end of a year. Other cities were slow to take up the idea of underground conduit construction on account of the high cost. Then, too, there was the ever present danger from water, snow, or ice getting into the conduit and causing a short circuit. New York and Washington are the only two cities in the United States which ever had extensive street railway systems with power supplied by underground conduits.

Two years after the Cleveland experiment, Leo Daft, who had designed a fairly successful third-rail line at Baltimore in 1885, built a short electric line at Orange, New Jersey, using an entirely different method of supplying electricity to the car. For this line, and some others which he built later, he employed a system of two overhead wires and a little four-wheeled carriage connected to the car by a flexible cable. This carriage was called a "troller" on account of the way it was pulled along the wires, and from this, by corruption, the word "trolley" developed as a general term for electric streetcars obtaining power from overhead wires. The most serious criticism of the operation was the unreliable behavior of the little four-wheel carriage on the overhead wires. Every once in a while it would jump off the wires and come crashing down through the car roof, to the consternation of the passengers.

John C. Henry, of Kansas City, had a somewhat similar idea. He built an electric railway there with two overhead wires and a trolley carriage held in place on the wires by lateral pressure. When this enterprise went bankrupt creditors received eight cents on the dollar.

Still another inventor was thinking about the electric railway problem in those days—a young United States Navy officer, Frank J. Sprague. While in London in 1882, acting as secretary of a section of the Jury at the Sydenham Electrical Exhibition, he had occasion to ride frequently on the dingy, smoky Metropolitan District underground railway. This—the only passenger-carrying subway in the world at that time—was operated with steam-locomotives, as the "fireless engine" originally proposed had never materialized. In spite of all the company could do to ventilate the subway, its atmosphere was decidedly sulphurous and soot-laden. Once, when a passenger died a few hours after having taken a ride, a coroner's jury declared that his death, while due to natural causes, had been "accelerated by the suffocating atmosphere of the railway."

Sprague thought the solution of the problem lay in electrification, and for a while he toyed with the idea of resigning from the Navy to undertake this laudable task. He did not resign immediately, but electricity had so taken hold of his imagination that he could think of nothing else. A year later, he sent in his resignation and went to New York to enter Edison's employ as a technical assistant. Convinced that the use of electricity for power would rival or surpass that for lighting, he left Edison in 1884 and organized a company of his own, the Sprague Electric Railway & Motor Company.

Before long opportunity came knocking at his door. A group of promoters invited Sprague to equip the Union Passenger Railway at Richmond. Although the road was non-existent and the route was only provisionally determined, Sprague, who was but twenty-nine years old at the time, was fascinated at the thought of this new adventure, and was willing to chance the outcome.

The Richmond contract provided for a power-plant, a complete system of current supply, and an equipment of forty cars, each with two motors. These cars were to be operated on grades and curves presenting unusual difficulties. The work was to be completed in ninety days, with a payment to the Sprague Company of $110,000 if the job was done to the "satisfaction" of the promoters.

When Sprague went to Richmond for the first time to look over the situation, and saw the hill which the cars were supposed to climb on Franklin Street, he was aghast. That an electric car could climb so steep a grade without damage to the motors seemed extremely doubtful. Returning to New

York he proposed a plan for a motor-driven cable operated in a conduit below ground as an aid to cars climbing the hill. Sprague's partner, Edward Johnson, pithily suggested that, before resorting to this costly expedient, the thing to do was to find whether it was necessary. Maybe the car could get up the hill on its own power, even if it did overtax the motors.

Sprague went back to Richmond to make a test. By this time most of the track had been laid. With General Manager Burt and a picked crew, Sprague started a car out from the end of the line and headed for Franklin Street hill. It was election night and the hour was late, but the streets were filled with hilarious people.

Sprague himself was at the controller. After successfully pulling out of a sharp curve on a six per cent grade, the car arrived at the foot of the Franklin Street hill. Sprague turned to Burt as the hill loomed up before them and shook his head.

"We won't make it," he said.

"If you could pull the car out of that curve-grade combination we just passed," Burt replied, "you could climb the side of a house with it if the wheels would hold."

Up the hill they climbed, slowly but surely, until the top was reached and they turned the corner into City Hall Square. They stopped near a theater which had just let out, and the car was immediately surrounded by an inquisitive throng. The motors had been under severe strain, and were very hot. Moreover, Sprague had noticed a peculiar chug which betrayed the fact that one of the motors was short-circuited. There was no need to tell the curious crowd exactly what had happened, but some sort of explanation had to be given for not continuing to the end of the route. They waited while the spectators spent considerable time admiring the lighted car and wondering how it had managed to get up the hill, then Sprague remarked rather loudly to his assistant,

"I think there is some trouble with the circuits and I'd like you to get the instruments so we can make a check."

The assistant nodded his head in understanding and departed. Sprague turned out the lights and lay down on a seat until the crowd got tired of looking at the darkened car and dispersed. A little later the "instruments" arrived—a team of Missouri mules, and the car was pulled back to the shed from which it had started earlier in the evening.

After this try-out, the promoters clamored for regular operation to begin, but one difficulty after another kept cropping up. A good deal of trouble was experienced with the motors, which were mounted under the car and connected to the axles by gears. There was trouble with the trolley, too. Legend has it that no less than forty designs of trolleys were tried out at various times, for it seemed impossible to make the pole stay in continuous contact with the wire. One day it was suggested that the solution lay in a swivel mounting that would permit the pole to swing freely to follow the trolley wire on curves or wherever it was not immediately above the center of the track. Pat O'Shaughnessy, one of the company's mechanics, then devised a rope arrangement by which the pole could be readily replaced in case it did leave the wire, or could be reversed at the end of a trip, thus solving another problem.

By the latter part of January events had taken a fairly even tenor, and the line was opened for regular service on February 2, 1888. On the first day children were carried free, but thereafter everybody had to pay to ride. Gradually the equipment increased until there were thirty cars in operation, and later ten more were added for good measure. An old Negro, watching with bulging eyes one of the mule-less vehicles steadily climbing a long hill, cried out:

"Fo' Gawd, what am de white folks a-gwine do nex'? Fust dey freed de darkey, an' now dey freed de mule!"

During those days Sprague was living in a room over a

saloon close to the center of the line. One cold morning he awoke to find that a misty rain had fallen during the night and the trolley wire was festooned with icicles. Hurriedly he set out for the car-house at the end of the line to see what, if anything, was being done to get the cars going. As he turned the corner at the head of the famous Franklin Street hill, he looked down the street and saw a car coming slowly up the track. On top of it was Pat O'Shaughnessy with a big broom, swatting the trolley wire, from which the icicles were dropping in a silver shower as his blows sent shivers through the wire. Behind Pat came the other cars making their regular runs.

The Richmond system had its most severe test on a warm night in the early summer of 1888. Henry M. Whitney, president of the West End Street Railway of Boston, was in town. His company operated one of the largest horse-car systems in the world, having been created by the merger of several older systems. Soon after this merger Mr. Whitney had begun to look around for a better form of motive-power. Horses had served well enough when the railways were comparatively small units and the routes were not too long. The new system, however, had long routes and the care of its eight thousand horses was a tremendous problem. The desirability of some other form of motive-power was obvious, but it was not easy to find a suitable substitute. At first the management favored the adoption of the cable system which was attracting much attention in Chicago. Mr. Whitney, however, had heard about the progress being made by the electric railway and he determined to investigate this form of motive-power before reaching a decision. Accompanied by his general manager, Daniel F. Longstreet, he visited a number of cities which had electric street-cars and finally arrived at Richmond.

Both men were a good deal impressed with what they saw there, particularly with the ability of the electric cars to climb the steep grades existing on the system, but Mr. Longstreet was worried about what would happen if a lot of cars became concentrated on a short section of track, as might easily occur in actual operation. It seemed to him that the single small wire suspended over the center of the street could not possibly furnish enough electric power to move such a concentration of vehicles. This situation had not actually arisen up to that time at Richmond, but Sprague thought that it could be handled.

Without telling Mr. Whitney what he had in mind, he laid his plans. First he went to the engineer of the power-station and explained that a critical test was to be made. He told him to raise the steam pressure in the boiler, fasten down the safety valves and keep all the generators running at full speed regardless of what happened. Then, at the outer end of one route, he began to collect a group of cars as they finished their day's runs. By midnight he had concentrated twenty-two cars on a section of track where there would ordinarily be only three or four.

At last everything was ready. Sprague dashed over to the hotel, routed Mr. Whitney and Mr. Longstreet out of bed, and took them out to witness a demonstration of the ability of electric power to move this concentration of cars.

"If you can start all those cars at once, I'll be convinced," said Whitney.

"We can and we will," Sprague replied.

Anxiously he waved a lantern as a signal for the cars to start. One by one they moved out, each getting into motion as soon as the car ahead gave it clearance. As more and more cars got under way, the lights in them began to grow dim, and it appeared that the power supply would be inadequate, just as Mr. Longstreet had predicted. Then the lights began to grow brighter and the cars moved faster. Before long the whole group passed out of sight down the street and both

Mr. Whitney and Mr. Longstreet had to admit that Sprague's little copper wire could do the job.

Returning home, Mr. Whitney startled the staid citizens of Boston with the announcement that the West End Street Railway had abandoned the idea of cable operation and would electrify its lines. Historic Beacon Street was soon festooned with trolley wires. Flashing and sparking, the little electric cars went hurrying back and forth at a speed far above that of their predecessors, the horse-cars.

Oliver Wendell Holmes at the age of eighty was greatly thrilled by the sight.

Look here! [he exclaimed in *Over the Teacups*] There are crowds of people whirled through our streets on these new-fashioned cars, with their witch-broomsticks overhead—if they don't come from Salem they ought to!— and not more than one in a dozen of these fish-eyed bipeds thinks or cares a nickel's worth about the miracle which is wrought for their convenience. We ought to go down on our knees when one of these mighty caravans, car after car, spins by us, under the mystic impulse which seems to know not whether its train is loaded or empty.

Later he wrote a rollicking poem about them for the *Atlantic Monthly*, called "The Broomstick Train, or The Return of the Witches:"

> They came, of course, at their master's call,
> The witches, the broomsticks, the cats, and all;
> He led the hags to a railway train
> The horses were trying to drag in vain.
> "Now, then," says he, "you've had your fun,
> And here are the cars you've got to run.
> The driver may just unhitch his team,
> We don't want horses, we don't want steam;
> You may keep your old black cats to hug,
> But the loaded train you've got to lug."
>
> Since then on many a car you'll see
> A broomstick plain as plain can be;
> On every stick there's a witch astride—
> The string you see to her leg is tied.
> She will do a mischief if she can,

But the string is held by a careful man,
And whenever the evil-minded witch
Would cut some caper, he gives a twitch.
As for the hag, you can't see her,
But hark! You can hear her black cat's purr,
And now and then, as a car goes by,
You may catch a gleam from her wicked eye.
Often you've looked on a rushing train,
But just what moved it was not so plain.
It couldn't be those wires above,
For they could neither pull nor shove;
Where was the motor that made it go?
You couldn't guess, BUT NOW YOU KNOW!

Repercussions in the transportation world were no less marked than in the world of letters. Richmond had proved, even more conclusively than Montgomery, that the electric railway was practical. The fever spread with lightning rapidity. Within two years there were hundreds of electric cars in Minneapolis, St. Paul, Cleveland, St. Louis, Pittsburgh, Tacoma, and other cities, all operating under the plan Sprague devised at Richmond. The era of the trolley had begun.

5

RAILWAY ON STILTS

The Story of the Elevated Railway

An editorial in the New York *Herald* of Oct. 2, 1864, said:

Something more than street-cars and omnibuses is needed to supply the popular demand for city conveyance. The cars are quieter than the omnibuses, but much more crowded. People are packed into them like sardines in a box, with perspiration for oil. The seats being more than filled, the passengers are placed in rows down the middle, where they hang on by the straps, like smoked hams in a corner grocery. . . . It must be evident to everybody that neither the cars nor the omnibuses supply accommodations enough for the public, and that such accommodations as they do supply are not of the right sort.

New York was then more like a struggling provincial town than a great city. The northerly limit of development was Forty-second Street. Beyond that was only a dreary waste of unpaved and ungraded streets with a scattering of squatters' shanties. Even in the built-up area there were many unpaved streets where passengers struggled through the mud to reach the horse-cars and omnibuses. Women wore hoopskirts and a six-story building was a "sky-scraper."

Even so, the city had a serious transportation problem, accentuated by the long, narrow shape of the island of Manhattan. Traveling by horse-drawn vehicle from the downtown business district to the uptown residential district was a slow and time-consuming process. Many people preferred to live in Brooklyn or New Jersey, which could be reached by short ferry trips, rather than make the long trek to upper Manhattan. Obviously, something would have to be done, or the growth of the city would stop.

The most obvious solution of the problem was to build an underground railway similar to that which had been in successful operation in London for more than a year. When this was proposed, however, it encountered strong opposition that succeeded in preventing the state legislature from giving the necessary authorization.

Meanwhile Charles T. Harvey had devised a plan for an elevated railway supported by iron columns along the curb, with the trains pulled by cables operated by steam-engines located at various points along the route. He persuaded the 1866 legislature to pass an amendment to the railroad law of 1850 permitting ten or more persons to form a company to build a railroad to be operated "by means of a propelling rope or cable attached to stationary power." In the heat of the debate about the underground railway proposal this amendment to the railroad law passed almost unnoticed. Nevertheless it paved the way for New York's first rapid-transit line.

No sooner had the legislation been passed than Harvey organized the West Side & Yonkers Patent Railway Company. Its capital was five million dollars and it proposed to build a line fifteen miles long from the Battery via Greenwich Street and Ninth Avenue to Kingsbridge and Yonkers. The building of the main part of the line, however, was contingent on the receipt of official approval of an experimental section one-half mile long, extending northward in Greenwich Street from Battery Place to Cortlandt Street.

By the summer of 1867 Harvey had succeeded in raising $100,000 among his associates, and work commenced. The first column was placed early in October, and the line had been completed for a quarter of a mile by December. A trial run so pleased the directors of the company that they authorized the construction of the second quarter-mile of the experimental section. That was completed by April, and on the first of May the directors took their first ride on the "Patent Railway," as it was called. Great was their excitement when they found themselves moving at a speed of fifteen miles an hour over the elevated track, propelled by an engine out of sight or hearing.

This was folowed by a long series of demonstrations. The railway was inspected by a commission appointed by the governor. Then the governor, Reuben Fenton, himself came down from Albany to look it over. Mayor Hoffman and other officials of the city of New York inspected it. So did the Governor of Minnesota, and a deputation from the Common Council of Boston.

It seems that the official demonstration was made on July 3, 1868. No wide interest appears to have been aroused, however, and no formal ceremonies marked the event. Under an inconspicuous heading the New York *Times* the next day said:

> The trial trip upon the elevated road in Greenwich Street, having been postponed on Thursday on account of an accident to the machinery, came off yesterday at noon and was very satisfactory. The car ran easily from the Battery to Cortlandt Street, starting at the rate of five miles an hour and increasing to a speed of ten miles. The company does not pretend with its present machinery to run the cars faster than fifteen miles an hour, but during the next two months will make arrangements for much more rapid motion.
>
> The chief engineer and inventor expresses the opinion that there is no engineering difficulty in the way of having the railway completed to the Hudson River depot at Thirtieth Street during the present year. Then the passage from Wall Street can be made in fifteen minutes!

Financial and legal difficulties, however, proved more formidable than engineering difficulties. After the first half-mile section had received official approval, arrangements were made with a prominent banking firm for a loan of $750,000 for the construction of the rest of the line. The job had been about half completed when the panic which started on "Black Friday," September 26, 1869, resulted in the failure of the company's bankers.

Then, too, the "Patent Railway" found itself involved in a mess of law-suits which sought to prevent the construction of the remaining part of the line. Some of the litigation was rumored to have been inspired by the street-railway companies, which did not fancy having the elevated railway as a competitor. Some was started by owners of real-estate along the line who feared that the elevated would have a harmful effect on their property.

Despite the legal difficulties in which it was involved the company received an offer of a loan from other financial interests to complete the road and get it running. The new plan is said to have involved a period of inactivity during which the "Patent Railway" was to appear as a failure so that the value of its securities would drop to a point where the new financial interests could buy them in for a song. Harvey refused to have any part in this deal and was displaced as chief engineer when the new interests acquired the property.

Nothing was done about construction until the following summer, when the line was extended north to Thirtieth Street. Attempts to operate it by the cable method proved a failure, however, and once more the property relapsed into idleness. During the winter the company was reorganized as the New York Elevated Railway, and permission was obtained to use steam locomotives instead of cables to pull the trains.

But now a new danger threatened the elevated. William M. Tweed, who was then Commissioner of Public Works of the city of New York as well as a member of the state senate, decided to introduce a different type of rapid transit known

as the "Viaduct Plan." This was to be an elevated railway
supported by huge masonry arches in the middle of the blocks
instead of iron columns in the street.

> In the days of the Tweed Ring [said the New York *Herald* a few
> years later], the corruptionists went so far as to try to indict the
> Greenwich Street Elevated railroad as a nuisance: they boasted that
> they would not only tear down the road, but would fine and imprison
> the enterprising citizens who advanced money to try this important
> and now entirely successful experiment. Engineers and newspapers
> were hired to assert that the road would not stand; that it was
> dangerous to the lives of the passengers; that it would cause constant
> runaways of horses; that it would destroy business; and attempts
> were even made at one time to incite mob violence against it.

The men in control of the New York Elevated Railway
were taken completely by surprise when Tweed, having obtained a charter for the twenty-five-million-dollar New York
Railway Company to operate under the Viaduct Plan introduced a bill in the senate authorizing him as Commissioner of
Public Works, to remove the Ninth Avenue elevated railway
within ninety days. At this point Charles Harvey came to the
rescue even though he no longer had any official connection
with the company. He went to Albany and talked with an old
friend of his, Erastus Corning, who had considerable influence
with the members of the legislature from the up-state coun-
ties. Though Tweed's bill passed the senate by a substantial
majority, it was decisively beaten in the house of assembly,
and the New York Elevated Railway continued to operate.
Nothing more was done about the Viaduct Plan as Tweed's
downfall came only a short time after the inception of the
plan.

Scarcely had the Viaduct Plan passed into oblivion when
the New York Elevated Railway found itself facing a new
rival. This was the proposal of a Dr. Rufus H. Gilbert. His
plan provided for tubular iron roadways suspended above
the streets by Gothic arches springing from the curb lines.

Cars were to be propelled through the tubular passageways by atmospheric or other power. A franchise was obtained from the legislature, but the financial panic of 1873 prevented the company from obtaining the capital needed to build the line. Some years later the Gilbert company was reorganized as the Metropolitan Elevated Railway and built the Sixth

Typical elevated-railway station in New York

Avenue line. This, however, followed conventional design instead of the Gilbert plan.

Threats of competition did not halt the expansion of operations by the New York Elevated Railway. By 1876 the company was proudly advertising that it ran forty trains a day from the Battery to 59th Street. The regular fare was ten cents, but a special rate of five cents was in effect between 5:30 and 7:30 in the morning, and between 5 and 7 o'clock in the evening. As the hour approached when the lower rate went into effect long lines of waiting people used to gather on the stairs leading up to the elevated stations. Then, when the price card was turned around at the ticket window, they surged forward with great pushing and shoving.

"It got so bad," according to A. L. Merritt, for many years general superintendent of the operating company, "that we couldn't close the gates on the cars. So I organized a squad of special officers—forerunners of the subway guards of a later day. I put them at the stations where the biggest pushes were, and gave them uniforms and helmets like those of the cops."

Elevated railways, in those days, were more popular with the people who used them than they were with the property owners. Whenever a new line was proposed, or an extension to an old one, strenuous opposition arose. The "horrors" of elevated railroad operation were eloquently described by the "antis." Horses would be frightened and run away. Fires would be started by sparks from the locomotives. People in the streets would be burned by hot ashes dropped down upon their heads. So to protect pedestrians from this danger a bill was introduced in the New York Legislature in 1885 requiring elevated railroads to place iron pans under the structures. With bored patience an officer of the Manhattan Railway Company commented:

It is the same bill that was presented last winter. It was sent to the Board of Railroad Commissioners for an opinion as to its practicability, with naturally an unfavorable result. Any sensible man would see at once that such a plan could not be carried into effect. In the first place the pans would seriously obstruct light, but in addition to that they would be practically useless, for they would be filled with snow and ice in the winter months, and in the summer every rain storm would overflow them. The bill is an old stand-by.

Boston began to think about building an elevated railway in 1879. Two groups of men petitioned the legislature in that year for acts of incorporation for elevated railways. But the committee to which the subject was referred did not think

An ingenious plan that never materialized—Swett's proposed elevated railway for Broadway, New York, 1853.

Trial ride on Charles T. Harvey's experimental elevated railway in Greenwich Street, New York, in 1858.

Boxlike bodies were built around the early locomotives for the "El"
lines to prevent scaring the horses in the street below.

Number 173, typical of the steam dummy that hauled the trains on
New York's Sixth Avenue "El."

In the 1880's Leo Daft proposed to run the elevated railways with
electric locomotives of this type instead of steam dummies.

Bicycle car used on the Ninth Avenue elevated line of the Interborough in 1897 had snubs on the floor to hold bicycles.

The high curve at 110th Street on the Ninth Avenue line was "Where you heard the angels sing."

A busy intersection of elevated-railway lines in Chicago's Loop district.

that the elevated lines in New York had yet demonstrated their safety and durability. Besides, stated the committee's report, "no complaints have been made that the citizens of the City of Boston and vicinity are not provided with reasonable facilities for getting to and from their places of business. ... The street-railway facilities of the City of Boston are exceedingly good, and no complaints were made against any of the companies for not performing their full duty to the public."

Five years after the legislature rejected the plans of the two groups just mentioned, it passed an act incorporating the Meigs Elevated Railway Company, which was somewhat vaguely authorized to build a line that would connect "some point in the city of Cambridge and Bowdoin Square in the City of Boston."

Joe V. Meigs was the designer of an extraordinary kind of rapid-transit railway, in which the wheels of the cars were tilted at an angle of forty-five degrees and rolled on similarly tilted rails at the bottom of a single truss supported on a row of iron columns. To give sidewise stability the trucks of the cars also had horizontal wheels which rolled on a rail at the top of the truss. These horizontal wheels were also the driving wheels of the steam locomotive.

A full-size, working model of this odd design for an elevated railway was built at East Cambridge. It received the approval of General George Stark, an eminent engineer appointed by the State Railroad Commission to investigate it. The law authorizing the organization of the company permitted it to "lease, purchase, own, and operate any lines of street or elevated railway which may be or become tributary to its lines." In spite of this great grant of privileges, the organizers of the company were unable to raise enough money to build more than the short experimental line. Not until 1898 was the construction of a real rapid-transit line started in Boston. Then it was under the auspices of the newly formed Boston Elevated Railway.

Chicago had elevated railway service before Boston. Preparations were being made for the World's Columbian Exposition in Jackson Park when the first train ran over the new "high-line" of the South Side Elevated Railroad on June 6, 1892. As on the "L" lines in New York the trains were hauled by small steam locomotives. In 1895 the Metropolitan West Side Elevated Railroad began operation in Chicago with trains composed of an electric motor-car and several trailers. Generaly speaking the electric equipment was similar to that in use at that time on electrified street-railways except that a third rail was used instead of an overhead wire to furnish the current.

Not to be outdone by its neighbor, the South Side company decided to electrify its line. The plan was to use electric locomotives to haul the same cars that were being hauled by the steam locomotives. In the course of carrying out this plan an opinion was sought from Frank Sprague, of Richmond fame, concerning certain aspects of the electric generating plant.

Sprague was working principally on the development of electric elevators at this time. For this purpose it was necessary to have a small control mechanism on the elevator car which would operate a main control adjacent to the electric motor at the bottom of the elevator shaft. One day, from curiosity, he connected the main controls of a number of motors to a single small control mechanism and found that there was no difficulty in getting them to operate in unison. This was an interesting experiment but seemed of no great practical value at the moment. Then, suddenly, Sprague had an inspiration. Why not, he thought, equip a train of cars with a motor and main control on each car and operate them all from a single master control at the front end of the train?

After settling the relatively unimportant power-plant matter on which he had been consulted, he made the startling suggestion to the South Side management that the idea of electric locomotives be abandoned, and instead that the cars be individually equipped with motors and control with a master control line running the whole way from end to end of the train.

This proposal seemed rather ridiculous to men experienced in the operation of elevated railways. As General Manager Hopkins of the South Side company explained the situation to B. E. Sunny of the General Electric Company, who hoped to get the contract for electrical equipment.

"Some fellow from New York with a military title, who has put in some electrically operated system of dumb-waiters in a hotel there, has proposed to apply the same principle to this operation of elevated trains."

"Who is he?" asked Sunny.

"I don't know his name, but I'll find out," replied Hopkins and both had a good laugh over the idea.

The next morning Hopkins telephoned to Sunny that the man with the novel idea was Lieutenant Frank J. Sprague, formerly of the United States Navy. Then it wasn't so hilariously funny. They realized that Sprague was well known for his successful electrification of the Union Passenger Railway at Richmond, Virginia, and Sunny saw a good chance of losing the expected contract.

But Sprague had no organization, no shop, no workmen—just an idea. Not unnaturally the Board of Directors of the South Side company asked what guarantee he could give for carrying out a scheme that had never been tried before, as compared with the guarantees of the established manufacturing companies making the original tenders.

"No guarantee," Sprague said, "except my past reputation and my prophecy that, if I get the contract, the manufacturing companies will be bidding on a subcontract for the motors within a fortnight."

That, in fact, was exactly how it worked out. The directors decided to try Sprague's method of "multiple-unit control," and the General Electric Company got a contract for 240 motors, two each for 120 cars. On July 25, a successful trial run was made with a six-car train at Schenectady. By a curious coincidence this date happened to be Sprague's birthday and the fiftieth anniversary of Moses Farmer's successful demonstration of the electric operation of a rail-car at Dover, New Hampshire, in 1847.

When the time came for a test on the elevated structure at Chicago, however, disaster threatened the whole undertaking. On the very first trip the control line became short-circuited and the six-car train was stalled in the heart of the downtown district, blocking the movement of all other trains. There was only one thing to do. The control line was cut, making useless the motors on all but the first car, and the train was moved away with the two motors of the first car carrying the entire load of the six cars.

Difficulties arose again when a severe sleet storm covered the third rail and interfered with the supply of current to some of the cars of the train. This was overcome by running a power line to connect the contacts of the several cars so that power was available to all as long as one was properly in touch with the third rail. Under this plan operation continued successfully throughout the winter. By the spring of 1898 the whole 120 cars were in operation. The stock of the South Side company trebled in value.

Brooklyn and Boston adopted the "multiple-unit" system for their elevated trains, and finaly New York followed suit. Eventually the system came into universal use for the operation of trains on elevated railways, subways, and electrified suburban railroads.

Construction of the famous elevated Loop—from which the downtown section of Chicago got its name—was completed in 1897. The business grew until each morning and evening during the space of a single hour, "L" trains entering and leaving the Loop literally formed a moving platform of cars that circled the downtown business district.

A few elevated railways were built outside of the United States, notably in Liverpool and Hamburg, but in the main the elevated railway, like the cable railway, remained a distinctively American institution.

As time passed, the original opposition to underground railways disappeared. Public opinion, in fact, completely reversed itself and became so opposed to elevated railways that some of them were actually taken down in New York and Boston. For more than thirty years, however, they reigned supreme as the only real means of rapid transit in American cities.

6

MILLIONS MOVE UNDERGROUND

The Story of Subways

When Jonas Hanway raised the first umbrella in England the people hooted and called him a "blooming Frenchman." But they quickly changed their tune when they found out how useful an umbrella could be. And when Charles Pearson suggested building an underground railway in London the people called him the fool who would undermine the most important buildings in the city. But, again, it did not take them long to change their tune. No sooner had the line started running than it became so popular that the trains could scarcely accommodate the great number of persons who wanted to ride.

The coming of the steam railroads to London in 1836 started the chain of events that led to the building of a subway. The city then had a population of more than two million, and its narrow streets were terribly congested. The railroads brought to the metropolis a great crowd of additional people from the provincial towns. It is estimated that these visitors numbered nearly eight hundred thousand a day. At noontime the sidewalks were almost impassable while the roadways were choked with thousands of horse-drawn omnibuses and drays of every description. It took longer to cross the city than to make a journey to Brighton or Oxford.

The first suggestion for relieving this situation came from the City Solicitor, Charles Pearson. His plan was to "encircle the metropolis with a tunnel to be in connection with all the railway termini without forcing the people to traverse the streets in order to arrive at their destination." This suggestion caused most of those who heard it to declare that the city solicitor had taken leave of his senses. "What a darned silly idea," they said, "a confounded lawyer trying to be a railway man." The "underground railway" became the best joke in town. The man in the street joked about it. Barmaids joked about it. Cabinet ministers joked about it. Finally the music-hall comedians joked about it and sang a song "Let's All Go Underground" that achieved wide popularity.

Along with the jokes there was also a good deal of serious criticism. Clergymen made dire predictions of what would follow from man's "burrowing like a mole beneath the feet of honest, God-fearing citizens." Householders who lived along the proposed route feared that their houses would collapse and the occupants tumble through onto the railway track. Other people said that the weight on the roof of such a tunnel would be so great that it would certainly fall in some day and bury alive the passengers on any train that happened to be passing. *Punch* called the proposed line a "Sewer Railway."

In the face of this criticism the City Solicitor made slow progress with his idea, but he never ceased to urge it. Year by year the congestion in the streets became worse. No one except Pearson seemed to have any constructive suggestions to offer. Finally the newspapers began to clamor for something to be done about the scandalous state of the city's transport facilities, and the authorities became convinced that the "Sewer Railway"" was the best solution of the problem.

In 1853 a bill was introduced in Parliament to permit the

construction of a three and three-quarter mile subway from Farringdon Street to Bishop's Road, Paddington. The walls of the structure were to be lined with brick and an arched roof was to support the pavement of the street. Trains were to be operated at five-minute intervals to carry both merchandise and passengers.

Opposition to the passage of the bill was long and bitter. All the old objections to the idea were reëchoed, and new ones voiced. It was argued that the foundations of important buildings in the city would be seriously weakened. Fears were expressed that the passengers would be asphixiated by the noxious fumes from the locomotives. Above all it was said that the operation of trains at such short intervals would be attended by horrible accidents. Despite these protests Parliament passed the bill and the Metropolitan Railway Company was incorporated in 1854 to build the subway for the transportation of passengers and merchandise.

Its construction was attended with great difficulty. A maze of water pipes, gas, and sewer pipes had to be moved without interrupting the services they rendered. Once a nearby sewer burst and flooded the newly dug tunnel to a depth of ten feet. The story is told that one night an excited newspaper reporter dashed into the editor's room just as the latter was preparing to go home.

"They say this new tunnel is too close to Fleet Street," he shouted. "The whole building is likely to collapse."

"That makes no difference," replied the editor. "We have already gone to press."

After several years of strenuous work the subway was completed. The original plan had been to pull the trains by "fireless engines" which would be charged with enough steam at one end of the line to carry them to the other end. This novel idea proved impracticable, and when operation began on January 9, 1863, the trains were pulled by coal-burning, steam locomotives. Mr. Gladstone, the Duke of Sutherland, Earl Grosvenor and the Chancellor of the Exchequer were among the celebrities who attended the opening ceremonies. More than thirty thousand people jammed their way into the cars when the line was opened to the public on the following day. A total of nearly ten million were carried during the first year of operation, but nothing ever was done about carrying merchandise.

While the subway was in course of construction, its builders worried a good deal concerning the way people would feel about traveling underground. They decided therefore, to make a special effort to distract the passengers' attention from the fact that they were riding in a tunnel below the streets. They decorated the car interiors in a most lavish manner. Seats were upholstered with finest plush. Floors were covered with heavy carpet. Walls were paneled with highly polished hardwoods. Mirrors were added for decorative effect. In short the passenger was intended to feel that he was in the parlor of an elegant private house instead of an underground railway car.

As it turned out there probably was no need for going to these extremes of decoration since the convenience and time-saving of the underground railway would very likely have caused people to ride in whatever kind of cars had been provided. Once this course had been embarked upon, however, there was difficulty in making a change, and London's underground cars have continued to this day to be characterized by greater luxury of appointments than those anywhere else in the world.

Visiting in London at the time of the opening of the first underground was an American railroad man, Hugh B. Willson of Michigan. He was much impressed by this new type of railroad. "Why not build something of the same kind in New

York?" he thought. On his return to the United States in June, 1863, he set to work to secure the aid of prominent New Yorkers for a subway project similar to that at London. As everyone was then deeply engrossed in the Civil War, he made slow progress. Finally, however, he succeeded in lining up enough support to permit the incorporation of a five-million dollar company. Like its prototype in London, it was called the Metropolitan Railway Company. Among the incorporators were many of the best-known men of the city.

New York at that time had a population of somewhat less than a million people. Its location on a long, narrow island between the Hudson and East Rivers, made it necessary for most people to travel considerable distances when going from home to work and back. Virtually, every north- and south-bound street was occupied by a horse-car line, but the utmost service these lines could render was insufficient to meet the transportation demands of the public. The only practical solution of the problem appeared to be a railway which could operate at speeeds higher than those of surface vehicles. This meant that it must be either above or below ground.

A. P. Robinson was the engineer of the Metropolitan Railway Company. He prepared a most ingenious design for a subway consisting of a more or less semi-circular, brick structure sixteen feet high and twenty-five feet wide, with two tracks in the center. Trains were composed of two cars, one of which would have a steam engine at one end, connected by short driving rods to the car wheels. Ventilation was to be arranged through pipes running laterally to hollow iron lamp-posts erected at intervals along the curb line of the street.

On account of the prominence of the incorporators the subway project received much attention from the newspapers and the public. Everybody began to talk about riding underground. Some timid individuals were fearful of catching cold by going suddenly from the warm temperature of the street on a hot day into the cold temperature of the subway. Others feared that the subway would be filled with fog and that the trains would run into each other. On the whole, however, the sentiment of the city was very favorable to the project.

Before construction could begin it was necessary to secure a charter from the state legislature. A bill to grant such a charter was introduced near the close of the 1864 session, but was rejected without explanation by the lawmakers. The public was highly indignant. According to the New York Times:

> The Underground Railroad promised to be an immense boon to the city. It was perfectly feasible; a similar road has been in successful operation in London for one year; it encroaches on no vested interest; takes no one's land or house; interferes with no traffic or thoroughfare; offers cheap, comfortable and speedy transit from one end of the island to the other; requires no money from the public; will add nothing to municipal taxation and is undertaken by men of the highest character and standing both social and commercial. In short, there is not a single objection to be made to it on the part of the public or the Government, and yet the Committee of the Senate has reported against it, under the lead of the Senator from this city, and it has been laid on the table, for what reason is not stated.

A second bill for the same purpose was introduced in the legislature the following year. After considerable argument it was passed by both houses; but it was vetoed by Governor Reuben Fenton. While the governor expressed the opinion that the subway was practicable and desirable, he raised a number of objections to the form in which the bill had been drawn. It might have been supposed that these objections could have been overcome by the drafting of a new bill, but the fact is that his veto gave the opponents of the scheme time to organize rival projects and actually postponed the establishment of underground transit in New York for almost half a century.

While wrangling continued over the question of granting a charter for an underground railway, the legislature of 1868

quietly passed a bill to permit the construction of a "pneumatic dispatch" line under Broadway. This was to consist of
two tubes of fifty-four-inch diameter through which letters,
parcels and merchandise were to be transported by pneumatic
power. Alfred Ely Beach, an engineer, and editor of the
Scientific American, was the designer of the pneumatic dispatch system, having demonstrated its possibilities the previous
year at the American Institute.

Beach really had his heart set on building a subway for the
transportation of passengers. "The pneumatic system appears
to be admirably adapted to the purposes of rapid city transit,"
he wrote, "since the ventilation is perfect and the freedom
from all jarring and dust is complete." As no practicable
means had yet been found to harness electricity to the task of
propelling railway cars, and the use of steam locomotives in
a subway had manifest disadvantages, Beach's idea of pneumatic propulsion was not without some distinctly attractive
features.

Under the authority granted by the legislature the Beach
Pneumatic Railroad Company went to work. The basement
of Devlin's clothing store at the corner of Broadway and
Murray Street was rented and digging started from there in
the fall of 1868. So discreetly was this work carried out that
the public remained in complete ignorance of it for several
months.

Instead of digging two small tunnels, however, the company
built a single large tunnel of nine-foot diameter, within which
the smaller tubes were to be constructed later. This extended
for a distance of about three hundred feet between Murray
and Warren streets. The company explained that, as the nine-
foot tube was found "to be strong enough for the transit of
passengers, the company laid down therein a railway track
and provided a passenger car for the purpose of temporarily
illustrating by an actual demonstration the feasibility of plac-

ing a railway under Broadway without disturbance of the street surface or injury to adjacent property."

The car had seats for twenty passengers. It was cylindrical in shape and fitted snugly into the tunnel, along which it was propelled by air from a huge, steam-operated blower at the Warren Street station. As the car approached the Murray Street end of the tube the conductor rang a bell, and the blower operator at Warren Street put his machine into reverse. This was designed to bring the car to a gentle stop and then suck it back to the starting point.

In February, 1870, a successful trial trip was made with the Mayor and a number of other notables. After that the tunnel was opened to the public for demonstration purposes. By paying twenty-five cents a person could ride back and forth between Warren and Murray streets for as long as he wished. One such passenger records that:

We took our seats in the pretty car, the gayest company of twenty that ever entered a vehicle; the conductor touched a telegraph wire on the wall of the tunnel, and before we knew it, so gentle was the start, we were in motion moving from Warren Street down Broadway. In a few moments the conductor opened the door and called out; "Murray Street!" with a business-like air that made us all shout with laughter. The car came to a rest in the gentlest possible style, and immediately began to move back again to Warren Street, where it had no sooner arrived than in the same gentle and mysterious manner it moved back again to Murray Street; and thus it continued to go back and forth for, I should think, twenty minutes.

Operation continued in this way for about three years, no effort being made to return to the original idea of letter and parcel transportation. On the contrary, the company tried its best to secure a franchise to build an underground passenger railroad. The desired permission was granted in 1873, but it was stipulated that operation should be with steam locomotives, the pneumatic method not being considered satisfactory. By this time, however, the Ninth Avenue elevated railway had been built and was operating with great success. Con-

sequently the Beach company was unable to interest investors
and raise enough money to build a subway.

The development of electric operation for street-railways
in the 1880's gave new impetus to the idea of subways. An
underground railway with electricity as a motive power was
a far more attractive proposition than one using steam or
pneumatic power as a means of propulsion.

It was Boston, however, and not New York, which took
the lead in building a practical subway. Here, again, Henry
M. Whitney and the famous West End Street Railway enter
the picture. Under the law which permitted the consolidation
of the various lines in Boston to form this big system, the company was authorized "to locate, construct, and maintain one
or more tunnels between convenient points in said city, in
one or more directions under the squares, streets, ways, and
places. . . ." This was in 1887, but no subway construction was
actually started until some years later. As a matter of fact
Mr. Whitney's real plan to meet the growing need for rapid
transit was to build an elevated railway, but the Massachusetts
legislature had considerable difficulty in making up its mind
about authorizing this step. When Boston's first subway was
planned, the purpose was to relieve street traffic congestion
rather than to provide rapid transit.

At this time the downtown traffic situation in Boston was
a serious problem. In 1871 the city's street-railway system carried some 34 million passengers; in 1881 the number was 68
million and in 1891 it had reached 136 million. In other words,
the number was doubling every ten years. To handle this
enormous business the West End operated more than 2,600
street-cars over some 300 miles of track. On Tremont Street
during the afternoon rush hour the cars were packed so close
together that one could almost walk from Scollay Square to
Boylston Street on the car roofs.

In an endeavor to relieve this condition it was decided to

build a subway under Tremont Street. Plenty of opposition appeared when the plan was proposed. A petition against the proposal, circulated in April, 1894, was signed by many prominent citizens and downtown merchants. It declared that they were "unalterably opposed to the construction of any subway in any portion of the City of Boston, whether for the alleged purpose of accommodating surface or elevated roads, or both, being convinced that such construction would seriously interfere with travel and traffic, proving ruinous to hundreds of merchants and in the end failing to relieve congestion or promote rapid transit." Public opinion, however, took a different view. The subway proposal fired the popular imagination, and the opposition was unable to stop its execution.

Built at a cost of $4,350,000, the Tremont Street subway was about one and two-thirds miles in length. For most of this distance it had four tracks, although there was one short section with only two tracks. It permitted an increase from 200 to 400 cars an hour in each direction in the peak period of the day, and materially reduced the running time in the downtown area of the city. Moreover, the removal of the cars from the surface of Tremont Street did much to relieve traffic congestion.

When it was opened for service in the fall of 1897 it was the first real subway in America and the fifth in the world. A structure somewhat similar to that in Boston had been completed a year earlier in Budapest, Hungary. London had three train-operated subways, and Glasgow one. The fact that the Tremont Street subway handled more than 50 million passengers during its first year of operation is the best proof of its practical usefulness. This number was about five times the first year's total at London.

Two years later the Tremont Street subway became part of Boston's first rapid-transit line; although it was still used also by street-cars. The rapid-transit line was mainly an elevated railway reaching Charlestown on the north, and Dudley Street on the south, but in the heart of the city it was linked up with two of the tracks in the subway. This was only a temporary expedient. Construction of a rapid-transit subway was started almost at once under Washington Street, and in 1908 the Tremont Street subway was restored to street-cars exclusively. In the same year a combination subway-elevated line began operation in Philadelphia.

The success of Boston's first subway gave encouragement to the advocates of a subway in New York, where discussion of the subject had continued intermittently since the first proposal for an underground railway had been made by Hugh Willson in 1864. The last political, financial, and legal difficulties, however, were not smoothed out until 1900. On March 24 of that year ground was broken for the first section of a subway line that was planned to extend from the City Hall to the northern limits of the city, a distance of about fifteen miles. This, naturally, was a much more elaborate project than the Tremont Street subway, as New York was a far larger city than Boston and its rapid-transit problem was even more acute. The estimated cost was in the neighborhood of 35 million dollars.

Despite the complicated problems connected with the digging of a subway through the busiest sections of the city the work progressed with great rapidity.

John B. McDonald, an experienced contractor who had built the Baltimore & Ohio Railroad tunnel under the city of Baltimore, was the successful bidder for the contract. Behind him stood August Belmont as the financial backer of the project. McDonald brought to the task an unusual combination of nerve and engineering experience. Belmont brought nerve and immense financial resources. All of these things were needed for the job, especially nerve, as no project of a similar kind had ever been attempted before, and nobody

Building America's first subway under Tremont Street, Boston, in 1897.

Times Square about 1900, when New York's first subway was being built. In those days little effort was made to keep a roadway open for street traffic during construction.

Acme

The subway at Tokyo is generally similar in design to subways in the United States.

A spacious station on the 110-mile system of the Chemin de fer metropolitaine de Paris.

Circular shape characterizes many of the underground lines of the London Passenger Transport Board.

Some of the rolling stock belonging to New York's billion-dollar subway system. The 209th Street storage yards.

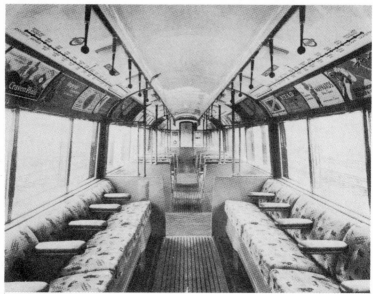

London Transport

Comfort characterizes the interior of modern subway cars in London.

knew whether or not it could be done for the price set. Attempts had previously been made to interest experienced street-railway and steam-railroad men in the subway project, but they had all shied away from it. But McDonald and Belmont thought the idea was sound and were willing to take the risk of attempting to carry it out.

Time proved that they were right. Construction work was completed in four and a half years at a cost reasonably close to the original estimates, and on October 27, 1904, the first trains were sent through. Everything ran like clockwork and the subway at once met with great popular favor. No difficulty was experienced in maintaining speeds of fifteen miles an hour for local service and twenty-five miles an hour for express trains. This, of course, was much faster than the surface-car lines, and somewhat faster, even, than the elevated railways, particularly the express service which had no counterpart on the "L" lines. People had laughed when the chief engineer of the subway had predicted during the construction period that it would some time carry as many as 400,000 passengers a day. Actually this figure was reached before the end of the first year.

The first subways in London, Boston and New York were all built by the "cut and cover" method. That is to say, the surface of the street was opened up, the necessary excavation made, the subway structure built, and the pavement restored. For the most part there was no effort to provide a temporary pavement while the work was in progress, and street traffic was almost completely stopped for a considerable period. The effect of blocking the roadway was extremely harmful, particularly in New York, where a number of merchants whose stores were located along the route were forced into bankruptcy on account of the difficulty of access to their places of business.

When it was decided to extend the New York subway

down Broadway to the Battery, the "cut and cover" method was again used for construction, but a temporary roadway of planks was built as rapidly as the work progressed so that there was no serious interference with surface traffic. This method was followed in virtually all of the subway construction carried out later in New York, Boston, and Philadelphia. As a matter of fact it would be virtually impossible to use any other method where the subway is built close to the street level, an arrangement that has usually been considered desirable in American cities, as it permits passengers to reach the station platforms from the sidewalk with a minimum of trouble. Some idea of what would be involved in a deep level subway can be had from the fact that it has been estimated that forty elevators with a capacity of sixty persons each would be needed at Times Square station to handle passengers to and from the train platforms if the subway were 100 feet below ground.

London, on the other hand, was more favorably inclined to low-level tubes. The second subway to be opened there, the Metropolitan District line, followed the shallow design of the first underground, but the City and South London Railway, opened in 1890, was placed in tubes ranging from forty-eight to 105 feet below the surface. It was built under the direction of James Henry Greathead, an engineer who perfected a method of digging originally devised many years earlier by Marc Isambard Brunel.

The latter had proposed, as early as 1824, the digging of a vehicular tunnel under the River Thames at London. Two previous attempts to accomplish this difficult feat had ended in disaster and the public was highly skeptical of the third proposal. But Brunel had figured out a new method of digging, which he thought would succeed where the others had failed. Several years earlier, while engaged on work at Chatham Dockyard, he had become keeenly interested in watching the boring activities of a ship-worm. A shell with parallel rows of teeth like the edges of a file forms the head of the ship-worm. As the animal digs its way into the wood, it passes the wood dust back through its body and deposits it with a carbonate-of-lime solution on the walls of the tunnel it has dug.

Brunel believed this principle could be employed in the construction of a vehicular tunnel under the Thames. His plan was to bore the tunnel by pushing forward, step by step, a rectangular casing, or shield, inside of which the workmen could dig in safety. Excavated material would be passed back through the casing to the tunnel entrance. As rapidly as the shield was pushed forward the walls of the tunnel behind it were to be lined with brick.

The approval of Parliament was finally secured, and work was commenced. The job proved to be a good deal more difficult than had been anticipated. Digging could proceed only slowly, and considerable time was required for the cement of the brickwork to set properly. At one point the river broke through and drowned seven workmen. Funds ran short and financial help had to be secured from the government. Brunel persevered, however, and the tunnel was finally completed in 1843.

Its fame spread rapidly. As one contemporary writer said: "This tunnel is the admiration of civilized Europe, and to many a stranger from afar the most wonderful of all the curiosities of England."

Though constructed to accommodate vehicular traffic, the Thames Tunnel was never used for that purpose. At first it was used by a good many pedestrians, but after the novelty wore off, the pedestrians seemed to lose interest in it. The greatest service it performed, in reality, was the demonstration it gave of the practicability of digging tunnels by the shield method.

A modification of Brunel's plan was used later by Peter Barlow and James Greathead in digging the Tower Tunnel. One difference was the use of a circular shield, rather than a rectangular one. Another difference was that the tunnel was lined with circular cast-iron segments bolted together instead of bricks. The diameter of the Tower Tunnel was about seven feet. Digging was begun from both ends at the same time and progressed at a rate of five feet a day.

Further improvements were made in the shield used by Greathead for the construction work for the City and South

Early electric train on City and South London line

London Railway. This line consisted of two tubes, each of ten-and-one-half-foot diameter running for a distance of three miles from Stockwell to King William Street. A shaft was sunk to a depth of eighty-two feet near London Bridge and boring started obliquely under the River Thames. Progress was made at a rate of about eighty feet a week, or more than twice that of the digging of the Tower Tunnel. Construction was finished by June, 1887, but the operation of the line did not begin until three years later. This delay made it possible to use electric locomotives to haul the trains instead of cables as had originally been planned. Thus the City and South London became the first electrically operated subway in the world.

Although "cut and cover" was the prevailing method of construction used in building the New York subways, digging by the shield method was employed for some sections such as the tunnels under the East River. The first of these under-river tunnels was started soon after the completion of the original line, as Brooklyn had by then become part of the city of Greater New York and was demanding its share of rapid-transit service.

This was an undertaking fraught with considerable hazard. Digging had to be done in a chamber filled with compressed air to keep back the water that would otherwise have seeped in. Sometimes the air pressure became too great and a blow-out occurred, with the air rushing through the thirty feet of sand and silt of the river bed to escape into the water and finally the outer air. When a blow-out of this kind started it was customary to plug the hole quickly with sand bags to stop the escape of the compressed air.

One day during the construction of the first tunnel from the Battery to Brooklyn the beginning of a blow-out was noticed, and Dick Creedon, a member of the gang working in the chamber, stepped up promptly with a sand bag to stop the leak. But he underestimated the strength of the uprush of air. Before he knew what was happening both he and the sand bag were carried into the hole, and up through the muck of the river bottom and the cold water of the East River. When he reached the surface Creedon started swimming, and a nearby tugboat picked him up none the worse for his experience. Finally the leak was closed by dumping tons of sand onto the river bottom above the air chamber.

The construction of New York's first underground railway ushered in a forty-year period of activity during which more than 150 miles of subway were built at a cost of over a billion dollars. During almost all of this period the construction work was under the direction of Robert Ridgway—perhaps the only man who has ever spent a billion dollars of public money without any criticism being voiced of the way it was done.

When Chicago started digging a subway in 1938 an innovation was made in American construction practice. It was decided to build twin tubes forty-four feet below the street level and excavate by tunneling rather than to follow the familiar "cut and cover" method used in Boston, New York, and Philadelphia. But, curiously enough, a different scheme was devised for the section under the Chicago River, the place more than any other where tunneling might most naturally have been expected. Here a double steel tube was built as long as the width of the river, covered with concrete and sealed at both ends. Then it was floated to a position directly above the line of the subway and sunk into a trench that had been dredged for it so deep that it came to rest with its top five feet below the normal bottom of the river. All that then remained to be done was to connect the ends with the adjacent land sections of the subway.

The influence that subways have had on the development of the cities where they are operated is almost incalculable. Yet it has been only what was predicted by the pioneers in this field. No one has ever expressed it any better than A. P. Robinson in describing the advantages of the subway he was not allowed to build in New York in 1864:

I can conceive of nothing so completely fulfilling in every respect the requirements of our population. . . . Passengers would not be obliged to go into the middle of the street to take a car. They would have simply to enter a station from the sidewalk and pass down a spacious and well-lighted staircase to a dry and roomy platform. . . . The passenger would . . . be carried to his destination in one-third the time he could be carried by any other conveyance. These would be the advantages to those who ride, and for the other great public in the streets. . . . Everything would be out of sight and hearing, and nothing would indicate the great thoroughfare below.

7

HEYDAY OF THE TROLLEY

The Story of Mergers and Expansion

In the 1890's and early 1900's a man could often make a pot of money for himself by watching where new electric railway lines were being built, and buying real estate along the proposed route. Property worth only $1,000 an acre before the building of a trolley line sold for $2,000 or $3,000 an acre afterward. Some people thought they could get rich with equal ease by putting their money into the companies organized to build and operate the trolley lines; for the most part they were disappointed. A few of the companies made fat profits, but many of them went bankrupt.

A craze for electric railways swept over the whole United States immediately after the Union Passenger Railway began operation at Richmond in February 1888. The *Street Railway Journal* was one of the most ardent advocates of electrification. An editorial in its May, 1888, issue stated positively that "the utility of electricity as a motive-power for the propulsion of street-cars is no longer a matter of question."

George Westinghouse, famous inventor of the air brake, held the same opinion. "The results of a comparatively short experience in the use of electricity as a motor for surface railway cars," he said, "have been such as to demonstrate beyond question its immense superiority for this purpose over any other known method of applying power."

Many others felt the same way; but there were plenty of dissenters. C. B. Holmes, president of the cable-operated, Chicago City Railway, was one of them. "There are the fixed laws of the universe," he cried, "which no ingenuity of man

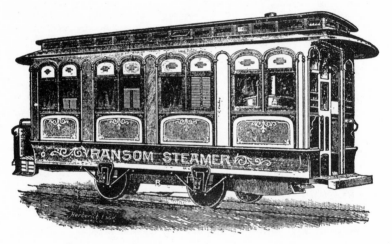

Steam-propelled car invented by Louis Ransom

can ever change. The electric car, like every other dependent on rail-traction, slips and labors in the effort to lift itself, but the cable-car glides up or down with an utter indifference to grades and gravity."

Another dissenter was Louis Ransom, of Akron, Ohio. "Who are these men who are so persistently and loudly crying that electricity is the motor of the future?" he demanded. "Are they men at all conspicuous for mechanical ability or mechanical achievement? Are they men whose declarations are invested with authority? After twenty-five years of the most careful study of the street-railway problem I am convinced that the motor of the future is steam." This view was not particularly surprising as Mr. Ransom was the inventor of a steam-propelled car.

Some street-railway men were sitting on the fence. Charles Atwell, president of the Pittsburgh, Allegheny & Manchester Railway, stated his position in these words:

> This company continues to operate its road with the somewhat discredited animal power. Slow and laborious the service may, indeed, be, but the horse is sure to get in his work in the given time. . . . Having a practical duty to perform in the carrying of passengers, we are not experimenting, simply holding ourselves in readiness to put aside our hitherto faithful servants as soon as a better motive-power becomes practical for us. Meanwhile I stroke my good horse's neck and call him my best friend.

This sentiment struck a sympathetic chord in the hearts of a majority of the men running the horse-car lines, but they could not afford to be swayed by sentiment. Electricity was rapidly proving that it was, indeed, "a better motive-power" for street-railways. Whether they liked it or not, the change to electricity was almost inevitable.

By 1890, when the first census of street-railways was made in the United States, the amount of electrified track had already reached the astounding total of 1,260 miles. At the same time there were 5,700 miles of track operated by animal power and about 500 miles operated by cable. Twelve years later, when a second census was taken, the total of electrified track had risen to nearly 22,000 miles, while animal traction had dwindled to 250 miles, and cable operation continued in only a few places.

The changeover to electricity was attended by a good many problems and difficulties. When the horse-car lines were built they were usually laid out to serve areas that were already well populated. Passengers presented themselves in large numbers as soon as the service started. Electrification was accompanied by an important change of policy. On account of the higher speed of the trolley a longer distance could be traveled in the same time. This led to the extension of lines into sparsely populated outlying districts. It was thought that when the trolley service became available, these districts would be built up rapidly and furnish a nice volume of business for the cars. Admittedly that was only a hope for the future. At the time the lines were built there were few passengers to be picked up in these outlying areas.

Sometimes the growth of population took place pretty much as anticipated. At other times it proved slower than the electric-railway promoters had figured. The result was that some electric railways prospered and some did not. Even when the population growth took place as hoped, it did not always produce big dividends for the electric railways. Electric power was cheaper than horses, to be sure, but this saving was often offset by other things.

In the days of the horse-car lines the fare had been fixed at five cents in most cities, regardless of the length of the ride. This was not always true, however, or Noah Brooks would never have been inspired to write his well-known verse:

> Conductor, when you receive a fare,
> Punch in the presence of the passenjare.
> A blue trip slip for an eight-cent fare,
> A buff trip slip for a six-cent fare,
> A pink trip slip for a five-cent fare,
> Punch in the presence of the passenjare!
> Punch brothers, punch with care!
> Punch in the presence of the passenjare.

The five-cent fare was all right at the time because nobody wanted to ride very far in the slow-moving horse-cars. After the introduction of the faster electric cars and the extension of service to more remote districts, it was not so satisfactory. Passengers had to be carried much greater distances, but the company got no more money for the long ride than it had for the previous short ride.

Then, too, there was the matter of fixed charges on the

investment, which was enormously greater for the electric lines than it had been with the horse-cars. Although the actual expense of operation took about sixty-eight cents of every dollar of revenue collected by the horse-car lines in 1890, and only about fifty-seven cents of every dollar of revenue of the electric railways in 1902, the fixed charges increased from fifteen cents to thirty-one cents. Profits, therefore, were smaller than they had been before electrification.

Taxes went leaping upward during this period. Electric railways were considered fair game by the taxing authorities, who displayed remarkable ingenuity in devising burdens that could be laid on them. In addition to the general taxes imposed on all corporations, the electric railways were subjected to a variety of special taxes, such as franchise taxes, vehicle licenses, taxes on gross earnings, paving taxes, and the like. Some cities required the street-railways to clean and sprinkle the streets on which they operated, and to remove the snow in winter. Others required policemen and firemen to be carried on the cars free of charge. Baltimore had the unique idea of collecting one cent out of each nickel fare to establish a fund for building a public-park system. Even the United States Congress got into the game by making the street-railways in Washington pay the salaries of traffic policemen. An act of June 24, 1898, specified that, "The Commissioners of the District of Columbia are hereby authorized and required to station special policemen at such railway crossings and intersections in the city of Washington as the said commissioners may deem necessary, the expense of such service to be paid pro rata by the respective companies."

Because extension of service had out-run the demand for it in many instances, a considerable number of electric railways found themselves in shaky financial condition. Thus the time was ripe for mergers. As a matter of fact, mergers had begun way back in the horse-car era. In the early days of the street-railways it was customary for each line to be organized as a separate corporation and operated under its own franchise. Then adjacent lines were combined to form larger systems. As merger followed merger, the genealogy of some American street-railway companies became as complicated as that of the old Norman families in England.

Take for example, the case of the Newark, Bloomfield & Montclair Horse Car Railroad Company. This was a six-mile line built in 1867 to connect Newark, then a city of about eighty thousand people, with the small suburban communities of Bloomfield and Montclair. In 1876 its property was sold to the Newark & Bloomfield Street Railway which, in 1885, was merged with others to form the Essex Passenger Railway, a system comprising a majority of the street-railway lines in Newark. Then in 1890 the Essex Passenger Railway became part of the Newark Passenger Railway, a still larger system. Two years later the New Jersey Traction Company leased the Newark Passenger Railway for 999 years. This arrangement was of short duration, however, for New Jersey Traction was absorbed by Consolidated Traction in 1893. As organized at this time, Consolidated had some 165 miles of track serving Newark and a large number of nearby communities. In 1898 Consolidated was leased to North Jersey Street Railway to create a system covering virtually all of the northern part of the state. Five years later North Jersey and eleven other street-railway companies were taken over by Public Service Corporation. The system thus created, covering not only the northern part of the state but most of the central and southern part as well, had nearly seven hundred miles of track and represented 108 different street and electric railway properties that had been organized at one time or another in the past.

Pretty much the same thing went on all over the country. Sometimes these street-railway mergers produced companies of considerable financial strength. At other times the larger company was as shaky as the various small ones had been. In any event the mergers added greatly to the attractiveness of the service, as free transfers were given from one line to another and a person could often ride all over the city for a single fare. They also permitted some economies in operation. This was particularly true with respect to power. One large generating station could furnish electric power for a number of street-railway lines at a cheaper rate than several smaller

Transfer of the nineties to be punched to indicate type of passenger

stations could do it. Everything considered, however, the mergers probably did more for the public than for the owners of the properties.

The era of mergers brought some colorful personalities into the limelight. One of the first was Henry M. Whitney of Boston who engineered the creation of the far-flung system of the West End Street Railway, later absorbed by the Boston Elevated Railway. As a young man he spent several years in the banking business. Then he became interested in shipping, and eventually succeeded his father as president of the Metropolitan Steamship Company. At this time he was living in Brookline and conceived the idea of uniting that village with Boston by means of a broad boulevard and a "superior system of street-railways." He even offered to pay one-third of the cost of the boulevard himself.

Arrangements to this effect had almost been completed when he ran into stiff opposition from the existing street-railways. Here his banker's training came to the rescue. He promptly organized a merger of the various horse-car lines in the city and had himself elected president of the new company. Then he went down to Richmond to look over Sprague's electric railway there. Convinced that electricity was the motive power of the future he built his line from Brookline to Boston and equipped it for electric operation— the first electric railway in Massachusetts.

There was also Charles Tyson Yerkes. He was born of Quaker parents at Philadelphia in 1839 and began working as a clerk in the office of a commission merchant. He soon tired of that, and at the age of twenty-one went into business for himself as a broker. In this he was extremely successful and acquired, among other things, a substantial interest in the Seventeenth & Nineteenth Streets Passenger Railway. He also organized the Continental Passenger Railway. Like many other eastern financiers he had large investments in Chicago. The disastrous Chicago fire of 1871 caused him heavy losses and compelled him to part with his street-railway holdings.

Then came the famous Jay Cooke failure and the consequent financial panic. This proved highly profitable to Yerkes as he had been on the short side of the market. Being back on his feet again financially, he moved to Fargo, South Dakota, in 1875. Six years later he moved to Chicago and started in business as a stock and grain broker, but always watchful for an opportunity to resume his interest in street-railways. In 1886 he secured control of the North Chicago City Railway which he reorganized with himself as president. Two years later he obtained control of the Chicago West Division Railway, which he also reorganized with himself as president. Immediately he set out to build other lines. Eight separate companies were chartered and 250 miles of track laid. All of these were then merged into the Chicago Consolidated Traction Company. By 1893 Yerkes was one of the biggest street-railway magnates in the United States. Later he sold his interests and moved to New York, but the Chicago street-railway system created through his efforts continued to hold a leading place among the street-railway systems of the entire world.

Another name famous in early electric-railway history was that of Thomas Fortune Ryan. He was the head of the important Metropolitan Street Railway of New York. With a group of associates, he had consolidated various properties by purchase or lease until there had been built up a system with 3,000 cars and 300 miles of track that gridironed the boroughs of Manhattan and the Bronx.

A great deal of money had been spent on improvements of one kind or another, and then, disconcertingly enough, the Metropolitan management found that its operation on the streets of the city was about to be subjected to serious competition from an electric railway built underground. This was something that the street-railway people had more or less feared and opposed for many years. But the talk of building an underground railway had dragged out over such a long period without anything coming of it, that the seriousness of the competitive danger had scarcely been realized.

The first actual subway construction in New York was started in the summer of 1900, as told in Chapter VI. As the work progressed there developed a better understanding of the kind of service the subway would render, and no transportation man could fail to see that it would take a good many passengers away from the street-railways. At this point the Metropolitan decided on a bold move. Ryan informed the city authorities that if they would lay out a second subway route, independent of the one already under construction, and so planned as to supplement the surface-car lines, the Metropolitan would bid for the franchise to build and operate it.

The fare was to be five cents with free transfers between street cars and subway.

This proposal caused a tremendous sensation. Here was the Metropolitan Street Railway, which had always been opposed to subways, offering to build and run one. Nobody was more startled than August Belmont whose money was financing the first subway, the Interborough Rapid Transit Company. The Metropolitan made every effort to build up popular sentiment for its plan. Many hearings were held to consider it. Countless articles were published in the newspapers.

All seemed to be going well, when, suddenly, the city received a second shock. This was the news that the Metropolitan and the Interborough companies had merged. Ryan's threat of building a second subway and giving free transfers to surface-cars had been too much for Belmont. "We couldn't stand that kind of competition, and so we combined with them," was the way the latter explained the situation. Needless to say, the Interborough-Metropolitan Company did not carry out Ryan's ambitious plan of building a second subway and interchanging transfers with the street-cars.

Electric-railway expansion continued rapidly for some fifteen years after taking of the second United States Census in 1902. By 1917 the industry had 80,000 passenger cars, operating on 45,000 miles of track. The trend toward mergers continued, too. Small systems were combined into larger ones, new lines were built and old lines were extended to serve additional territory.

In Massachusetts there grew up the huge system of the Bay State Street Railway with more than 3,000 cars and 500 miles of track serving all of the eastern part of the state except Boston. In Connecticut Charles S. Mellen, president of the New York, New Haven & Hartford Railroad, organized a street-railway system with more than 800 miles of track and 1,800 cars serving virtually every important city in the state.

Open-car days in British Columbia. The advertising on the roof was common practice in Canada, but was seldom seen in the United States.

A trolley picnic of the Gay Nineties on the Boston & Worcester line.

In the heyday of the trolley the usual practice was for passengers both to board and alight at the rear end.

Tops in carrying capacity—this double-deck open car at Pittsburgh had seats for 182 passengers.

The light-weight, one-man Bierney car, developed in 1916, promised
for a time greatly to alter the economics of street-railway operation.

The Broadway Battleship—an unusual type of double-deck car
supported on trucks at the extreme ends.

Three-car train operated in Boston in the 1920's.

Street-cars ran fender to fender on many streets like this in Los Angeles in the heyday of the trolley.

Market Street, San Francisco, one of the few places with four parallel
tracks for street-cars.

Westminster Bridge, with the Houses of Parliament in the background
—an important artery of tramway traffic in London.

The Scots, like the English, have favored double-deck tramcars as
indicated by this scene from Edinburgh.

In Mexico City the tramcars follow closely the design of American vehicles.

Street-cars in Puerto Rico are not unlike those in the United States, except that they have no windows.

Hongkong's double-deck tramcars reflect the British influence.

In Buenos Aires the Anglo-American Tramways formerly operated
a large street-railway system, using mostly small, single-truck cars.

Clear across the continent, Henry Huntington, nephew of the great railroad builder, Collis P. Huntington, was creating the Pacific Electric Railway system. By the time he was finished his company had more than 1,000 miles of track radiating out of Los Angeles to Pasadena, Glendale, San Pedro, Santa Anna, Redondo, and a host of other towns.

In the heyday of the trolley you could go all the way from Boston to New York by street-railway. A party of street-railway officials actually made this trip in March 1912 in the private car "Hugenot" of the Worcester Consolidated Street Railway. Park Square, Boston, was the starting point. The route was westerly through Worcester to Springfield and thence south to Hartford, New Britain, and New Haven. From there the car followed the shore of Long Island Sound through Bridgeport, Norwalk, and Stamford until it met the tracks running up into Westchester County from the City of New York. The officials making this trip were headed by Thomas N. McCarter, president of Public Service Railway of New Jersey and also, at that time, president of the American Electric Railway Association. Having a private car was a great advantage, of course, because meals could be served as the car rolled along. With somewhat less comfort and speed, however, the same trip could have been made by anyone who had enough nickels to pay an aggregate of $2.40 in fares and enough patience to ride for twenty consecutive hours on more than a dozen different street-car lines.

One could even go from New York to Chicago by electric railway in those days. That involved the use of some lines that were not trolleys in the ordinary sense, but were rather electric interurban railways. It is not of record that this trip was ever made by anybody except one of the editors of the *Electric Railway Journal*, that being the new name which had been adopted by the *Street Railway Journal* after the general changeover to electric motive-power.

While the track layers were busy extending the electric railway lines, the car builders were equally busy improving the vehicles. The first electric cars, like their predecessors, the horse-cars, were quite short, with the body carried on a single framework, or truck, mounted on four wheels. Seats were provided for about twenty passengers. As the wages of motormen and conductors gradually increased, the operating companies found that they had to carry more passengers per car if they expected to keep their budgets in balance. That meant larger cars, but the limit of length with a four-wheel car was soon reached. If the axles were placed too far apart the car could not go around the sharp curves existing on many street-railways. If the car body extended too far beyond the axles, the vehicle was likely to develop a galloping motion.

The car builders had an answer for this. It was a car with the body supported on two independent four-wheel trucks, pivoted near the ends of the car. Such an arrangement had been in use for many years on the steam-railroads, and proposals had been made from time to time to use it for horse-cars, but the general feeling had been that such a car was too big for the power available. A few double-truck cars had been tried by the cable lines, where there was no question about the adequacy of the motive power, but at the time of the introduction of electricity the single-truck vehicle was in use virtually everywhere.

The J. G. Brill Company, veteran car builders for the street-railway industry, designed the first double-truck electric cars. They had seats for about thirty-six passengers. Lengths were gradually increased, however, until the ordinary city car had upwards of forty seats. Sometimes these cars were coupled together in trains of two or three, operated by one motorman for the whole train and one conductor for each car, substantially reducing labor costs with respect to the number of passengers carried.

In 1916, Charles Birney, engineer of Stone & Webster, to
meet the growing shortage of labor, developed a small, light-
weight, single-truck car equipped with safety devices to permit its operation by one man. This immediately put the small
car back on the map. A street-railway company could give
more frequent service with these light, one-man cars without
having excessive labor costs. The Birney car sprang into immediate popularity. Thousands of them were built for street-
railways all over the United States. But their popularity did
not last very long. They were somewhat dumpy in appearance and rather prone to gallop. The public soon began to
make fun of their looks and gait. This inspired the car designers to develop a light-weight, double-truck car, provided
with the same safety devices so that it, too, could be operated
by one man. It was more commodious and had better riding
qualities than the small car, so most railways returned to the
use of double-truck vehicles.

Tramway operators in England solved the problem in a
different way. When they wanted to get more seats per
vehicle they added an upper deck instead of making the car
longer. This had been proposed by George Francis Train
when he was seeking to get permission to build the first street-
railway in London. His project was not a success because the
rails projected above the pavement and interfered with other
traffic, but double-deck cars eventually became very popular
in England, and British colonial cities. A few double-deck
horse-cars and cable-cars were built in the United States and
attempts were made at various times to introduce double-deck
vehicles on the electric lines, notably in New York City and
Pittsburgh. They did not meet with much favor, however,
as the passengers disliked to climb up and down the stairs to
the upper deck.

Open cars were very popular for summer service during

the horse and cable eras. As cars were simple and inexpensive affairs in those days, the operating companies could afford to have different sets of vehicles for winter and summer. Electric cars were more expensive, and most of the early ones were of the closed type, suitable for use throughout the year. But the open car had great popular appeal, and soon came back into

Large open car of a type widely used about 1910

general use. In the early 1900's nearly twenty-five thousand of them were in operation in cities all over the country. The introduction of the pay-as-you-enter method of fare collection, which was not very practical on open cars, caused a swift decline in their use.

Compromise designs between open and closed cars were tried now and again. One of these was the "convertible car" with removable side panels, developed about 1895. Later came the "semi-convertible car" with permanent side panels below the seat level and windows that could be pushed up against the roof, leaving a large part of the side open. At one time a "half-and-half" car was tried in New York, with one section open and one section closed. This compromise pleased nobody. In fair weather, every one wanted to be outside, and in bad weather, every one wanted to be inside. Another compromise was the "California-type" car, with a closed section in the center and more or less open sections in the ends. In the famous California climate this type of car proved quite satisfactory.

Abraham Brower's first omnibus, operated in New York in 1831, had a single door at the center of the rear end of the vehicle. This eventually became the general practice for all horse-drawn omnibuses. But the first street-railway car, the "John Mason" of the New York & Harlem Railroad, followed the design of the early steam-railroad cars with doors on the sides to provide access individually to each of the compartments into which the vehicle was divided. This was a handy plan so far as the passengers were concerned and also handy in that it permitted the car to run in either direction.

When street-railway building began in earnest in the 1850's and 60's the car designers reverted to the omnibus idea with a single door at the back. This immediately introduced a problem of how to turn the car around at the end of the line. Some cars were built so that the body would rotate on a pivot at the center of the truck. When the end of the line was reached the wheels remained standing in the same position on the rails while the body was reversed. A more usual plan, however, was to have a turn-table at the end of the line and reverse the car, wheels and all. These tables were turned by hand and were regarded with strong distaste by the car crews who were expected to push them around.

The first great departure from omnibus design was to bring the driver down from a seat on the roof to a standing position on a platform at the front of the car. Then a second platform was added at the other end, and once more the car could be run in either direction by simply unhitching the horses, taking them around to the other end, and hitching them up again.

Practically all of the early electric cars were built with platforms at both ends, so they could be run in either direction. By this time it had become customary to have a conductor on each car as well as a driver or motorman. Passengers

Car with reversible body for changing direction at end of line

usually boarded and alighted at the rear. Fares were collected by the conductor who went through the car from time to time trying to identify the passengers who had paid and those who hadn't. What proportion of fares the average conductor succeeded in collecting when the car was crowded is not a matter of statistical record, but the number that were missed was a continuing source of sorrow to all street-railway managements.

Then, in 1905, an idea was born that changed the whole situation. It was nothing less than to collect the fare from the

passenger as soon as he boarded the car, and before he min-
gled with the other passengers. This change had a profound
effect on car design, as it was found desirable to have a rear
platform with plenty of room for a group of passengers to
stand while waiting to pay their fares rather than for them to
wait on the street and delay the starting of the car. To avoid
confusion the outgoing passengers were expected to leave by
the front door. Here, again, was a return to the old idea of a
car that would run in only one direction. As the cars were
now too big for turn-tables, track loops or "wyes" were built
to permit them to turn around. Where these could not be
built the use of double-end cars continued after the introduction of the pay-as-you-enter system of fare collection.

As their properties expanded many electric railways en-
deavored to build up riding by the operation of amusement
parks. Norumbega Park, run by the Middlesex & Boston Street
Railway, Willow Grove Park, run by the Philadelphia Rapid
Transit Company, and Sacandaga Park, run by the Fonda,
Johnstown & Gloversville Railroad were among the best
known.

Roller-coasters, merry-go-rounds, toboggan slides, swings,
zoos, and band concerts were among the attractions offered.
"The amusement park that doesn't have a baseball gallery
will be a year behind the times" said an advertisement in the
Electric Railway Journal in 1905. Another advertisement
described a "bump-the-bumps" as the king of fun-makers.
"It will do more in making your park attractive than any
other amusement device costing twice as much."

"Anything from a White Mouse to a White Elephant,"
was offered by one advertiser. "All kinds of native and foreign
wild animals—birds, swans, geese, ducks, cranes, eels, beaver,
buffalo, deer, raccoons, squirrels, bears, monkeys, eagles, owls,
seals, sea-lions, and so on. A few attractive animals to rent
for the season."

From the standpoint of trackage, 1918 was the peak year of electric-railway development. At that time the motor-bus was still in its infancy, but it was rapidly becoming a pretty lusty infant. Many rail extensions were made after 1918, but they failed to balance the abandonments of unprofitable lines. In some instances these were lines that had been built in hopes of business that never materialized. In other instances they were lines that had been able to operate with a small margin of profit in days when costs were lower but could not make the grade in the post-war era. For many of the latter the solution of the problem was found in a changeover from electric railway to motor-bus operation involving a much less expensive physical plant.

Riding on the electric railways continued to increase for a time after the trackage began to shrink, but the rate of growth was comparatively slow. Between 1917 and 1923, the peak year of riding, the number of passengers increased only from thirteen billion to fourteen billion, or about seven per cent. This was in sharp contrast to the increase from two billion in 1890 to more than five billion in 1902, a gain of 160 per cent, and the further increase to eleven billion in 1912, a gain of 120 per cent. After 1923 the number of electric-railway passengers began to decline as more and more companies adopted the motor-bus or the electric trolley bus as a substitute for the trolley car.

Such changes were not made without some feeling of sadness on the part of the men who managed the companies. Most of them had grown up with the trolley lines, and they had bitterly opposed the bus when it first appeared. They were not highly enthusiastic over the early development of the trolley bus, either, although they felt that it was rather closer kin to their first love, the trolley car. But they soon recognized that the newer types of service had much to recommend them —were, in fact, definitely superior to the electric railway under certain conditions. There was only one thing for them to do, and they did it. They ceased to be trolley operators and became transit operators, ready to render service by electric railway, motor-bus or trolley bus, whichever offered the best solution in each individual instance.

8

FIRE AND STORM

The Story of How Emergencies Are Met

"Get going, boys!" bellowed the heavy-set man at the desk. "Box twenty-three's ringing from Main and Market. We roll on that."

Clang, clang——clang, clang, clang, sounded the gong for the second time. Down the brass pole from the second floor slid a couple of half-dressed men.

"All right, Mike. We're here," exclaimed the first as he hit the rubber pad at the bottom of the pole.

But Mike was no longer at the desk. He had run to the back of the building to rouse a team of sleeping horses. In a moment they were lumbering out of their stalls toward two sets of harness suspended from the ceiling. A bright red wagon bearing the legend "City Railway Company—Emergency Number One" was the equipment the horses would draw. The harness dropped on their backs; Mike climbed up to the front seat; one of his companions climbed up beside him and grabbed the reins while the other pushed open the wide front doors and swung onto the rear step of the wagon as it dashed into the street.

"Giddap!" shouted the driver, and away they went, horses

at full gallop and bell ringing a clamorous warning. The time
that had elapsed since the big brass gong began to sound had
been less than three minutes. Not even a city fire-department
company could have got in motion much faster.

Three blocks run and the emergency wagon was in Main
Street, where Saturday night crowds were thronging the sidewalks, watching with keen interest the fat pumping engines
and the sleek ladder trucks of the fire department getting to

Horse-drawn emergency wagon answering a hurry call

work on the fire. The railway's emergency wagon dashed on
another block to Market Street.

As the driver reined in his team, Mike saw that Engine
Number Ten was connected to a hydrant on the east side of
Main. The engine's three white horses were being unhitched
so that they could wait comfortably under their blankets a
short distance away, undisturbed by the vibration of the
pumps. Firemen with helmets bearing the numeral "10" were
laying a hose from the engine across the car tracks toward
"The Cotton Bazar," from the upper windows of which dense
clouds of smoke were rolling out into the night air. Engine
Number Three was getting ready to lay a second hose across
the car tracks.

"Jumpers!" yelled Mike, climbing down from the seat of

the emergency wagon and running around to the back. Out came the long slender iron frames known as "hose-jumpers," and used to make a bridge for the car tracks over the hose lines. In a couple of minutes the men had the "jumpers" in place, and the first of the cars waiting on Main Street was able to proceed on its way despite the fire department's hose. The engines might stay there for hours pumping water into the burning building, but the Saturday night crowds could go home whenever they wished.

Handling emergency calls for the street-railway involved picturesque equipment in the days of horse-drawn apparatus. The emergency wagon was usually provided with a movable tower that could be raised to a convenient height to permit work on the overhead trolley wires. For this reason it was called a "tower" wagon. It was housed in much the same way as a regular fire-engine. Sleeping quarters were provided for the crew on the second floor with the same kind of a shiny brass pole to provide a means of rapid descent. Horses were stabled immediately behind the wagon with spring doors at the front of their stalls so that no time would be lost in their getting out. Special harness was arranged on frames suspended from the ceiling so that it could be dropped quickly on the backs of the horses as soon as they had come out of their stalls, and snapped fast with a minimum of effort. The frames were counter-weighted so that they rose out of the way to the ceiling as soon as the harness was released. With the advent of the automobile, of course, the horse-drawn vehicles were replaced by motorized "tower" wagons.

On the wall was a big brass gong connected on the fire department alarm circuit so that every alarm of fire was repeated in the railway's emergency station. Not every alarm, however, meant a run for the emergency wagon. Unless the call came from a box, on, or very close to, a street where the railway's cars ran, the emergency crew paid no attention to

An early type of electric-railway tower wagon

it, as it threatened no interference with the company's service.

History does not record the exact place or date of the first use of hose-jumpers, but they were well known way back in the horse-car days. When the New York *Morning Journal* of July 15, 1885, referred to a delay of an hour and a half to Broadway street-cars caused by hose used in fighting a fire on Liberty Street, the editor of the *Street Railway Journal* was prompted to remark:

> The idea suggests itself to us that there must have been a good many fares lost to the street-car lines, by reason of the hose impeding the traffic, and that this loss is one that is very often repeated on a greater or less scale, from the same cause. If the evil were irremediable this loss would be a fit subject for bewailment; but the fact of the matter is, that simple and effective hose-jumpers are so cheaply made and so easily carried, that companies deserve the losses that they incur from such blocks at fires. Most of us remember when hose-bridges and jumpers were regularly carried and used; and we believe that the reason for their discardal was a silly squabble as to whose place it was to pay for them and carry them; the firemen's or the street-railway men's. The railroads insisted that it was the place of those who laid the hose lines across the street, to prevent them obstructing travel. The fire department, on the other hand, claimed that it was the duty of those who didn't want to be bothered by such delays, to obviate them. Perhaps the railway men had the right of it, but the firemen have the best of it; and we suggest that it will pay the railways to carry hose jumpers.

Many of the calls for the emergency wagon had nothing to do with the fire department. They came in by telephone, occasioned by such diverse causes as a broken trolley wire, a wagon broken down on the track, a derailed car, or anything else that might disrupt the normal operation of the cars.

No one ever knew just what was in prospect when answering a call with the emergency wagon. A fire might involve a big job for the railway's men or it might involve nothing at all. Hose-jumpers, of course, were needed only when the fire was of considerable size. A small fire could usually be put out with chemicals, or if hose was needed, enough could be laid from hydrants on the same side of the street as the burning building so that the car tracks were not blocked. But a big fire almost always meant hose across the tracks, and might even mean cutting down a section of trolley wire to permit greater freedom of action for the fire department's aërial ladders and water-towers.

The job might last a few minutes or many hours. For example, an alarm sounded one day for a warehouse fire on North Broad Street, Philadelphia, shortly after seven in the morning. Scarcely had the first fire-engines arrived, when a second and then a third alarm were rung in. This was soon followed by a fourth. A total of forty-four pieces of fire apparatus were assembled in the streets adjacent to the warehouse. Hose across the tracks completely blocked the street-cars of Routes 20 and 54. But the Philadelphia Rapid Transit Company's emergency crews had reached the scene only a little later than the first engines. The hose lines across Route 20 were brought together in one place, and hose-jumpers installed over them for both tracks. On Route 54 a different procedure was followed. Instead of laying hose-jumpers over the fire department's lines, the railway emergency crews arranged two "tower" wagons opposite each other, one on each side of the tracks and carried the hose lines clear over the trolley wires so that the cars could pass under them without interruption.

Well before eight o'clock, when the morning rush started, the cars were running through according to schedule on both routes, and the 40,000 people relying on them reached their work without delay. Late that afternoon they headed homeward, and again they found the cars running on time though the fire department's hose lines still sprawled across the streets. It was not until nearly eight o'clock that night, more than twelve hours after the start of the fire, that the railway crews were able to lower their "tower" wagons, remove their hose-jumpers and betake themselves back to their stations.

Sometimes, of course, even the hose-jumpers were not enough to enable the cars to keep going. A fire that started in the heart of Baltimore's business district on the morning of Sunday, February 7, 1904, spread so rapidly that it soon became impossible to get the cars through the main downtown streets of the city by any means. All of the United Railways Company's cars, however, were of the so-called "double-end" type, so that it was possible to switch them back at any place where there was a crossover from one track to the other. So the cars were run from the outlying sections as far in to the heart of the city as they could go, and then turned back. As the fire area grew larger and larger the railway lines, converging on the business district, grew shorter and shorter.

At this time the company's offices were on the ninth floor of the Continental Building. Even though it was Sunday the cashier and some of his assistants were working in the offices. By dusk the fire had come so close to the building that he began to get worried. A couple of flat-cars were hurriedly summoned and the office force began to take its books and precious records downstairs to the street. All of them were loaded on to the flat-cars. Every bit of available money was then stuffed into a suitcase which was put on one of the flat-cars, too, where the cashier sat on it for safekeeping until a new headquarters had been established at the Madison Avenue car-house.

Next morning the fire was still burning but Frank Badart, the dispatcher at Madison Avenue car-house wasn't going to be stopped by that. At 5 A.M. he started the first cars downtown on the old "business as usual" principle. He didn't know it, but he was licked before he started. The fire had reached the company's main power-house and it was not long before the electric current supply failed on virtually all of the thirty-four lines of the system, leaving cars stranded all over the city.

Emergency crew of the Westfield & Elizabeth Street Railway putting
a derailed car back on the track—1900.

North Jersey Street Railway's tower wagon at Elizabeth in 1902.

Hose-jumpers keep the street-railway line open during a four-alarm fire at Philadelphia.

Tower wagons carry the hose over the tracks of P.R.T.'s route 54 during a fire.

Street-car service was resumed in Baltimore while the ruins of the
great fire of 1904 were still smoking.

Street-car operating on an emergency trestle during a flood
at Cincinnati.

One of Baltimore's thirty-seven snow sweepers that fought the big storm of Thanksgiving Day, 1938.

Car 5921—mobile patrol unit of the Department of Street Railways at Detroit equipped for two-way radio communication.

But the fire was being brought under control by the heroic efforts of the Baltimore firemen and those of other cities as far away as New York who had come to aid in the fight. Before Tuesday dawned the battle had been won. More than one hundred blocks in the heart of the city had been burned with a loss of 125 million dollars. Street-railway tracks were buried under a mass of debris. Eight miles of trolley wire were down. The supporting poles were twisted and broken. The main power-house was destroyed. One hundred and twenty-six cars were stranded at various points on the system. The company's offices had been completely burnt out with nothing saved but what the cashier had been able to salvage Sunday evening on the flat-cars he had hurriedly requisitioned to carry his money and records.

Here was a staggering task for the emergency crews. With indomitable energy they set to work to clear the tracks, and re-string the wires. On Wednesday the company was able to operate about 10 per cent of its normal service. Cars were rolling through Baltimore Street while the ruins were still smoking. Each day the volume of service increased. The end of February saw it back to sixty-five per cent of normal, and a few weeks more sufficed to complete the restoration.

Storms often give the street-railway crews worse trouble than fires. When snow begins to fall every company prepares for battle. The first flakes may turn out to have been a false alarm, but, on the other hand, they may turn out to have been the beginning of a blizzard. In any event the snow-fighters must be on their toes, and the equipment must be ready for whatever demands are made upon it.

Arriving on Thanksgiving Day, 1938, a heavy snow came as a startling surprise to people in many cities in the eastern part of the United States. Thousands of automobiles were stalled in the drifts that formed, but transit service was maintained with relatively few interruptions. Early though it was for a snowfall of this severity, the transit companies were ready for it when it came.

The way the situation was handled at Baltimore was typical of the procedure in a score of other places. According to the log-book of the Baltimore Transit Company's superintendent of transportation a light rain commenced about seven o'clock in the morning. There was nothing particularly alarming in that, but when the rain began to turn to sleet around noon-time, the outlook was more ominous.

Orders were issued to put chains on the wheels of suburban buses. A few motorized sand-spreaders were sent out to work on hills that were apt to get slippery. At five in the afternoon the sleet was still falling, but no trouble had been reported. By six o'clock the company had all of its fifteen sand-spreaders at work, and an order had gone out to put chains on the city buses as well as those in suburban service.

At six-thirty the company's weather bureau warned the superintendent of transportation that heavy snow was moving eastward. Then things began to hum. The track department was told to get out its men to keep the switches clear. The equipment department was told to have men ready to repair any vehicles that became crippled. All over town transit men were getting up from their Thanksgiving dinner tables. Tur-keys and mince-pies were forgotten when the call came to do battle with the elements.

It was hailing fiercely with some snow by half-past seven. The superintendent of transportation had sent for a second telephone operator to handle the rapidly increasing number of calls. All transit lines were still running pretty nearly on schedule time.

By eight o'clock the snow was a little more than an inch deep and coming down harder than ever. The weather bureau reported that the storm would probably continue all night. Number 8 car line was having a little trouble. The line supervisor was told to have his snow-sweeper crew stand by. During the next hour the snow increased to a depth of nearly three inches. Life-guards on all cars were ordered hooked up against the under side of the car floor to avoid getting tangled in the rapidly accumulating snow. Sweeper crews all over the system were told to stand by for orders.

These orders were not long in coming. At nine-thirty the word was broadcast, "Send out all sweepers!" Almost before the last call had been made for them to go out, came reports that they were on their way:

9:39—Sweeper 3210 out on Line 4
9:44—Sweeper 3220 reported out
9:48—Sweeper 3209 gone to Windsor Hills
9:50—Sweeper 3223 gone to Hinton Street
9:52—Sweeper 3218 out on Eastern Avenue

By ten o'clock the big rattan brooms on all of the company's thirty-seven sweepers were whirling the snow off the car tracks. Fifteen motorized snow-plows were working to keep the bus routes open. Then came a slight lull—not in the storm, but in the frenzied activity at the office of the superintendent of transportation. At 10:12 a frozen switch was reported. At 10:37 came word of another frozen switch. These were jobs for the men of the track department. Except for these minor difficulties, the system was running satisfactorily.

So far the demands on the emergency wagons had not been particularly heavy, but trouble was not far away. Just before eleven a report came in that two automobiles were stalled on the car tracks on Park Heights Avenue. An emergency wagon was sent out. A little after eleven a stalled auto near Cold Spring Lane was reported to be holding up a snow sweeper. Another job for the emergency wagon. Within five minutes word was received that a stalled auto was blocking the sweeper on Liberty Heights Avenue. "Emergency wagon called," says the record.

The snow was now over five inches deep. Snow-sweepers were making their second trips over their assigned routes. Cars were ordered to run all night on lines which did not ordinarily have all-night service, as a heavy snow accumulates behind the sweepers, and unless something is done to keep the rails clear, the next trip of the sweeper finds the going tougher than before. Running passenger cars up and down the line, even though nobody is riding in them, tends to keep the tracks open.

Midnight found the snow getting deeper and drifting a good deal. The equipment department was notified to get the big rail-snow-plows ready. These plows cannot get the snow off the tracks clear down to the rail, but they can buck the deep drifts. Orders were issued that the sweeper crews be fed as they came back to their stations, and that the sweepers then be sent out as quickly as possible for a third trip over their assigned routes. Three rail plows were reported ready and were sent out. Sweepers 3209 and 3220 needed new brooms; as soon as they could be installed, the sweepers were to go out again. Another call came for the emergency wagon—this time the message was the laconic statement: "Sweeper derailed on Pratt Street."

At two o'clock the company's weather bureau reported "no change" in the situation. At 3:10, however, came word that the storm seemed to be abating. Nevertheless all sweepers and plows were kept going. At four o'clock the record says "the stars are out." At 4:30 the order was issued, "Pull in all sweepers and plows."

When morning came there were long, clear ribbons from one end of the city to the other where the transit routes had been swept clean. At seven o'clock radio-station announcers began telling thousands of listeners, "All street-car and bus lines are open. Baltimore transit men worked all night to keep the cars and buses running. If your automobile is snowed under, don't worry—take a street-car or bus downtown this morning."

The development of short-wave radio broadcasting opened the door to a new method of handling emergency calls on transit systems. The municipal street-railway at Detroit was the first to establish a two-way system of communication. An emergency dispatcher's office was established early in 1940 on the thirty-seventh floor of the Barlum Tower in the heart of the downtown business district, and equipped with short-wave radio apparatus. It was known as Station WALJ. At the same time ten small automobiles were equipped for operation as mobile patrol units with two-way communication apparatus.

The emergency dispatcher's office was provided with direct telephone connection with all the divisional headquarters of the system. It also had a fire-alarm recorder—not a big brass gong as in the old days, but a neat little telegraph arrangement showing the number of the fire-box by printing purple dashes on a paper ribbon. Behind the dispatcher's desk hung a huge wall map of the city of Detroit, divided into the sections in which the mobile patrol units were operating.

As the fire-alarm began to click the dispatcher watched the dashes being printed on the paper ribbon. Then he consulted a printed list to find the location of the box from which the alarm was rung. A quick glance at the map showed him that the fire was on a street where four bus lines operate and not far from a car line. Instantly he closed the switch of the transmitter and began to send out his call:

"Station WALJ calling Car 5921—Station WALJ calling Car 5921—go to fire at Cass and Davenport Avenues."

Back came the answer within five seconds, "Car 5921 calling Station WALJ—o.k. on the way."

A minute later came the next report, "Car 5921 calling Station WALJ—fire looks bad—will have to reroute buses."

"Station WALJ to Car 5921—o.k.—reroute buses—I will notify patrol cars in adjoining areas."

"Car 5921 to Station WALJ—fire getting worse—we may need hose-jumpers."

"Station WALJ to Car 5921—o.k. will send emergency wagon with hose-jumpers."

But, as it turned out, the hose-jumpers were not needed. The bus lines had been rerouted at almost the same moment that the first engines arrived at the scene, so that there was no delay to bus operation and no interference with the fire-department's activities. The fire had then been brought under control before it had become necessary to lay any hose across car tracks.

Day in and day out the emergency dispatching system at Detroit handled about 300 calls a month for fires, accidents, and other happenings threatening the regular continuity of the transit service. The actual time that Station WALJ was "on the air" averaged somewhat less than one minute per episode. How much time was thus being saved by the system's cars and buses could not be measured definitely, nor could the time-saving to the people riding on these vehicles, but the total certainly reached a tremendous figure.

Tower wagons, hose-jumpers, sand-spreaders and snow-sweepers may not be the stuff from which popular romance and drama are woven, but they have their parts to play, and they play them well. It would not be too much to say, indeed, that they permit the carriers of passengers in city transportation to repeat the boast of the ancient postmaster general of France, Cardinal Richelieu, "Neither rain nor snow nor heat nor gloom of night stays these carriers from the swift completion of their appointed rounds."

9

UNUSUAL TYPES OF TRANSIT

The Story of Novel Means of Rendering Service

"Load a Ransom Steamer heavily, steam it up a grade of 300 feet to the mile—it will shake under the action of its engines then, if ever—and it will be as smooth as a horse-car rolling down the grade by its own weight. I think this cannot be said of any other steam street-car in existence."

The advantages of a type of vehicle which he believed to be a vast improvement over the horse cars which were then the ordinary means of city transportation were argued by Louis Ransom of Akron, Ohio, in 1884. His arguments fell on deaf ears, however. No street-railway company ever adopted this form of motive power. He went on:

"The engine is attached directly to the driving axle—no growl of gears, no rattle of sprockets. It is capable of any speed, up to twenty miles an hour.

"Place the car on any horse-railway track and it is ready for work. Each car is independent of all other cars and all other machinery—a self-contained, powerful monarch of the road. The cost of equipping a road with Ransom Steamers is limited to the cost of the cars. It burns seven pounds of coal to the mile of travel."

About this same time George A. Clark, of Cincinnati, put forward a plan for operating street-cars by compressed air. According to an article in the Cincinnati *Commercial Gazette:*

Cars are constructed with double metal bottoms for air chambers. Compressed air, which is known to be about ten per cent more efficient than steam at the same pressure, will be utilized to run the car both forward and backward and stop and start it on any grade. By a simple contrivance the motion of the car continually replenishes the constantly exhausting air, but, of course, only partially. Means must be provided for refilling.

At each end of the line is a simple twelve horse-power engine. The entire length of the line, between the tracks if double, or at the side of a single track, is laid fifteen inches beneath the surface, an iron pipe four or five inches in diameter. This is perfectly jointed, and every piece tested to stand a pressure of 125 pounds. The engines keep this pipe constantly filled with air at a pressure of about 100 pounds. At intervals of a square, this pipe will be tapped, and it is estimated that connection can be made with the car and pressure taken on in six seconds time. A pressure of 80 pounds to the square inch in the air chambers of the car will give a propelling force equal to six horses. This will always be sufficient to drive the car through snow and slush, or assist it on the track should it be derailed.

The advantages claimed over horses, steam, electricity, or cable are considerable. The inventor claims that any line which is now in operation can be equipped with compressed air cars, air pipe-line, engines and all complete for less than $7,000 per mile; that the change can be made without stopping travel for a single hour, or obstruction of the street; that once equipped, the expense of running is reduced to the minimum. No horses to buy and feed, no cable to renew, no stables to rent or stablemen to pay. The engines are so small and simple that any man competent to run a car can tend one. There is no steam to frighten horses, no disagreeable dust, no fire and no smoke; there is no tearing up streets for repairs as with the cable, and expresses and wagons can use the track as now, which can not be safely done on the cable. There are no electrical shocks during a storm, as is the case on electric roads, to frighten ladies and endanger life.

A number of compressed-air cars were operated for short periods in various American cities. None proved satisfactory and the idea was soon given up.

In 1886 a test was made at New Orleans of a car using ammonia gas as the propelling agent. This gas, weighing a little more than one half as much as air, was known to be powerfully expansive, and when passed through the cylinders of a steam-engine "would operate the same as steam in moving machinery." In order to carry enough of the gas to drive the machinery for any considerable time, the gas was forced by powerful pumps into a reservoir on the car until a pressure of from 180 to 200 pounds to the square inch was reached. Each car was supposed to carry enough gas to make a trip back and forth between Carrollton and Canal Street.

The argument in favor of this form of power was, that

there being no fire, no smoke, no steam, no heat, there is no need to have the propelling power separate from the cars that carry the passenger (as with the so-called steam "dummies" used on some street-railways), but, on the contrary, the propelling appliances are compactly stored beneath the floor of the car, which, in external appearance or internal accommodation, is in no way different from the ordinary street-car, save that it stands a little higher on its wheels, to make room for the machinery underneath. The engineer or driver sits on the front platform, which is no more encumbered than is the platform of a horse-car, and by means of a couple of levers he reverses or forwards the engine movement at will, while a throttle valve controls the admittance of gas to the engine in much the same way as steam is managed. Right here comes in a great item of economy. The ammonia gas after passing through the engine and doing its work is not lost by being allowed to escape into the atmosphere, but is saved simply by turning it into the airtight water-tank carried under the car. The gas has such an affinity for the water that the latter will absorb 700 times its bulk, ten cubic feet of water taking up 7,000 cubic feet of the gas, which is extracted from the water and is again utilized for driving a car.

As in the case of the Ransom steam-car, however, the streeet-railway industry remained cold to the idea.

The era of street-railway electrification marked the end of numerous unusual transportation schemes, but at the same time, it fostered some new ones. A certain amount of prejudice against electric railways was occasioned by the presence of overhead wires in the streets, and much ingenuity was devoted to the development of other forms of current collection. Some cities adopted the underground conduit system and a considerable number of surface contact schemes were tried. The theory behind all surface contact systems was that a collector underneath the car should slide over a continuous row of electrified studs in the pavement. Systems of this kind were tried in a number of cities in England and the United States.

In general the plan was to place the studs about three feet apart and to equip the car with a "skate" or other contact mechanism of sufficient length to cover at least two studs at the same time. This assured an uninterrupted supply of electric energy. Sometimes the car was equipped with a magnet which lifted a movable contact piece inside the stud so that the stud became electrified only when the car was immediately above it, and no danger existed for other users of the street. At other times the contact pieces inside the studs were moved by an arrangement of electromagnets and relays under the pavement. Some of these surface contact systems gave fairly satisfactory results, but the idea never attained any wide popularity.

Electric-railway operation in what is now the city of New York began in 1891 when an overhead trolley line was built in Brooklyn. On the island of Manhattan, however, the authorities were unwilling to permit the erection of the poles and wires necessary for an overhead trolley system. At the same time it was felt that there was room for improvement in the existing methods of city transportation.

For that reason, H. H. Vreeland, president of the Metropolitan Traction Company, offered a prize of $50,000 in November, 1893, to the person who should submit a practical plan for operating street-cars, "superior or equal to the overhead trolley, but without its objectionable features." The Railroad Commissioners of the State of New York were asked to be the judges of the contest.

There were in operation at this time a number of electric

Electric surface-contact system with movable studs

railways operated by means of power obtained from an underground conductor instead of the usual overhead trolley. The North Chicago Street Railway had tried this experiment with some success in 1892. The next year a portion of the Rock Creek Railway at Washington, D. C., was electrified in the same manner. At Budapest, Hungary, an underground conduit electric-railway system was operating quite satisfactorily.

The prize offered by the Metropolitan Traction Company inspired the submission of a large number of plans. Some of them were ridiculously impractical, but others had considerable merit. Many of them were variations of the underground conduit systems in use in other cities.

In fixing the conditions of its contest the Metropolitan had set March 1, 1894, as the closing date. Before the Railroad Commissioners could serve as judges, however, it was necessary to secure from the state legislature an amendment to the Railroad Law permitting them to act in this capacity. The expectation was that this could be done very quickly, but that proved to have been an overly optimistic idea, and it was actually May before the permission was granted. When the Commissioners told the company on May 3, that they were prepared to proceed, Charles E. Warren, company secretary, replied that when it had appeared that

long delay was likely to occur in the passage of the act, which has since occurred, this company proceeded to employ experts and conduct the investigations which it was originally proposed to have the Railroad Commissioners conduct, and has spent a large sum of money exceeding the $50,000 which the company proposed to award in determining the question which was to be the subject of investigation and award.

This company is about to enter upon a large expenditure based upon the results of its inquiries and should prefer to await the results of some practical experiments which it is now entering upon as the result of contracts with one or two electric companies, before deciding to go on with the matter of the award.

In other words, the company has itself conducted the investigation and has passed beyond the stage of inquiry and has determined for itself upon an improved motive-power and is about to put it in.

The upshot of all this was that the Metropolitan proceeded to electrify its Lenox Avenue line by the underground conduit system. The General Electric Company got the contract on the basis of being paid at the end of twelve months if the experiment was a success or having to remove the equipment if it was a failure. The design was a great improvement over the conduit systems previously used. Operation began in the summer of 1895 and proved to be entirely successful.

Under this plan the two rails of each track were supported on the shoulders of cast-iron yokes having the general shape of the letter U with the tops bent inward toward each other, but not far enough to meet and form the letter O. These yokes were spaced about five feet apart. Between the yokes ran a brick conduit of the same U shape, with a continuous open slot in the paving surface. On the inside of the bottom of each yoke were a couple of so-called "chairs," on which rested a pair of contact rails, one to supply current and the other to act as a return circuit to the power-house. Each car was equipped with a "plow" projecting downward through the slot and having two contact shoes sliding along the rails in the conduit.

The chief advantages of the underground conduit system of current collection were that it eliminated all overhead wires in the street, and that one of the two rails in the conduit provided the return circuit instead of having one of the running rails used for that purpose. Against these advantages, however, stood some very serious disadvantages. The original construction was far more costly than that of an overhead trolley system. At locations where two tracks crossed there were "dead spots" where the power rail in the conduit had to be broken so that it would not touch the return circuit rail of the intersecting track. Cars had to coast over these "dead spots" in the same way the cable-cars had to coast around curves. Worse still was the tendency for water, snow, ice, and refuse to collect in the conduit. A piece of metal falling through the slot onto the rails often caused a short circuit.

On account of these disadvantages only two cities in the United States ever adopted the underground conduit system of electric railway operation on any large scale. They were New York and Washington, the former with something over

200 miles of such track and the latter with a little more than 100 miles. In Washington, it was a young, Connecticut-born engineer, Albert N. Connett, who was in charge of most of the construction beginning with the electrification of the Metropolitan Railroad in 1895. He had been employed on the construction of one of the early, experimental, electric-railway lines at Kansas City, and had then become associated with the firm of Bentley & Knight, builders of the famous underground conduit electric railway at Cleveland in 1884. Because the Metropolitan was a horse-car line, this job was more complicated than that at New York, where much of the track which was electrified had previously been operated by cable. A much larger amount of excavation was needed for the conduit and the expense was correspondingly greater. Later, Connett built underground conduit systems in London, Paris and other European cities.

Diametrically opposite to the underground current-collection systems installed at New York and Washington, was the two-wire overhead system at Cincinnati. A controversy with the local telephone company was the cause of the adoption of this unusual system.

The first electric-railway service at Cincinnati was started with a single overhead trolley wire. Because the track rails were not well connected electrically where they joined, however, the track was a poor return circuit to the power-house. There was some sparking at the joints, and a certain amount of the current wandered away to follow paths other than the track.

In those days the telephone circuits used a ground return instead of a wire return, and the return current of the trolley line caused a great deal of interference with the telephone service. This got so bad that, in 1889, the telephone company secured an injunction against the street-railway's use of its track for its return circuit. The best way out of that situation seemed to be the construction of a two-wire overhead system, one wire to supply electricity and the other to serve as a return circuit.

Later the Supreme Court of Ohio reversed the lower court which had granted the injunction, and permitted the use of a single trolley by the street-railway. Nevertheless, in view of the possibility of stray electric current causing electrolytic damage to water and gas pipes in the ground, the railway continued to use a double trolley-wire system.

For many years Cincinnati, and Havana, Cuba, were virtually unique in using this two-wire trolley system. With the development of the trolley bus, however, the novelty of the double trolley began to disappear. Since the trolley-bus had no track which could be used for a return circuit, there was no alternative to using two trolley wires, and this type of overhead became a familiar sight in many cities throughout the world.

One of the difficulties with early electric cars was that they did not always have power enough to get up steep hills. Frank Sprague had had considerable trouble of this kind at Richmond and others had experienced it elsewhere. At Providence, Rhode Island, the fifteen per cent grade on College Street hill presented a particularly knotty problem until a most ingenious solution was worked out. This was nothing more than a heavy counter-weight operating in the old cable conduit between the rails. At the bottom of the hill the car was hooked on to one end of a long cable running over a wheel at the top of the hill. Attached to the other end of the cable was the counter-weight, slightly lighter than the car. As the car went up the hill the counter-weight slid down the conduit. Being lighter than the car it served only as an aid to the movement of the car, the car's own electric power being required to do the rest of the work.

Having reached the top of the hill, the car was unhooked

from the cable and continued its run. Then the next car headed in the opposite direction picked up the end of the cable at the top of the hill and proceeded down under electric power, thus pulling the counter-weight up again to its original position. This system was installed in 1895 and remained in use until 1915. But they had been building a tunnel through the hill and when this was completed the tough climb for the trolley was over. In operating the counter-weight system, great care was required to make sure that the mechanism was adequately secured when the weight was left in the up-hill position. Otherwise it might come loose and start down of its own accord. When that happened the hook at the other end of the cable, which projected above the pavement, went sailing up the hill. In spite of all precautions this sometimes happened. It was entertaining to watch, but was occasionally dangerous to the other users of the street. Once when the weight broke loose, the rapidly moving hook neatly removed the rear wheels from a wagon crossing the street at an intersection part way up the hill.

Another solution of the problem of steep grades was the inclined railway, or, as it was sometimes called, the wagon elevator. First introduced in horse-car days, this device was adopted in a number of cities including Cincinnati, Pittsburgh, and Duluth, and two were installed on the west shore of the Hudson River opposite New York, at the foot of the precipitous Palisades. But the most famous of all the inclined railways was the Mount Adams route at Cincinnati, rising 270 feet in a length of 980 feet, for a 28.9 per cent grade. The city was growing rapidly at this period and could not accommodate its increasing population without spreading to the hills that surrounded it. The grades were too steep for horse-cars, so it was decided to build an inclined railway equipped with two platforms connected by cables. The platforms were mounted on flanged wheels with the axles at different distances

Walking-beam car at New Orleans, one of the early unsuccessful
experiments.

Connelly gas-motor system was tried at Elizabeth, New Jersey, but
did not prove very practical.

Philadelphia's famous funeral car, The Hillside. The opening near the front is for the coffin.

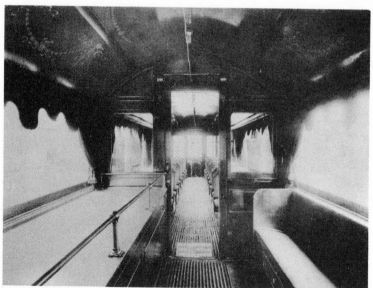

Interior of The Hillside. Floral tributes were placed on top of the compartment for the coffin at left. The family occupied the bench at right.

A combination mail and passenger car operated by the Boston Elevated Railway.

An electric-railway tank-car for street sprinkling, formerly a common sight in many cities.

Sightseeing car of the Cincinnati Street Railway on its way up the famous Mt. Adams incline.

Battery-operated automobile which first provided transportation in the Senate Subway at Washington in 1908.

below the floor to compensate for the slope of the incline and keep the platform level. A steam-engine at the top of the hill furnished the power for pulling the platforms up the hill, but this was not an extremely difficult undertaking as one went down as the other went up, and the weights more or less counter-balanced each other through the connecting cable.

The first inclined railway at Cincinnati was built to the top of Mt. Auburn in 1872. A second was built up Price Hill and

Mt. Adams Incline Railway and Highland House

a third on Elm Street before the Mt. Adams incline was completed in 1877.

These new "elevator" railways not only opened up new residential areas but they provided unsurpassed locations for amusement centers. At the top of the Mt. Adams incline was the elegant Highland House, one of Cincinnati's show places in the late 1870's and 1880's and famed throughout the county. Its host, Frank Harff, made entertainment history in 1877 when he arranged a three-week series of concerts by Theodore Thomas in the outdoor pavillion on the hilltop. As many as 8,000 people climbed the hill for some of the concerts.

Since the incline railway could handle only 2,000 people per
hour, the newspapers warned the concert goers to make an
early start if they wanted to be sure of getting to the Highland House on time. The charms of this hostlery have been
thus described:

Mein Host, Fred Harff, invites you and your lady friend to stroll
on the veranda of his celebrated Highland House and listen to the
entrancing music offered by Theodore Thomas' world-renowned
orchestra. It will be a rare treat for you and any of your friends
who happen to be visiting our fair city. The view of the river,
spanned so recently by John Roebling's suspension bridge, and of
the beautiful hills of Kentucky and Ohio from this high-class resort
is beyond comparison, while the ride up Mount Adams Incline will
give a new thrill to your out-of-town guest.

When first built, the Mt. Adams inclined plane carried only
passengers. Horse-car lines connected with it at top and bottom. Later rails were laid on the platforms and the horse-cars
were taken up and down the inclined railway so that the riders
did not have to make any change of vehicle. When the Cincinnati street-railway system was electrified, the platforms
were strengthened a little so the electric cars could travel up
and down just as the horse-car did.

In the heyday of the trolley there were many unusual kinds
of vehicle to be found running on the electric-railway tracks.
Not only were there some extremely odd varieties of passenger cars, both open and closed, but there were also a wide
variety of cars for special purposes. Trolley mail-cars were
operated in many cities. Sometimes these were special cars
for that particular purpose; sometimes they were combination
cars with one compartment for passengers and one for mail.
Trolley express cars were widely used, too. Naturally their
utility was greatest on systems which had numerous suburban
lines radiating out of urban centers. Milk-cars were sometimes
operated under similar circumstances. Before the day of modern pavements many electric railways operated sprinkler cars

spraying water over a wide area of the street to lay the dust.

Oddest of all, perhaps, was the electric-railway funeral car; the "Dolores," put in service in 1900 by the United Railways & Electric Company of Baltimore, was a splendid example of this type of vehicle. According to Raymond S. Tompkins, official historian of the company:

The Dolores was designed for the purpose of furnishing transportation service for bereaved persons who desired a quick, comfortable, convenient, and tasteful method for transporting the deceased from home to cemetery. Her carrying capacity was 32 persons. She was divided into two compartments—the rear compartment seated 24, and the front compartment seated 8. This front section was known as the "casket compartment" so it may be said that it seated 8 in addition to the deceased. The car was particularly valuable in case the funeral was held from a house on a car line; but if the house were off the car line, a pneumatic tired casket carriage, which was part of the equipment of the Dolores, was brought into play. This casket carriage was quiet and smooth in operation, and with its assistance little effort was necessary to convey the deceased in the casket almost any distance from the house to the funeral car Dolores, or at the end of the journey from the car to the grave.

An interesting and spectacular feature of the Dolores was the fact that the casket was placed in the car from the outside through a large glass door built into the casket compartment; thus the casket was visible from the street as the car rolled along to the cemetery. A nickel plated rail extending around the casket compartment was used for placing the floral designs. The car was equipped with 16 electric heaters which made it very comfortable for funeral parties during winter months, and it was sometimes difficult to get the funeral parties to leave the car when the funeral was over on very cold days. The seats in the car were upholstered in leather and the windows were draped with heavy black curtains so that the interior presented a very neat appearance.

Charges were very reasonable—for a funeral within the city limits of Baltimore, the cost of the service of the Dolores with neatly dressed motorman and conductor was $20. Outside the city limits in the second fare zone the fare was $22, in the third fare zone $24 and in the fourth fare zone $26. Sometimes the family made arrangements for the car directly with the company, but in most cases arrangements were made by the officiating mortician.

So popular was the Dolores that quite often two funerals would be taken care of in one day. If the demand was greater than this, then the handsome parlor car "Lord Baltimore" was pressed into service. This was a luxurious vehicle and differed little from the Dolores, both being painted black. However, as the Lord Baltimore had no casket compartment, the deceased was not visible from the street. This made it less attractive to customers than the Dolores.

Hundreds of Baltimore's best citizens were hauled to their last resting place on the Dolores, including a great many old Confederates from the Soldiers' Home in Pikesville. On such occasions, the Dolores, the Lord Baltimore, the Chesapeake and a large number of regular trolley cars would be chartered to accommodate the crowds of guests.

A unique type of city transportation service is given by the suspended mono-rail system at Elberfeld, Germany. This is an eight and one-half-mile line with two running rails, one for each direction, suspended from steel arches spanning the streets over which the line operates. The ends of the cars are hung from the running rail by brackets provided with two wheels in tandem.

This pair of wheels more or less resembles one side of a conventional car truck, being provided with an arrangement of springs and an electric motor to propel the car. The vehicles themselves are like ordinary electric railway cars except for their running gear. Each is about thirty-seven feet long, seven feet wide, and weighs twelve and one-half tons. They are run in two-car trains, one motor-car pulling one trailer. The trailers seat fifty passengers, while the motor-cars, on account of provision for the operator and operating mechanism, seat only thirty-two passengers. Each motor car is provided with a contact shoe which slides along a power rail placed above the running rail.

Part of the line is over the streets of the city and part above the River Wupper. Altogether there are twenty stations located about half a mile apart. On Sundays and holidays when crowds are going to the Zoölogical Gardens, the trains are operated on headways as close as two and one-half minutes. Construction of this line cost only about $200,000 per mile—far less than the cost of the ordinary elevated railway. Its operation has been successful for many years, but the idea has never been adopted in any other city.

Probably the most unusual subway in the world—certainly the shortest—is the mono-rail line which operates through the 760-foot tunnel between the Capitol and the Senate Office Building at Washington, D. C. This is one of a pair of tunnels constructed in 1908 when the Senate and House office buildings were built. At first a battery-powered Studebaker automobile provided service through the Senate tunnel, but in 1912 a double-track mono-rail system was installed. The House tunnel has never been equipped with any sort of transportation vehicles.

Two eighteen-passenger cars are operated in the Senate subway. Each rests on two two-wheel trucks running on the single rail. Unlike most car wheels these have double flanges. They are rubber cushioned to prevent noise and vibration. On each truck is mounted a small electric motor connected to one of the wheels. Overhead an arrangement of horizontal trolley wheels in a substantial mounting serves the double purpose of holding the car upright and providing for current collection. With a top speed of eighteen miles an hour these cars can make the 760-foot trip from end to end of the subway in about one minute. A total of 225 trips are made every day to transport an average of some 3,000 persons.

The development of rubber-tired highway transportation vehicles inspired many attempts to perfect a combination of wheels that could be run on tracks or pavements as might be desired. One of these experiments was the "road-railer" operated by the Arlington & Fairfax Railway in suburban Virginia territory adjacent to the city of Washington. This railway started as an ordinary trolley line which made connection with the Washington street-car system at a transfer point across the Potomac River from Georgetown. The suburban line fell upon hard times, however, and an attempt was made to revive it through the use of the "road-railer."

The idea was to operate it as a rail-car with flanged wheels over the route where the company had its tracks, and then to continue downtown to the center of the city of Washington as a bus on pneumatic tires. The transition was accomplished by an arrangement that retracted the flanged wheels at will, allowing the vehicle to rest on its rubber tires. An automotive engine was the propelling agent both on the rails and on the highway. This made it possible for the operating company to get rid of its trolley wires and all questions of electric power supply.

From a mechanical standpoint the design was reasonably satisfactory, but the desired permission to continue the route downtown was not secured, and the main theoretical advantage of the combination could not be obtained. Then, too, there remained the economic problem of the upkeep of track, a relatively expensive matter considering the small number of passengers the company carried. Eventually the "road-railer" idea was given up and ordinary motor buses were used, operating on the highway for the entire length of the route.

10

ROLLING ON RUBBER

The Story of the Motor Bus

"If the City Council or Board of Public Utilities can't or won't tame the Trolley Trust there is something else that can and will. And that is the 5-cent fare autos."

So said the Los Angeles *Record* in an editorial in its issue of October 1, 1914. A few days later the paper again addressed itself to this subject:

> The Trolley Trust will not succeed in throttling the People's Five-cent auto car service. The masses are aroused on this question and they will come to the front in such numbers and in such vigorous fashion in defense of the auto men that it will result in a greatly extended auto service in behalf of the public. That's the *Record's* prediction.

The owners of these small machines operating as common carriers could make as much as ten dollars a day, according to the *Record*. They had built up a fine and lasting business, the paper said. All that was needed to make the service a complete success was a system of universal transfers.

Events, to some extent, confirmed the *Record's* prediction. The first of the five-cent fare autos had made its appearance on the streets of Los Angeles on July 1, 1914. Before the end of the year there were more than 700 in operation in the city. Certainly it did not look as though anyone had succeeded in "throttling" them. The name "jitney" was bestowed on these vehicles because of their five-cent fare, but how "jitney" first came to be used as slang for five cents is not altogether clear. One explanation is that it came from the name of a Negro jail

Jitneys in Los Angeles in 1914

trusty called Jedney, who used to smuggle tobacco into the prison for his fellow inmates. For every dime he received he delivered a nickel's worth of tobacco. So the term "a Jedney's worth," later corrupted to "a jitney's worth," became a way of referring to five-cents' worth of anything.

In other respects the ideas of the *Record* were not so close to the mark. Its prediction concerning the prosperous and lasting character of the jitney business did not come true. The universal transfer system, which so appealed to the newspaper, ate a big hole in the income of the jitney operators. The business was pretty shaky anyway from a financial stand-point, as the five-cent fare did not really cover the cost of giving the service, and when a free transfer was added there just wasn't enough left to pay operating expenses in many instances. Lots of the operators quit, but, for a while, other optimists were not lacking to take their places.

Los Angeles, the birthplace of the jitney, was not the only city to have this kind of transportation. The craze spread rapidly. Jitneys were soon in operation in cities all over the country. California and New Jersey had them most plenti-fully. Every sort and condition of vehicle was brought into use, from the nondescript flivver to the decrepit limousine that had seen better days. It seemed as if every man who had no steady job and could get the use of an automobile went into the business. Sometimes the vehicle owner and an other-wise unemployed chauffeur worked on shares, one furnishing the car and the other furnishing the labor. In other instances the owner of the automobile had regular employment and used his vehicle at the close of his ordinary day's work to make a little extra money. Everywhere the impression ap-peared to exist, as it had with the Los Angeles *Record*, that there was a fortune to be made in the local transportation of passengers at five cents a head.

Street-railway men were very bitter about the jitneys. Al-most without exception the jitneys operated along established street-railway routes and skimmed off the cream of the busi-ness. In most cities no effort was made to compel the jitney men to adhere to an orderly procedure. It was a case of every man for himself, drivers jockeying with each other, cutting in to the curb to pick up passengers and then scurrying away on their self-chosen routes as far as was necessary to get rid of their loads. Then they would hurry back to the heavy loading areas to repeat the operation. There was no such thing as a schedule nor were the individual operators particular about holding to definite routes. The jitneys were most numerous in the morning and evening rush hours and roved where the pickings were most plentiful without regard to public convenience or necessity.

In considerable measure it was the growing popularity of the automobile that was responsible for the enthusiastic reception accorded to the jitney. Everybody who could afford to own an automobile and many who only thought they could, had one. Still there were a lot of people whose resources would not permit their indulging in such a luxury, and they turned to the jitney as a substitute. Actually it did not provide a more comfortable mode of transportation than the street-car, but it did offer the opportunity of an automobile ride. This was particularly attractive to the younger element of the population who constituted the majority of patrons of the early jitney.

No reliable figures exist to show how much the jitneys cost the street-railway industry. According to an estimate made by Edwin L. Lewis, superintendent of the Los Angeles Railway, the loss of revenue in that city was more than three million dollars a year at the height of the jitney craze. The "Trolley Trust," it would seem, had been effectively "tamed." R. E. Danforth, general manager of the Public Service Railway of New Jersey, estimated that the jitneys operating in the territory served by his company were costing it about four million dollars a year.

What particularly irked the electric railway men was that their jitney competitors were not only free of regulation regarding standards of service, but were free of the license fees and most of the taxes the railways had to pay. This was not particularly surprising since the jitney never had been thought of when the laws and ordinances governing street-railways were written. But it rankled with the men running the established companies, and there began a battle to place the jitney under what the street-railway men considered adequate regulation.

"Either similar burdens should be imposed upon the new transportation system," said Franklin T. Griffith, president of the Portland Railway, Light & Power Company, "or the existing company should be relieved of further obligations in the matter of such charges and be reimbursed for what it has heretofore expended for the benefit of the public."

Practically the entire street-railway industry was of this opinion. An editorial in a contemporary issue of the *Electric Railway Journal* said:

One feature of the jitney bus situation that stands out above all others is the need for regulation. Primarily the new conveyance aims only at competition with the much-regulated street-railway for the cream of its traffic—a fact borne out by the naive testimony of a jitney operator in one of the western cities to the effect that he couldn't operate on streets other than those occupied by railway tracks because he could keep his car full only by picking up groups of people who were waiting for the street-cars.

From the standpoint of ethics it is manifestly impossible to enforce the principle of regulation for the electric railway and to permit its competitor to go free of all restraint. Unfortunately, however, ethics are frequently a poor basis for argument, and regulation of the jitney, at least during its early stages, will probably come about not so much through a spirit of fair play as through the realization by the affected cities that the advent of the unrestricted jitney involves more direct dangers to the community than merely the abandonment of outlying and unprofitable electric railway lines. Already reports of extreme vehicular congestion are heard from the western towns where appreciable numbers of jitneys are operating, and fatalities to pedestrians struck by the recklessly driven vehicles have brought home generally the need for imposing responsibility by means of indemnity bonds.

This matter is a serious one for every citizen to consider. If a man is injured while on the public thoroughfares he can look for damages only to the owner of the vehicle that hits him, and if the owner's only asset is a second-hand automobile, the victim is not likely to be well compensated. This is a point which might well be emphasized in communities where the advent of the jitney has been hailed as a complete solution for the transportation problem. Another is that, to the jitney, a schedule has not even the value of a "scrap of paper," one driver admitting with perfect frankness that he never completed his advertised route in rush-hours because it wasn't profitable.

Meanwhile the newspapers were able to get a little fun out of the jitney situation. The Dallas *Dispatch* offered prizes of two dollars each for the best jingles about the jitney. One of the prize-winning rymes ran as follows:

> Hush, little Ford,
>> Don't you cry,
> You will be a jitney
>> Bye and bye.

The competition between the street-car and jitney inspired a jingle in the Fort Worth *Telegram* running:

> If a street-car meets a jitney
> Coming down the lane,
> And the street-car hits the jitney,
> I wonder who's to blame.

Efforts to secure regulation of the jitneys made comparatively slow progress. The feeling in many cities was the same as that expressed in a report of the Public Utilities Committee of the Los Angeles City Council, which stated: "We hold as a sound economic principle that every mode of transportation in operation prior to the advent of the motor bus should sustain its appeal to popular favor and profit making upon its intrinsic merit and not upon protective legislation."

Chaos continued; street accidents increased. Instances multiplied where jitney patrons suffered injury or death as the result of collisions, and they and their dependents were left without redress because of the financial irresponsibility of the jitney owners and their lack of accident insurance. There was also a high percentage of turnover among those who had gone into the jitney business. Instead of the fat profits their imaginations had pictured most of them had found that when the old car was completely worn out they did not have money enough to replace it. So they disappeared from the field, but others, unaware of the financial tribulations of their predecessors, took their places.

As time went on the necessity for adequate regulation became apparent to even the most enthusiastic jitney advocates. Even before this the first signs of the development of the jitney into a real transportation vehicle were making their appearance. The nondescript passenger automobile was giving way to a larger vehicle. The first step was to place a box-like body on a light truck chassis. This provided increased carrying capacity. Operators of this type of vehicle met with financial success in many cities. In design these vehicles were more or less of a makeshift, but they did fulfil the immediate need fairly well. It was not, however, until the vehicles were designed from the ground up that motor-bus operation became a real success.

The jitney bus, which had its birth in Los Angeles in 1914, was not the first common-carrier motor vehicle in American cities. Credit for taking the initial step belongs to the Fifth Avenue Coach Company which imported and put on their route in 1905 a single twenty-four-passenger, double-deck motor-bus. This was in addition to the company's horse-drawn omnibuses and proved so successful that fourteen additional buses were bought within two years. The chassis were built by De Bion-Bouton in France while the J. G. Brill Company in Philadelphia built the bodies. A year later twenty more chassis were imported and all of the company's horses were sold at auction.

Curiously enough, the use of horse-drawn omnibuses continued in London for some years after they were abandoned in New York. An experimental motor-bus had appeared on the route between Kensington and Oxford Circus as early as 1900 and many others quickly followed. Thomas Tilling and other independents adopted the motor-bus but the London General Omnibus Company refused to be hurried, and it was not until 1911 that the last L.G.O. horse-bus was withdrawn.

In 1912 the Cleveland Railway purchased three motor-buses for service in an outlying section of the city. This was the first time any street-railway company in the United States had operated motor-buses. There was no rush to follow the example of the company at Cleveland. As late as 1920 there were only about sixty motor-buses operated by ten electric railways in the whole United States.

By that time it had become clear that a specially designed vehicle was necessary if motor-bus operation was to be a real success. The converted motor-truck had never made a thoroughly satisfactory motor-bus. Its power-plant was not suitable for the demands put upon it, and the riding qualities were extremely poor. Safety, early recognized as a vital factor in bus design, demanded a low center of gravity. This, in turn, meant a lower floor level, making possible a reduction in the step height at the door, an important factor in speeding up loading and in reducing the number of boarding and alighting accidents.

Two brothers, Frank and William Fageol, were the builders of the first bus designed from the ground up for that particular purpose. This was at Oakland, California, in 1920. Frank was already a veteran of the bus business, having driven a crude steam-bus between downtown Des Moines and the fair grounds as far back as 1899. It was not much of a bus, judged by later standards, but it was a great thing in its day. Seats were provided for only seven passengers in addition to the driver. The roof was only a canopy, and the sides were only roll curtains. There was no windshield of any kind.

This primitive vehicle, however, gave Frank Fageol an interest that never waned in the bus business. Fifteen years later he saw the jitney craze spread throughout California. Then he saw the makeshift buses that followed in the wake of the first seven-passenger autos. These, he realized, were not the kind of vehicles to render satisfactory service. So he sat down at his drawing-board, and with the help of his brother, began to design the first built-for-the-purpose bus.

The result was the Fageol Safety Coach. It was built close to the ground, giving it a low center of gravity and a low entrance step. The springs were a great improvement over those in the truck chassis then widely used for buses. The engine was more powerful and the interior fittings much more attractive. Altogether it was such an advance over previous designs that its principal features soon became almost standard for buses in the United States and to some extent in Europe.

Six years later the Fageol brothers brought out another innovation in bus design—a vehicle with a body like a street-car, the engine being placed inside the body instead of under a hood at the front. This design, too, was almost universally adopted for city buses in following years.

Once again, in 1938, the fertile brains of the Fageols were responsible for a new development in bus design. This was the result of a desire to provide a greater number of seats without going to the extent of making the vehicle a double-decker. By joining two ordinary bus bodies together with a flexible coupling, and mounting the unit thus created on four axles they had a bus with seats for fifty-eight passengers, the largest number ever accommodated in a single-deck vehicle on rubber tires.

The development of the built-for-the-purpose bus came at exactly the right moment for the progress of bus transportation. Regulation that had so long been a crying need, was gradually being adopted. Mr. Danforth, of hard-hit Public Service Railway of New Jersey, told the midwinter meeting of the American Electric Railway Association in 1922 that he thought he could see daylight ahead in the proper coördination of bus and trolley services. Paul Shoup, head of the Southern Pacific Railroad and affiliated electric railways, was pessimistic about the situation in California. Elsewhere regulation was making good progress. "The question now is," said an editorial in the *Electric Railway Journal*, "will the railways grasp the opportunity while it exists? Neither coördination nor monopoly is likely as a natural course unless the development of the bus is guided in that direction. This 'guiding' means that the railways should inaugurate the use of buses themselves where there is a field for them. This will avoid the development of a competitive situation, costly to all, and will satisfy the desires of the public."

This idea seemed to appeal to the street-railway companies. All over the country they began buying buses. Some they bought new from the various manufacturers who had gone into the bus building business. Others they bought second-hand from the operators who were already running them. At the end of 1922 there were about fifty street-railways operating 400 buses. The next year saw the numbers increased to 121 companies and 1,200 vehicles. By January 1, 1925, there were 220 companies operating about 7,000 buses. Five years later some 390 street-railways were operating more than 13,000 buses.

Most spectacular was the vigorous entry of Public Service Railway of New Jersey into the bus business. This followed quickly after the passage of legislation limiting the number of buses that could be operated on the same street with trolleys. The buses operating at the time of the passage of the legislation were allowed to continue, but any one else desiring to get into the game had to obtain a certificate of convenience and necessity from the Public Utility Commission.

While this did not do anything directly to diminish the uneconomic competition that had been going on for years, it did at least stabilize the situation somewhat by preventing continued increase in competition. At that time there were some 1,200 independently owned buses competing with Public Service Railway, taking the cream of the business and carry-

Frank Fageol's steam-bus operated at Des Moines in 1899.

One of the earliest types of gasoline motor-bus operated in the
United States.

London Transport

London Transport

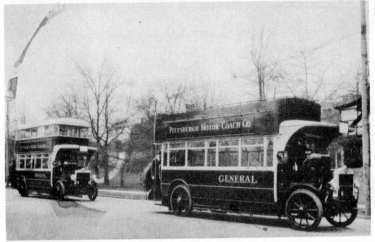

Upper Left: A converted horse-drawn omnibus in London.

Lower Left: This model was popular in London in 1910.

Upper Right: An early type of motor-bus used in the United States.

Lower Right: Double-deck bus which was imported from England.

A great variety of vehicles was to be seen on the streets of Camden about 1920.

Newburgh, New York—one of the first cities to have all local transportation service rendered by bus.

Bumper to bumper—an almost continuous line of buses on Broad
Street, Newark, in the rush hour.

Small buses on short headways became a major factor at Detroit in the 1930's.

Large capacity, single-deck motor-bus with six wheels operated in Paris in 1924.

A large capacity motor-bus with articulated body, seating fifty-eight passengers, developed in 1938.

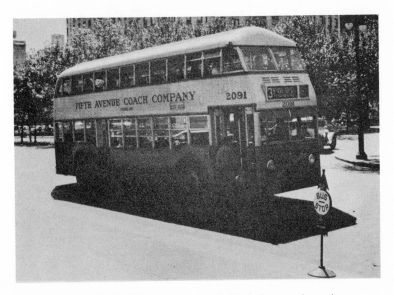

On New York's Fifth Avenue the double-deck motor-bus reigns supreme.

Motor-buses in 1935 replaced the street-cars which had been operating for more than a hundred years on Madison Avenue, New York City.

ing a total of 200 million passengers a year. Their usual practice was to run immediately ahead of the street-cars and pick
up waiting passengers. Thus the service was essentially no
more than a duplication of that being rendered by the street-
cars. When the situation became stabilized the company decided to buy out the buses operating in direct competition
with its service, and to try to effect some sort of coördination.

To carry out this plan the Public Service Transportation
Company was formed, because the railway company's charter
did not permit it to engage in bus operation. More than five
hundred independent operators were bought our during 1924.
As fast as the buses on a given line were taken over, the
schedule for buses was coördinated with the trolley schedule,
so that each vehicle had its own duty to perform and the
former duplication was to some extent eliminated.

On a line where the independent buses had been operating
on an eight-minute headway and the street-cars had been
doing the same thing, the riding public was receiving an eight-
minute service—two vehicles together and then an eight-
minute wait. After the railway purchased the buses both cars
and buses were operated on a twelve-minute headway, arranged so that there was one vehicle every six minutes instead
of one every eight minutes as formerly. The public received
more frequent service, while a saving was made in the number
of car miles and bus miles operated.

In the course of a few years, Public Service had acquired
the permits of more than one thousand of its competitors.
This was a rather costly procedure as the price paid seldom
covered much more than the permit to operate, the vehicle
itself usually being too old and decrepit to have any considerable value. The company, therefore, was obliged to embark
on a huge program of new bus buying.

The plan of alternating trips by street-car and bus over
the same route did not prove altogether satisfactory, as the

cars did not earn enough under this arrangement to pay an adequate return on the investment in track and power facilities. Line by line, therefore, Public Service began to discontinue the car service on routes where both types of service were being operated, and leave the whole job to be done by the buses. The substitution of buses in place of cars was later extended also to lines on which there was no competitive service. In the case of some of the later substitutions the cars were replaced by a unique type of vehicle equipped to operate either as a motor-bus or an electrically driven trolley-bus.

Eventually Public Service had only a handful of street-railway lines in operation and had the largest fleet of motor-buses in the United States. Numbering more than 3,000 vehicles, this fleet was exceeded in size only by that of the London Passenger Transport Board, numbering over 6,000, and that of the Transports en Commune de la Régione Parisienne, numbering some 4,000 vehicles.

The first bus operation in the United States, that of the Fifth Avenue Coach Company in New York, was with double-deck vehicles, but this type of vehicle never achieved any wide popularity in America. It was used to a limited extent in Philadelphia, Cleveland, Pittsburgh, Baltimore, Washington, Kansas City, Atlanta, and Los Angeles, but had been given up in all of the cities mentioned except Philadelphia and New York before the beginning of 1940. It was used to a much greater extent in Chicago where the routes of the Chicago Motor Coach Company along the shore of Lake Michigan offered the unusual scenic attractions that always seemed necessary to make double-deckers a success. This was the reason for their continued popularity on Fifth Avenue, too, in combination with the fact that many passengers rode a long enough distance to make it worth their while to climb to the upper deck.

A notable by-product of the double-decker was the so-called "gas-electric" bus. In 1924 the engineers of Mitten Management, running the transit companies in Philadelphia and Buffalo, began making an extensive study of bus operation on their own properties and in various other cities. They found the life of the average bus was about five years—a startling figure when compared with the life of a street-car, which was admittedly not less than twenty years. Something should be done, they thought, to give the bus a longer span of life. The gas-electric design, developed in conjunction with the General Electric and Yellow Coach companies, was the outcome.

Fundamentally the gas-electric principle was simply this: A gasoline engine was directly connected to an electric generator. This generator provided electric current for electric motors which drove the rear wheels. Into the scrap-heap went the gear-shift, with its tremendous wear and tear upon the bus and the equal strain upon the driver. Along with the gear-shift went the grinding gears, the jerking, as the bus was slammed from one speed to another, and much of the delay due to the necessity for changing back and forth from one gear to another when operating through congested traffic conditions.

The advantages of electric drive were especially marked in the operation of heavy, double-deck buses, where mechanical shifting gears involved a lot of hard physical work, but they were considerable also in the operation of single-deck buses of large capacity. Then, too, it was felt that the elimination of the jars incident to gear shifting would prolong the life of the vehicle, one of the primary objects of the study made by the Mitten engineers.

Immediately after the design had been worked out, the Philadelphia Rapid Transit Company ordered 125 double-deckers and eighty-five single deckers with gas-electric drive. Other companies quickly followed suit. Within two years they were operating in Albany, Atlanta, Buffalo, Kansas City, Los Angeles, Miami, and Portland, Oregon. Then came the startling announcement that Public Service of New Jersey had placed a record-breaking order for 330 new buses all to be equipped with gas-electric drive. Thomas N. McCarter, president of the company, commented: "It will make possible a wonderful improvement from the standpoint of the riding public in the local transportation system and will, I hope, aid very materially in the fulfilment of our efforts for a properly coördinated bus and trolley service."

A variation of the "gas-electric" design was the "diesel-electric," introduced in the 1930's. The development of this type of vehicle was greatly accelerated as the result of a trip to England in 1928 made by M. R. Boylan, vice-president, and Martin Schreiber, chief engineer, of Public Service of New Jersey.

In England the high cost of gasoline had early resulted in the extensive use of diesel engines. Enthusiastic Britishers emphasized the advantages of the diesel to the visitors from the United States. Like most American bus operators, however, Boylan and Schreiber had the feeling that the characteristics of the diesel engine were not well adapted for driving a bus through mechanical transmission. But Public Service was already operating a large number of buses with electric transmission. If combined with electric transmission, they thought the diesel engine might become an efficient and economical source of power. So they imported a couple of Mercedes-Benz diesel buses in 1929, which were equipped with electric drive. These gave very satisfactory service, but the need to send to Europe for replacement parts was a serious drawback. Then came the introduction of the Hercules diesel engine built in the United States. Immediately Public Service and Yellow Coach went to work on a new design of diesel-electric bus, and in 1937 a fleet of twenty-seven units made their appearance on the streets of Newark, the first such fleet in the world.

The British, while recognizing the desirability of getting away from mechanical transmission, never became very enthusiastic about electric drive. Instead, they tried a number of forms of hydraulic transmission. Here the basic principle was that of the turbine. At the back end of the engine shaft was placed a disc or plate which rotated with the shaft, throwing jets of liquid against a facing disc provided with receiving cups. This second disc was connected with the rear axle. As the speed of the engine increased the impact of these jets increased, and the second disc was forced into rotation. So, here again, it was necessary for the driver to do no more than speed up his engine to increase the speed of his vehicle.

There was only one trouble with this otherwise attractive scheme—when the engine speed got too high, the jets failed to drive the second disc at the same rate as the first. The Britishers tried to get around this difficulty by having the driver effect a mechanical interlocking of the discs when a certain predetermined speed was reached, but had only moderate success.

Out at the huge plant of Yellow Coach at Pontiac, Michigan, sat the company's chief engineer, Colonel George Greene, pondering this problem. He had been a motor-transport officer in the British Army and had been connected for some years with the London General Omnibus Company before coming to the United States. He recognized the possibilities of hydraulic transmission provided some effective way could be found to make the interlock when the proper speed was reached. This, of course, was easier said than done. Month after month he struggled with this problem until eventually he discovered a way to do it automatically, without the aid of the driver, when a certain speed was reached. Buses equipped with this type of transmission were first put in service on the Eighth Avenue line in New York City, April 19, 1939. They proved very successful and "hydraulic transmission" was soon in demand by bus operators all over the United States.

When Cleveland's street-railway broke the ice by starting the operation of buses way back in 1912, the new vehicles were used only to carry passengers from an outlying district to the nearest car line—a type of operation known amongst transit men as "feeder service." For some years that was considered by street-railway management as the only proper field for the bus. Gradually, however, the idea began to grow that maybe the bus could do more than merely render "feeder service."

Running street-railways was not a very profitable business in small towns as there usually were not enough passengers to pay the cost of operation, plus the interest on a pretty heavy investment in track and electric-power facilities. Moreover, the best service these companies could render was not particularly attractive, as their routes were mostly single track with turn-outs, resulting in frequent delays. Operation of buses in place of street-cars, it was recognized, would eliminate these delays and would probably attract more passengers. Then too, the cost of providing the service would be less than with street-cars.

To say just when various cities in the United States began to have all local transportation service rendered by motor-buses is not as easy as might appear. Street-railways often continued to operate one or two cars a day long after the major part of the traffic was being handled by bus. Bay City, Michigan, Everett, Washington, and Newburgh, New York, were among the first all-bus cities in the country. This was about 1923.

Street-railway men at that time were inclined to feel that the bus might be able to do the whole job in cities of under

50,000 population. Soon they raised the figure to 75,000. Then it became 100,000. But the limit would not stay fixed. In 1933 the city of San Antonio, with well over 200,000 inhabitants changed over to all-bus operation. Up to the beginning of 1940 this was still the largest city relying wholly upon motor-buses for transportation. Along with it were some 170 other cities ranging between 25,000 and 200,000 in population. By that time the number of buses in transit service in the United States had grown to nearly 30,000, or slightly more than the number of street cars, though the buses were carrying only about half of the number of passengers carried by the street cars.

Even the changeover to buses at San Antonio left room for debate about what the motor-bus could do on city routes with extremely heavy riding. The city of San Antonio had a large population, all right, but its people were not very active transit riders. Many street-railway men shook their heads in doubt concerning the ability of the bus to meet heavy demands. But enthusiasts, on the other hand, were sure the bus could do it.

Early in 1935 the matter was put to a decisive test when buses were substituted in place of cars on the New York & Harlem route, the world's first street-railway, which had then been in operation for more than a hundred years. This was one of a number of street-railway properties that had been purchased some time before by the Omnibus Corporation with a view to converting them to bus operation. February 1, 1935, was the date of the changeover. The conditions under which the new buses started operation were extremely unfavorable. Heavy snows followed by long periods of freezing weather had made Madison Avenue a sea of ice from one end to the other, criss-crossed by every conceivable kind of rut and ridge.

"Nevertheless," according to Hugh Sheeran, president of

the company, "from the outset the new operation was a re-markable success and increased its popularity with the passage of time."

The motor-bus, considered an upstart a few years earlier, had conquered the patriarch of the street-railway industry.

11

TROLLEYS WITHOUT TRACKS

The Story of the Trolley-Bus

A frown wrinkled the brow of E. S. King, manager of the Merrill Railway & Lighting Company, every time he thought of the problem of providing transportation service to the Sixth Ward in the western section of that Wisconsin city. If he built a street-car line to serve the people living there, he would have to construct expensive crossings at three places where steam-railroad lines intersected the proposed route, and he would have to arrange for reinforcing a bridge over the Wisconsin River, which was not strong enough to carry the weight of street-cars. All this seemed to promise a lot more expense than was likely to be repaid by the operation of a car line to a newly developed section of the city.

Then one day Manager King made a trip to Chicago, where he saw an electric-storage-battery bus operated by one of the large department stores. That gave him an idea. Why not an electric bus operated by power obtained from overhead trolley wires instead of storage-batteries? Electric power so obtained would be more plentiful in amount and lower in cost than that obtained from storage-batteries. The vehicle itself could be light in weight as no batteries would have to be carried. A trolley-bus of this kind, he thought, would neatly solve his troublesome problem of providing transportation service to the Sixth Ward of the city of Merrill. As compared with a street-car line, the trolley-bus would save

Trolley-bus at Merrill, Wisconsin, in 1913

all the cost of track construction and bridge strengthening, though it would be necessary to string two trolley wires as there would be no rails to act as a return circuit.

Losing no time, he got in touch with the Feld Electric Bus Company, builders of the vehicle he had seen, and commissioned them to build him a bus similar in design, but equipped with two poles so that it could be operated by central-station power obtained through overhead trolley wires. When completed, it had seats for eighteen passengers and weighed only 6,000 pounds—much less than a street-car. A single fifteen-horse-power motor drove the rear wheels by a complicated system of shafts, gears, sprockets, and chains. The trolley poles were arranged to swivel so that the vehicle could move some distance on either side of the trolley wires.

King's combination trolley and bus began operation at Merrill in the summer of 1913. It worked quite satisfactorily and remained in operation for about a year. Then it was sold to a Massachusetts concern which proposed to run it on Sconticut Neck Road, near New Bedford, to carry summer colonists between their cottages and the main highway where there was a trolley line operated by the Union Street Railway of New Bedford. The latter company had no desire to venture into a seasonal business of this kind, but gave its blessing to the idea of some one else doing it, and lent some assistance in the stringing of the overhead wires. Operation was started on October 8, 1914, according to report, "so late, indeed, that there was practically no travel at all upon it yesterday." It was further stated that "until next summer the line will only be operated about one mile or so down the road." By the next summer, however, even this operation had been given up and the vehicle spent the rest of its days in a barn on Sconticut Neck.

The system at Merrill was not, strictly speaking, the first commercial trolley-bus line in the United States. The initial venture was made in 1910 when the Laurel Canyon Utilities Company installed a mile and a half line between the tracks of the Pacific Electric Railway at Hollywood and a small settlement in Laurel Canyon, known as Bungalow Town.

Service over this route had been started originally with

Laurel Canyon's converted auto-bus in 1910

crude gasoline buses, but they did not perform very satisfactorily on the steep grades encountered, which were as much as twelve per cent in places. So the company removed the engines and transmissions from two of its buses and substituted electric motors. Wooden trolley poles were then installed on the roof of the vehicles with aluminum contacts to slide along the underside of the trolley wires which were strung along the route. This system operated for some months before it was abandoned in favor of an improved type of gasoline bus.

As a matter of fact the idea of combining some of the features of the trolley car with some of those of the omnibus had been in men's minds for a long time. The ability of the trolley to draw upon the almost unlimited supply of cheap electric current obtainable from a central generating station was one of its greatest advantages. On the other hand, the necessity to follow a fixed steel track was a distinct drawback in comparison with the flexibility of other highway vehicles. In early days, of course, the trolley's steel wheels and steel track had been in its favor, as they gave a more comfortable ride than wooden wheels bumping over cobblestone pavements, but the coming of rubber-tired vehicles and smooth pavements changed that to a very considerable extent.

A certain Doctor Finney of Pittsburgh seems to have been the first man in the United States who thought of running an omnibus by electric power obtained from overhead wires. He devised a system of this kind as far back as 1882. It was not very different from the two-wire systems then being tried for street-cars, except that the vehicles did not run on rails. Dr. Finney's plan, however, got no further than preliminary drawings.

About this time the German firm of Siemens and Halske brought out what they called *Fahrdrahtbus* which, literally translated, means "trolley wire bus." This was a kind of open wagon equipped with an electric motor and a little overhead trolley carriage attached to the wagon by a flexible cable.

Some years later a trial run was made in Germany with a vehicle called an *electromote*. It was not a trolley without tracks in the sense that it operated as a road vehicle with electric central station-power, but was rather a combination electric railway car and omnibus, operating on electric central-station power while running on the rails and on storage-battery power when running on the road. Flanged wheels that could be raised and lowered at will were the means by which the transition was occomplished.

Early in 1900 an experimental trolley-bus line 3,000 feet long was built in France by M. Lombard-Gerin. It ran on a

Trolley-bus design patented by Harvey D. Dibble in 1889

road along the Seine just outside of Paris. A four-wheel over-running carriage was used on the overhead wires to collect the current. This was, in principle, not unlike the little carriage used by Leo Daft for the early electric cars he designed.

In the early 1900's A. B. Uphan of Boston, president of the Eastern Trackless Trolley Company, undertook to demonstrate the practicability of the trolley-bus in the United

States. His vehicle somewhat resembled the lightweight street-car of early days, had rubber tires, an outside platform for the driver, two motors and two trolley poles. The seating capacity was twenty. An unusual feature of the design was the use of trolley wheels in a horizontal plane, pressed apart and against the sides of the wire by a spring.

Plans were made by this company to install a line in Franklin, New Hampshire, between two railroad stations some distance apart, and in April, 1902, a franchise for operating the system was granted by the city council. A little later an announcement was made by two Lowell, Massachusetts, capitalists that they were backing Mr. Uphan for a line between Franklin and Franklin Falls, New Hampshire, and that permission had been secured to install systems in Lowell and other New England cities. None of the contemplated installations was actually made. In 1903, however, the same company, with its name changed to the American Trackless Trolley Company, demonstrated its vehicle in New Haven, Connecticut, before a group of capitalists who desired to try the vehicle in that city.

Finally, on November 2, 1903, the American Trackless Trolley Company formally opened an experimental line in Scranton, Pennsylvania. This line, 800 feet in length, ran over private property. The route traversed was neither smooth nor hard, but approximated the conditions that would be encountered on many country roads. The vehicle used was the same one demonstrated on the two occasions previously discussed. It was operated for a few months at Scranton and then abandoned.

Feeble as were these efforts, they prompted the *Street Railway Journal* to remark in Nevember, 1904, that trolley buses held forth real possibilities and the "unseemly merriment which the proposition provokes from the average street-railway man," was unjustified. The editorial went on to state that the excessive cost of tires, averaging around three cents per mile for light automobiles, and the rough streets and roads, causing uncomfortable rides, excessive maintenance, and high consumption of energy, were the chief obstacles to be overcome.

Commenting again in June, 1905, on proposed systems in Nahant and Brookline, Massachusetts, the *Street Railway Journal* stated: "The trackless trolley, whatever may be one's judgement as to its commercial merits, is not a thing to be turned down offhand in these days of automobiles. It is an automobile system with a continuous source of energy, being thereby limited in its sphere of action, but relieved of the necessity of carrying a prime mover with it." The editorial further pointed out that the existing rolling stock was at a serious disadvantage, being much more expensive than streetcars of similar carrying capacity, and that the tire problem was "especially grave."

About the time of the Laurel Canyon experiment in California, local transportation men in England became interested in the trolley bus and made extensive studies of its possibilities. As a result of these studies operations were started in the cities of Bradford and Leeds on June 20, 1911. They were the forerunners of numerous other systems started in England during the next few years.

In the early 1920's a wave of keen interest in the trolley-bus spread over the United States. The General Electric Company demonstrated a vehicle built by the Atlas Truck Company at Schenectady. Then Detroit tried two types of vehicles, one with a J. G. Brill body and Packard chassis, and the other built by the Trackless Trolley Corporation of New York. The Brill company also developed a complete vehicle and experimented with it at Philadelphia. The Toronto Transportation Commission placed four vehicles in service and the Staten Island Midland Railway inaugurated two lines, totaling

Crude trolley-bus with boxlike body operated on Staten Island lines in the 1920's.

An early trolley-bus of the United Traction Company, Albany, New York.

Original type of Oregon Avenue trolley-bus in Philadelphia. This is the oldest line in continuous operation in the United States.

Salt Lake City trolley-bus instalation in 1928 inspired a revival of interest in this form of transportation.

Broad Street, Newark, thronged with the combination motor-bus
type and trolley-bus type of vehicle developed by Public Service
Coördinated Transport.

On the road to Waikiki—a modern trolley-bus of the Honolulu Rapid
Transit Company.

Hose-jumpers used to maintain trolley-bus service at Cincinnati.

seven miles, with eight trolley-buses manufactured by the Atlas Truck Company. Later purchase of fifteen additional vehicles made this for a time the largest trolley-bus system in the United States.

Following years saw systems established at Minneapolis, Windsor, Ontario; Baltimore, Rochester, and Philadelphia. All this, however, was only a flash in the pan. Interest in the trolley bus died as quickly as it had begun. By 1925 the urban transportation industry in the United States was just about ready to bury the trolley-bus as a dead issue. That did not mean that the basic idea of the trolley-bus was unsound. Electric power obtained from a central generating station of almost unlimited capacity still had some marked advantages, and the familiar electric trolley-car didn't any longer seem to be the complete answer it had once been to the problem of carrying people to and fro in cities.

These were the thoughts chasing around in the mind of Edward A. West as he looked over the exhibits at the annual convention of the American Electric Railway Association at Cleveland in 1927. Brilliant sunshine flooded the colorful array of vehicles standing in the open space alongside the Grecian columns of the huge Auditorium building. A cool breeze blowing in from Lake Erie tempered the heat of an Indian summer afternoon.

West was the general manager of the Utah Light & Traction Company of Salt Lake City. Along with some thousands of other men engaged in the business of operating city transportation services in the United States and Canada, he had come to Cleveland to see the latest developments in equipment applicable to the operation of a business such as the one for which he was responsible.

Here was a shiny new trolley built by the St. Louis Car Company for the Northern Texas Traction Company. Here was one built by the J. G. Brill Company for Oakland, California. Eight tracks were full of them—big and small—for Brooklyn, Baltimore, Houston, Milwaukee, and other cities. But alongside the trolleys was an equally interesting display of motor-buses. One was an unusual twin-motored vehicle developed by Frank Fageol. Another was a six-wheel design brought out by the Versare Company. Both of the latter buses employed the then rather novel type of drive wherein the wheels were turned by light-weight electric motors which obtained their power from a generator coupled directly to the gasoline engine. Known familiarly as "gas-electrics," these buses had the advantage of eliminating the shifting of gears, a considerable burden on the driver of a vehicle stopping and starting again at nearly every street intersection.

Looking at these big buses with their electric drive, Ed. West conceived the idea of combining their desirable features of flexibility and comfortable riding with the old, outstanding advantage of the trolley-car—an unlimited supply of inexpensive electric power obtained from a central generating station. "Put trolley poles on those buses so you can get current from overhead wires," he exclaimed to his chief engineer, Jed Woolley, "and you'll have something pretty hard to beat as a vehicle for city transportation."

That, of course, was not a new idea. It was, indeed, quite similar to others that had been proposed at various times in the past. But if West's idea was an old one, it was an old one with a difference which was just enough to revive successfully a type of vehicle which was virtually dead.

The problem facing the Utah Light & Traction Company at this time was not the same as that which had worried Manager King of the Merrill Railway & Lighting Company on an earlier occasion, but it was even more serious. The municipal authorities of Salt Lake City had decided on an extensive program of paving improvements, largely on streets where the tracks of the trolley company were located. According to the franchise under which the company operated it was obliged to pay from one-third to one-half of the entire cost of this paving work.

That would have been bad enough by itself, as it meant additional investment without any additional earnings to pay interest charges, but that was not all. Paving improvement was likely to result in greater use of private automobiles, and the average auto driver, wishing to show himself a good fellow, was inclined to pick up any one he passed who was waiting for a street-car. Thus the trolley company was being asked, in effect, to furnish a large part of the means of destroying its own business.

The immediate problem centered in the reconstructing and repavement of four miles of single track. There were also future paving liabilities which would have aggregated about $174,000. The particular car line affected was well patronized. It served a closely built-up district where there was no paralleling car line on either side for more than a quarter of a mile. It was paying as well as any of the traction company's lines. Abandonment of the route seemed to be out of the question.

Considerable study was given to determine the most economical transportation medium with which to give the service. If the tracks were rehabilitated and paved, street-car operation could be continued with the same rolling stock as that serving the patrons on other lines. But that, of course, would mean undertaking the costly paving job. The company's experience with gasoline-propelled vehicles indicated that the available types of buses were not altogether satisfactory substitutes for the street-cars under the existing conditions. Sound transportation merchandising policy dictated the furnishing of something attractive, comfortable, safe, and speedy. Could some type of transportation vehicle be found that would not run on rails and yet would utilize the power-plant, substations and overhead investment, with a property write-off that would not be excessive?

Ed. West thought the trolley-without-tracks which he visualized while looking at the convention exhibits at Cleveland might be the answer to the problem facing his company at Salt Lake City. This was such a radical idea that he hardly dared mention it out loud in the presence of his fellow delegates at the convention. Whenever the words "trackless trolley" were mentioned in those days the average street-railway man's nose turned up a little, as though he detected a slightly unpleasant smell, and he glanced quickly at the speaker to see if he appeared to be in his right senses.

But West was not thinking of the kind of trackless trolley they had in mind—a makeshift sort of vehicle that looked awkward and was hard riding because of solid rubber tires, poor spring design, and short wheelbase. It was bulky and cumbersome because it was equipped with heavy, street-railway motors, the only ones available at that time. This made the floor heights too great for comfort. Relatively low power limited the speed. The body had an ungainly appearance. Its lines were blunt and broken with sharp angles.

The kind of vehicle West had in mind was an up-to-date, pneumatic-tired bus with electric drive—just what was on display at the convention—except that it would get its electric power from overhead wires instead of an engine-generator set on the vehicle itself. West talked with C. A. Burleson and other engineers of the General Electric Company who thought his idea was practical. Meanwhile Jed Woolley, who had gone to Rochester to look over the system there, came back with an enthusiastic report.

Certain difficulties then presented themselves. It was necessary to make application to the city commission for a franchise amendment permitting operation of trolley-buses in Salt Lake City. Some of the city commissioners were rather hesitant about granting permission for the operation of this strange and unknown type of vehicle. They were unable to grasp the idea of a trolley without tracks. A hurry-up request was sent to Rochester for a motion-picture of the trolley-buses operating in that city. This seemed to be the most effective way to present the idea to the municipal authorities even though the vehicles were not what Ed. West had in mind.

The Rochester trolley-bus system was then the largest in the United States, the one on Staten Island having been abandoned. Philadelphia's trolley-bus system was a little older than Rochester's, since it had been started on Oregon Avenue in October, 1923. It had been a trolley-bus operation since its inception, the trackless vehicle having been selected because there were already steam-railroad tracks on Oregon Avenue which prevented the construction of a street-railway line. The operation at Rochester, on the other hand, had been begun with twelve gas buses. Five had been changed over to electric operation as an experiment, and had proved so successful that the other seven were converted soon afterward.

When the moving-picture was received at Salt Lake City from Rochester a few days later it was shown to the heads of the city government. The officials were quick to see the advantages of this mode of transportation. At a hearing held on the following day an amendment to the Utah Light & Traction Company's franchise was granted, permitting operation of trolley-buses. An order was then placed for ten vehicles and operation was started on September 9, 1928. Within a year the company ordered sixteen more.

Although it was the installation at Salt Lake City that inspired a revival of interest in the trolley-bus, it was the much larger installation made two years later at Chicago that really drove the lesson home.

Five routes were started by the Chicago Surface Lines during 1930 and a sixth in 1931. All of these routes were in the

northwest section of the city, a residential district which had
been built up extensively in the 1920's. It was felt by the management, in view of the Salt Lake experience, that the necessary service could be rendered more economically by trolley-
buses than by extending the tracks of neighboring street-car
lines. This was particularly true of the Central Avenue line.
Although its riding was heavy enough to justify street-railway
operation under ordinary circumstances—a total of 50,000
passengers a day with 4,000 in one direction during the busiest
hour—the route included a long bridge over steam-railroad
tracks which was not strong enough to carry street-cars. To
strengthen it sufficiently would have been extremely expensive. Trolley-bus operation was, therefore, selected as the best
solution of the problem.

Chicago's Central Avenue line, a fifteen-mile crosstown
route intersecting many of the trunk lines of the street-railway
system at points seven miles or more from the center of the
city, soon became a Mecca for interested transit executives
from all over the country. Operating smoothly and efficiently
on a headway as short as forty-five seconds in rush hours, it
showed conclusively that the redesigned trolley-bus was a
vehicle with real possibilities in city transportation service.

During the ten years following Salt Lake City's establishment of a new type of trolley-bus operation, the use of this
vehicle spread rapidly. More than 2,000 were put in service
on 1,500 miles of route in some sixty cities of over 25,000
population in the United States and Canada. In England the
number of trolley-buses grew to more than 2,600. Elsewhere
throughout the world a little more than 1,300 were put in
service.

A novel variation of the trolley-bus idea was introduced by
Public Service Coördinated Transport of New Jersey in 1934.
The management of this company had long felt that the elec-
tric motor possessed marked advantages for the propulsion of

transit vehicles, rubber tired as well as rail-operated. Having found the motor-bus with gas-electric drive to be highly satisfactory, especially from the standpoints of ease of operation and low maintenance cost, the management reasoned that it would be desirable to go a step further and equip the gas-electric bus with two trolley poles so that electrical energy could be obtained from the overhead trolley wires where they were available. Thus the vehicle could be operated either on central-station power or as an independent unit, as might be desired. The changeover from one type of operation to the other was made easier by an ingenious device developed in conjunction with the Ohio Brass Company which enabled the driver to press a button and start a pair of small electric motors to pull the trolley poles down to the roof.

An experimental vehicle of this kind was rebuilt from an old gas-electric bus and tried out on the steep Pershing Road hill at Weehawken early in 1934. This combination gas-electric and trolley-bus negotiated the six per cent grade at substantially higher speed than either the ordinary motor-buses or the street-cars operating on adjacent tracks.

On the basis of this result the company placed orders the following year for sixty-two built-for-the-purpose units of the combination gas-electric, trolley-bus type, to which it gave the name "all-service" vehicle. The performance of these vehicles was so satisfactory that additional units were purchased and more of the existing units were converted until Coördinated Transport had built up a fleet of 566 units, the largest fleet of vehicles equipped for trolley-bus operation in the United States. A notable advantage of the "all-service" vehicle was felt to be its ability to operate on a route partly equipped with wires and partly without.

In its reincarnation the trolley-bus had many desirable qualities. Its operating cost was relatively low. It was quiet and comfortable to ride in. It was fast, but smooth in starting and stopping. Small wonder, then, that it proved very popular everywhere it was tried.

At Portland, Oregon, one of the cities where a large installation of trolley-buses was made, the newspaper, *The Oregonian*, conducted in the spring of 1940 a front-door ballot-box poll in which a scientifically stratified sample of the adult population was asked what kind of city transportation service they liked best. Four out of five, according to D. E. Clark II, director of the poll, said they "would rather ride the trolley-buses than either street-cars or gasoline buses."

A type of vehicle once discarded as unsatisfactory in virtually all ways, had, through improvements in design, been restored to a high place in popular favor.

12

TRANSIT IN THE MODERN AGE

The Story of Urban Transportation, To-day and To-morrow

In the fall of 1929, a small group of electric railway executives met at the Marlborough-Blenheim Hotel in Atlantic City, trying to figure out what to do about the rising costs and declining revenues of their business. These men constituted the Advisory Council of the American Electric Railway Association. A total of some four and a half billion dollars of good money was tied up in street-railway facilities—an investment not lightly to be cast aside. But they knew that the slow, noisy street-car of the past held no appeal for Americans living in an automotive age, and a majority of their vehicles certainly were "street-cars of the past." More than 22,000 of them had reached the age of twenty years and most of the others were little younger.

What, specifically, was wrong with these cars? What, if anything, could be done about it? Could a street-car be built that would recapture the favor of the public? These were the questions they asked themselves.

To find the answers they appointed a committee of two, Dr. Thomas Conway, Jr., president of the Philadelphia &

Western Railway, and Charles Gordon, managing director of
the association. These two quickly decided that the way to
get real answers to such questions was to do a thorough job
of scientific research. So they proposed the formation of
what became known as the Electric Railway Presidents' Conference Committee, consisting of the heads of some twenty-
five electric railway companies, who, along with manufacturers of cars and equipment, were to subscribe enough money
to do the job. This idea was approved and Professor C. F.
Hirshfeld, research chief of the Detroit Edison Company, was
selected to undertake the work.

First a series of tests was begun in Brooklyn to determine
the good and bad features of existing cars. Street-railways all
over the country sent their cars to Brooklyn to be tested.
The volume and character of noise was measured on the
street and inside the cars. Tests were made of the amplitude
and frequency of vibrations, and their effect on the passenger.
At Ann Arbor, Michigan, experimenters began tests on human
"guinea-pigs" standing on platforms moved at varying rates
of acceleration. Slow-motion pictures were taken of each test
to show how the guinea-pigs held their balance or lost it
during acceleration.

After eighteen months of hard work, Professor Hirshfeld
and his engineers had found some of the answers to what was
wrong with the street-car. The fastest street-car of that day
could travel only seventy-six feet in the first five seconds;
the fastest automobile left it twenty-five feet behind. From
a speed of thirty miles an hour, the fastest-braking street-car
took 144 feet to make a stop; the automobile required only
fifty feet. Worst of all, the cars' solid steel wheels conducted
impacts, noises, and vibrations into the structures above, neces-
sitating great sizes and weights in trucks and car bodies.

The engineers began by evolving a resilient wheel with
vulcanized "sandwiches" of rubber and steel forming a cush-

ion between rim and hub. Next they set about lightening the truck, cushioning on rubber all parts that caused noise or vibrations. Surprisingly enough, the Michigan experimenters found that the rate of acceleration did not matter much, provided the pickup was smooth. This made it seem obvious that to start and stop cars more rapidly, new and smoother control mechanisms were needed. Shelving control methods which brought a car from standstill to full speed in nine steps, Professor Hirshfeld's staff, in conjunction with engineers of the Westinghouse and General Electric companies, developed types of control with 61 to 260 steps, converting acceleration from a series of jerks to a smooth, powerful sweep that would upset nobody. Similarly, new types of magnetic track brakes made fast, smooth stops easy to achieve.

Seats, lights, heaters, ventilators, windows, and a host of other details were made matters of careful study. Finally the committee got substantially what it wanted in a sample car completed in the fall of 1934. Running tests with passengers in Brooklyn proved the merits of the design. Early in 1935 the committee was ready to write commercial specifications for the new vehicle. In July, the Brooklyn & Queens Transit Company placed an order for 101 of these cars with the St. Louis Car Company. Because nearly a million dollars had been spent on research and development the newspapers hailed the new vehicle as "the million-dollar street-car." Within the transit industry it became known as the P.C.C. car, a condensation of the initials of the committee which had created it. The following February, Chicago Surface Lines ordered eighty-three; and Baltimore Transit Company, twenty-seven. In August, Pittsburgh Railways ordered a hundred; Los Angeles Railway followed with sixty, and San Diego with twenty-five. By the beginning of 1940 more than eleven hundred of the new street-cars had been bought by transit companies throughout the United States and Canada.

The public's response to this modernization of street-car design was prompt and unmistakable. On every line where the new "million-dollar" cars were operated, the riding showed a marked increase. The committee had proved what it set out to prove—that a street-car could be designed and built that would recapture popular favor. This did not mean that the electric railway would regain its former monopoly of the business of public passenger transportation in cities. The development of economical and efficient motor-buses and trolley-buses precluded the return of any such monopoly. But it did mean that a type of car was available that could be used effectively where conditions favored the continued operation of electric railway service. The prevalence of these conditions varied, of course, in different localities.

If cities have developed distinctively individual characteristics with respect to atmosphere and local color, they have developed even more distinctively individual characteristics with respect to the nature, extent, and use of their transit facilities. For example, New York and London, the two biggest cities in the world, have adopted widely divergent methods of solving their transit problems. So, too, have Paris, Buenos Aires, and Chicago, cities of fairly comparable size in the next smaller population group. Even between American business centers as similar in size as Philadelphia and Detroit the contrast in transit methods has been extremely marked. In fact, looking at the general pattern of transit in various large cities, the conclusion is inescapable that it has developed differently in each individual city.

While a great many cities throughout the world have considered establishing underground or elevated rapid-transit service, the high cost of building the necessary structures has almost always stood in the way unless the population served was well over a million people. Of the world total of twenty-

two cities which had service of this kind at the beginning of
1940, all but four were listed as having more than a million
inhabitants, and three of the four exceptions were the centers
of metropolitan areas which put them in the same population
class for all practical purposes.

New York was far in the lead in respect to the extent of
its rapid-transit facilities and in respect to the use of them
by its seven million people. "Bagdad on the Subway," the
city had been labeled by O. Henry in earlier years, and the
passage of time had served only to emphasize the appropriate-
ness of this label. Three out of five of the three billion annual
riders on transit vehicles, dropped their nickels in the clicking
turnstiles of the subway and elevated railway lines. For this
modest sum it was possible to purchase a ride of more than
twenty miles from Coney Island to the Bronx, though actually
there were few, if any, people who wanted such a ride. The
remaining users of transit service were divided about equally
between street-cars and motor-buses, with an increasing trend
toward the buses.

Londoners, whose disgust with the slow speed of surface
transportation originally led to the building of the world's
first subway in 1863, never developed as much enthusiasm for
their own invention as did the residents of New York. In
the aggregate the eight million inhabitants of the British capital were taking, at the beginning of 1940, a slightly larger
number of transit rides every year than were the dwellers in
the American metropolis, but seven-eighths of them were
being taken in surface transit vehicles, five-eighths being in
motor-buses and the rest divided more or less evenly between
trolley-buses and tram-cars.

More remarkable, perhaps, than the differences in the use
of the several types of transit service, was the fact that all of
London's more than three billion annual riders were being

handled by a single organization, the London Passenger Transport Board, while New York had some thirty separate organizations to handle its riders. At the head of London Transport, the largest passenger-carrying business in the world, was the dignified Lord Ashfield who, as Albert Stanley, had previously been general manager of the street-railways in Detroit, Michigan, and later in Newark, New Jersey.

In Glasgow the canny Scots, who won for their city the distinction of being the second in the world to have underground railway service, learned a lesson from the smoky condition of the early steam-operated Metropolitan in London, and decided to operate their subway by cable. It operated successfully in this way for many years, but eventually was electrified. Liverpool, which had a small elevated-railway system, was the only other city in Great Britain which had established rapid-transit service up to the beginning of the year 1940.

On the continent of Europe there were at that time nine cities having rapid-transit systems of one sort or another; Berlin, Paris, Moscow, Barcelona, Hamburg, Madrid, Vienna, Warsaw, and Elberfeld. All were subways except those at Hamburg and Elberfeld, which were elevated railways, and those at Vienna and Warsaw, which were mainly on private right-of-way on the surface.

Parisians were the most enthusiastic users of rapid transit. More than 800 million riders a year were patronizing the Chemin de Fer Métropolitaine, as compared with less than a third of that number using the more extensive underground railway system at Berlin. Russian authorities estimated that some 135 million Moscovites were using the Soviet capital's elaborate new subway system, which, with its marble columns, chromium trimmings and indirect lighting was the most elegantly decorated underground railway in the world.

To supplement its "Metro," Paris relied wholly upon motor-buses, while Berlin had an extensive street-railway system with a moderate number of buses. Moscow, to meet the conditions resulting from an astonishingly rapid increase in population, was busy with the creation of a vast trolley-bus system, and was, at the same time, building new streamlined street-cars more or less suggestive of the latest designs in the United States.

Spain's two largest cities, Barcelona and Madrid, were the only other places in Europe where subways were in operation. To some people they were better known, probably, as air-raid shelters during the Spanish Civil War than as means of transportation. At Madrid the almost complete cessation of the normal life of the city during the civil war included the stopping of the subway for a long period. At Barcelona, on the other hand, the bombs that rained on the city for many months failed to halt the operation of the subway. Only at the very close of the war, when the subway's somewhat distant power-station was engulfed in the tide of battle and the supply of electric energy failed, were the trains compelled to stop running.

Rapid-transit facilities in South America were confined to that continent's largest city, Buenos Aires. For many years the surface lines of the Anglo-Argentine Tramways—one of the largest street-railway systems in the world—were the main reliance of the inhabitants of the Argentine capital. Then several short subways were built. By 1940 they were handling about 100 million passengers a year. At the same time a host of small motor-buses had sprung into operation. Confusion reigned until the formation of the Corporación de Transportes de la Ciudad de Buenos Aires to control and coördinate all forms of public passenger transportation within the city. Under its auspices plans were made for extensions of the subway system and for improvement of the street-railways through the introduction of new streamlined cars. Elsewhere in South America the trend was generally toward replacement of street-cars by motor-buses, with a limited use of trolley-buses in some places.

The Japanese, not to be outdone by the peoples of the western nations, had built themselves subways in two of their principal cities, Tokyo and Osaka. At the beginning of 1940 the system in the latter city was still of comparatively small extent, but the Tokyo subway had grown to a point where it was carrying some seventy million passengers a year.

Sydney, metropolis of Australia, was the only other city on that side of the world to have a subway. It had also an extensive system of electrified suburban railways which gave service closely approximating that of rapid-transit lines. Melbourne, too, had service of this kind.

In the larger cities of the United States rapid transit has probably been the subject of more debate than any other municipal question. Twenty years of discussion preceded the building of the first elevated railway in New York. Another thirty years passed before the first subway started running. In none of the other three cities which had acquired extensive rapid-transit facilities by the beginning of 1940 had that goal been reached without prolonged argument.

Boston started with the idea of building a subway, changed its mind and organized the Boston Elevated Railway Company, and then proceeded to dig a subway before it built its elevated line. Chicago began quite early with elevated railways but did not get around to starting to dig a subway until 1939. Philadelphia began operation of a combination subway-elevated system in 1908, to which extensive additions were made in later years.

The only other real rapid-transit system in the United States was the dream of the fabulous Van Sweringen brothers at Cleveland. They wanted to develop a large tract of land at Shaker Heights, and they felt that some means of quick and

New York streamlined articulated unit for service on either subway
or elevated lines.

Electric Railway Presidents' Conference Committee car operated with
double overhead-wire trolley system at Cincinnati.

On a congested thoroughfare one lane of street-cars carries more than six times as many passengers as two lanes of automobiles.

$6,600,000 worth of transit plant and equipment at the North Avenue Station of the Chicago Surface Lines.

Motor-bus with sloping windshield and standee windows brought out in 1940.

A modern streamlined car of the Transport Corporation of
Buenos Aires.

Trolley-bus of the tramway company of Lausanne, Switzerland.

New buildings along Toronto's Yonge Street Subway.

A municipally owned parking lot built over the subway tracks at St. Clair station on the Yonge Street Subway in Toronto. Motorists who park here can ride downtown in 10 minutes by subway, a trip that takes twenty to thirty minutes by car.

Modern rapid transit in the reserved strip, in the center of a super-highway in Chicago.

Park and Ride Field for 353 cars at 69th and Market Streets in Philadelphia. Believed to be the oldest park-and-ride field in the United States.

easy transportation to the center of the city was necessary. Another of their plans was to divert the trunk-line railroads from their location along the lake front to a route which would pass through a great, new Union Station immediately adjacent to the Public Square. So they built a pair of tracks for rapid-transit service in the same wide cut they dug for the tracks of the trunk-line railroads and established a local line to carry the residents of the Shaker Heights development to the heart of Cleveland in half the time they could make the trip by any other means.

Strikingly different methods have been followed in providing surface transportation service in American cities. "One man's meat is another man's poison" has been the rule with respect to the selection of vehicles by transit operators.

"Electric rail cars seating sixty passengers can render better mass transportation service than any forty-passenger vehicle," according to the head of a large transit company which took an active part in the work of the Electric Railway Presidents' Conference Committee. "Trolley-buses are preferred for lines where traffic requires a forty-passenger vehicle and gasoline buses for light lines."

"We prefer the trolley-bus to the street-car," said the head of another company, "because it offers relief from track and paving maintenance. Moreover, it is faster, smoother, and more economical."

"Mr. and Mrs. America won't stay put," according to a third. "The centers of population in our community shift around like billiard balls. Only the motor-bus can keep pace with these gyrations at reasonable cost."

Thus surface transit development has followed three lines— street-car, trolley-bus, and motor-bus. At the beginning of 1940 most of the larger American cities had at least two of these forms of transportation, and many had all three.

Among the cities where street-cars were handling the great

majority of the surface passengers were Chicago, Philadelphia, Pittsburgh, Baltimore, the Minnesota twin cities of Minneapolis and St. Paul, and San Francisco in the United States; as well as Montreal and Toronto in Canada. On Chicago's street-railway system with more than 1,100 miles of track and 3,600 cars—the largest system in the world—you can travel for thirty-seven miles on a single fare with transfers. In New York, Detroit, Los Angeles, Cleveland, St. Louis, and Washington, D. C., there was a more or less even division of business between street-cars and motor-buses. Boston, Milwaukee, Kansas City, and Indianapolis were definitely in the "all-three" class. At Newark, Seattle, and Portland, Oregon, the trolley bus had assumed a predominant position. San Antonio was the largest city in the United States relying entirely on motor-buses, but there were many others of smaller size where this type of service had been adopted to the exclusion of all others.

Of the 376 cities in the United States listed by the 1930 census as having more than 25,000 inhabitants, there were actually fewer with street-railways at the beginning of 1940 than there were fifty years earlier. In 1890 some 230 of these cities had horse-cars or cable-cars and a few had electric cars. By 1912 the horse-cars and cable-cars had virtually disappeared and electric railways had been built in 370 of the 376 cities. In only one of them, New York, was there any bus service.

Then began a period of far-reaching change. The development of the motor-bus and the trolley-bus provided the transit industry with new types of vehicles having marked advantages under many conditions. By 1940 the number of cities relying exclusively on electric railways had dropped from 369 to eleven, while in 171 others the service was given by electric railways in combination with motor-buses or trolley-buses or both. In 200 cities the rubber-tired vehicles were furnishing all local service.

The history of transit during this fifty-year period, however, represented evolution rather than revolution. The horse and cable railways, for the most part, were not driven out of business by the electric railways. On the contrary, the managements recognized the advent of an improved method of rendering transit service and proceeded to take advantage of it in their own operations. Similarly, the electric railways in more recent years recognized the advantages of the bus and the trolley-bus under many conditions and proceeded to make use of them on a broad scale. Evidence of this is found in the fact that at the beginning of 1940 more than eighty-five per cent of the buses used in cities over 25,000 population were operated under the auspices of organizations which were, or had been, electric-railway companies. In only three of the ninety-three large and medium-size cities of the country had the established electric-railway companies passed out of the picture to be replaced by independent bus companies.

What had happened was that the "trolley-minded" attitude of transit managements had been replaced by a broader conception.

"The traditional street-car operator has practically disappeared," said Walter Draper, president of the Cincinnati Street Railway, in discussing this subject in the *Transit Journal*, "and in his place stands an operator ready to render service by surface railway, subway, elevated, motor-bus or trolley-bus—in short, a merchant of transportation."

When the private automobile first came into widespread use in the United States it was expected by many people to spell the doom of the companies furnishing local common carrier service for passengers.

"In five years," said a prominent manufacturer of private automobiles back in the 1920's, "every one will own an automobile and there won't be any need for street-cars or buses."

Those five years passed, another five years, too, but people continued to use transit service—to use it, in fact, in greater numbers than before the advent of the private automobile. In 1940 the transit industry was carrying passengers at a rate of over thirteen billion a year. This was about twenty times as many as were being carried by intercity buses, twenty-five times as many as by taxicabs or the Class I steam-railroads and about six thousand times as many as by the air-transport lines. It meant that every man, woman, and child of the entire urban population of the country was using transit service on the average more than 200 times a year.

To handle this immense volume of business the transit industry in the United States was operating some 30,000 electric surface-railway cars, 11,000 rapid-transit cars, 2,200 trolley buses and 30,000 motor-buses. The track and route over which these vehicles were in operation totaled nearly 60,000 miles. Annual revenues were running about 800 million dollars, making transit one of the largest industries in the United States. Approximately half of the revenue was being paid out in wages to some 200,000 employees.

If this seemed a far cry from the prediction of the automobile manufacturer who prophesied an early funeral for the transit industry, there was a good reason for it. Without transit service to carry the bulk of the riding the streets of every sizable city would have become so congested that virtually all movement would have been impossible.

Even with the aid of transit vehicles handling hundreds of millions of passengers the situation in the streets of many a city was not unlike that foreseen by Nahum, the Elkoshite, who predicted in the eighth century, B.C., that "The chariots shall rage in the streets, they shall justle one against the other in the broad ways; they shall seem like torches, they shall run like the lightnings."

Traffic engineers figure that a sixty-foot pavement will accommodate only three lanes of automobiles, carrying 3,700 people per hour in each direction. With buses using one lane the carrying capacity of the street is increased to 11,130 people per hour in each direction. With street-cars the capacity becomes 15,630. One express-local subway will carry 100,000 passengers per hour in one direction on two tracks. Twenty-one four-lane elevated highways would be required to carry the same load in automobiles.

Then, too, there is the problem of vehicle storage. Transit vehicles are returned to their car houses and garages in outlying districts when their work is done, but the private automobile used to carry people to shop, office, or store must be parked somewhere until the owner is ready to return, unless he can afford a chauffeur to drive it away. Certainly there is not enough room in the streets to store everybody's automobiles. For off-street parking the space required to store a private automobile is almost exactly the same as the working space required by the workers it carries. Each office building, or factory therefore would have to be accompanied by a garage of the same size as the original building if enough off-street storage space were to be provided for every one to use private automobiles as a means of getting there. This might be possible in outlying districts, but the idea of devoting half the ground area of downtown districts to garage purposes is obviously impractical.

It would undoubtedly be the ideal standard of travel [according to Philip Harrington, Chicago's commissioner of subways and superhighways], if every one were able and could afford to execute all his movements in his own car, with complete safety, free from all traffic annoyance and delay and have a doorman take and deliver the car whenever the need for parking arose. But unless it is proposed that we first wreck from stem to stern the present pattern of city streets which we have inherited, we know that no such traffic Utopia is possible even if our national economy could afford it. I conceive the only adequate approach to a lasting solution of the problem to be a comprehensive attack upon the broad and fundamental, though basically unsound practice which brings about this condition. The guilty culprit is the excessive and uneconomical use of the private automobile for daily travel to and from home and place of work or other occupation. It is not my idea that there should be less ownership of automobiles, but that those who have no need for their cars for their daily activities should leave them at home, and avail themselves of public carrier facilities.

American cities may never reach the condition that prevailed two thousand years ago in Rome when the private vehicles of all but the most important people were banned from the congested streets in the center of the city, but neither are they likely to reach a condition when they can dispense with the service of the common carrier transportation vehicle, and the old cry of "Fares, please!", which has been a characteristic feature of transit service since its earliest days, will continue to echo down the years.

BIBLIOGRAPHY

ARCHAMBAULT, E. J., "Improving Methods of Track Construction," *Transit Journal*, September 15, 1931.

BLAIN, HUGH MERCER, *A Near Century of Public Service in New Orleans* (New Orleans, New Orleans Public Service, Inc., 1927).

———— *History of the Chemical Bank* (New York, The Chemical National Bank, 1913).

BROWN, HENRY COLLINS, *Brownstone Fronts and Saratoga Trunks* (New York, E. P. Dutton & Co., 1935).

BURCH, EDWARD P., *Electric Traction for Railway Trains* (New York, McGraw-Hill Book Company, 1911).

CROSBY, OSCAR T. and BELL, LOUIS, *The Electric Railway in Theory and Practice* (New York, W. J. Johnston Co., 1892).

DRAPER, WALTER A., "Trolley Operators Become Transit Merchants," *Transit Journal*, September 15, 1934.

EASTON, ALEXANDER, *A Practical Treatise on Street or Horse Power Railways* (Philadelphia, Crissy & Markey, 1859).

FABER, LOUISE E., "California Gold Rush Days."

FAUST, CLIFFORD A., "The Trolley Bus," *Electric Railway Journal*, September 15, 1931.

Fifty Years of Unified Transportation in Metropolitan Boston (Boston, Boston Elevated Railway, 1938).

HANNA, JOHN H., "Changing from Cable to Electricity," *Transit Journal*, September 15, 1934.

HARTE, CHARLES RUFUS, "Boom Days of the Electric Railways," *Transit Journal*, September 15, 1934.

McCARTER, THOMAS N., "From Jitney Competition to Bus Co-ordination," *Transit Journal*, September 15, 1934.

MILLER, JOHN A., "In Every Place It's Different," *Transit Journal*, March, 1940.

Ohio Brass Company Traction News, February, 1939.

PASSINGHAM, W. S., *Romance of London's Underground* (London, Sampson Low Marston & Co., 1932).

QUIETT, GLEN CHESNEY, *They Built the West* (New York, D. Appleton-Century Co., 1934).

RIDGWAY, ROBERT, "Rapid Transit Enters a New Era," *Transit Journal*, September 15, 1934.

RYDER, E. M. T., "Improvements in Track," *Electric Railway Journal*, September 15, 1931.

SPRAGUE, FRANK J., "Birth of the Electric Railway," *Transit Journal*, September 15, 1934.

———— "How Multiple-Unit Control Originated," *Transit Journal*, September 15, 1934.

STOCKS, CARL W., "The Modern Motor Bus," *Electric Railway Journal*, September 15, 1931.

STRATTON, EZRA M., *The World on Wheels*, published by the author (New York, 1878).

The News, Cincinnati Street Railway, July, 1930 and February, 1940.

TOMPKINS, RAYMOND S., "Horse Car Days," *Transit Journal*, September 15, 1934.

———— "Horse Car Days," *American Mercury*, April, 1929.

WALKER, JAMES BLAINE, *Fifty Years of Rapid Transit* (New York, Law Printing Company, 1918).

WEST, EDWARD A., "The Trackless Trolley—Has It A Place?" *Electric Railway Journal*, September 8, 1928.

WHIPPLE, FRED H., *The Electric Railway* (Detroit, 1889).

WRIGHT, AUGUSTINE W., *American Street Railways* (Chicago, Rand McNally & Company, 1888).

INDEX

(1)

CATALOGUE OF DOVER BOOKS

Books Explaining Science and Mathematics

WHAT IS SCIENCE?, N. Campbell. The role of experiment and measurement, the function of mathematics, the nature of scientific laws, the difference between laws and theories, the limitations of science, and many similarly provocative topics are treated clearly and without technicalities by an eminent scientist. "Still an excellent introduction to scientific philosophy," H. Margenau in PHYSICS TODAY. "A first-rate primer . . . deserves a wide audience," SCIENTIFIC AMERICAN. 192pp. 5⅜ x 8.   S43 Paperbound **$1.25**

THE NATURE OF PHYSICAL THEORY, P. W. Bridgman. A Nobel Laureate's clear, non-technical lectures on difficulties and paradoxes connected with frontier research on the physical sciences. Concerned with such central concepts as thought, logic, mathematics, relativity, probability, wave mechanics, etc. he analyzes the contributions of such men as Newton, Einstein, Bohr, Heisenberg, and many others. "Lucid and entertaining . . . recommended to anyone who wants to get some insight into current philosophies of science," THE NEW PHILOSOPHY. Index. xi + 138pp. 5⅜ x 8.   S33 Paperbound **$1.25**

EXPERIMENT AND THEORY IN PHYSICS, Max Born. A Nobel Laureate examines the nature of experiment and theory in theoretical physics and analyzes the advances made by the great physicists of our day: Heisenberg, Einstein, Bohr, Planck, Dirac, and others. The actual process of creation is detailed step-by-step by one who participated. A fine examination of the scientific method at work. 44pp. 5⅜ x 8.   S308 Paperbound **75¢**

THE PSYCHOLOGY OF INVENTION IN THE MATHEMATICAL FIELD, J. Hadamard. The reports of such men as Descartes, Pascal, Einstein, Poincaré, and others are considered in this investigation of the method of idea-creation in mathematics and other sciences and the thinking process in general. How do ideas originate? What is the role of the unconscious? What is Poincaré's forgetting hypothesis? are some of the fascinating questions treated. A penetrating analysis of Einstein's thought processes concludes the book. xiii + 145pp. 5⅜ x 8.   T107 Paperbound **$1.25**

THE NATURE OF LIGHT AND COLOUR IN THE OPEN AIR, M. Minnaert. Why are shadows sometimes blue, sometimes green, or other colors depending on the light and surroundings? What causes mirages? Why do multiple suns and moons appear in the sky? Professor Minnaert explains these unusual phenomena and hundreds of others in simple, easy-to-understand terms based on optical laws and the properties of light and color. No mathematics is required but artists, scientists, students, and everyone fascinated by these "tricks" of nature will find thousands of useful and amazing pieces of information. Hundreds of observational experiments are suggested which require no special equipment. 200 illustrations; 42 photos. xvi + 362pp. 5⅜ x 8.   T196 Paperbound **$2.00**

*MATHEMATICS IN ACTION, O. G. Sutton. Everyone with a command of high school algebra will find this book one of the finest possible introductions to the application of mathematics to physical theory. Ballistics, numerical analysis, waves and wavelike phenomena, Fourier series, group concepts, fluid flow and aerodynamics, statistical measures, and meteorology are discussed with unusual clarity. Some calculus and differential equations theory is developed by the author for the reader's help in the more difficult sections. 88 figures. Index. viii + 236pp. 5⅜ x 8.   T440 Clothbound **$3.50**

SOAP-BUBBLES: THEIR COLOURS AND THE FORCES THAT MOULD THEM, C. V. Boys. For continuing popularity and validity as scientific primer, few books can match this volume of easily-followed experiments, explanations. Lucid exposition of complexities of liquid films, surface tension and related phenomena, bubbles' reaction to heat, motion, music, magnetic fields. Experiments with capillary attraction, soap bubbles on frames, composite bubbles, liquid cylinders and jets, bubbles other than soap, etc. Wonderful introduction to scientific method, natural laws that have many ramifications in areas of modern physics. Only complete edition in print. New Introduction by S. Z. Lewin, New York University. 83 illustrations; 1 full-page color plate. xii + 190pp. 5⅜ x 8½.   T542 Paperbound **95¢**

Classics of Science

THE DIDEROT PICTORIAL ENCYCLOPEDIA OF TRADES AND INDUSTRY, MANUFACTURING AND THE TECHNICAL ARTS IN PLATES SELECTED FROM "L'ENCYCLOPEDIE OU DICTIONNAIRE RAISONNE DES SCIENCES, DES ARTS, ET DES METIERS" OF DENIS DIDEROT, edited with text by C. Gillispie. The first modern selection of plates from the high point of 18th century French engraving, Diderot's famous Encyclopedia. Over 2000 illustrations on 485 full page plates, most of them original size, illustrating the trades and industries of one of the most fascinating periods of modern history, 18th century France. These magnificent engravings provide an invaluable glimpse into the past for the student of early technology, a lively and accurate social document to students of cultures, an outstanding find to the lover of fine engravings. The plates teem with life, with men, women, and children performing all of the thousands of operations necessary to the trades before and during the early stages of the industrial revolution. Plates are in sequence, and show general operations, closeups of difficult operations, and details of complex machinery. Such important and interesting trades and industries are illustrated as sowing, harvesting, beekeeping, cheesemaking, operating windmills, milling flour, charcoal burning, tobacco processing, indigo, fishing, arts of war, salt extraction, mining, smelting iron, casting iron, steel, extracting mercury, zinc, sulphur, copper, etc., slating, tinning, silverplating, gilding, making gunpowder, cannons, bells, shoeing horses, tanning, papermaking, printing, dying, and more than 40 other categories. 920pp. 9 x 12. Heavy library cloth. T421 Two volume set **$18.50**

THE PRINCIPLES OF SCIENCE, A TREATISE ON LOGIC AND THE SCIENTIFIC METHOD, W. Stanley Jevons. Treating such topics as Inductive and Deductive Logic, the Theory of Number, Probability, and the Limits of Scientific Method, this milestone in the development of symbolic logic remains a stimulating contribution to the investigation of inferential validity in the natural and social sciences. It significantly advances Boole's logic, and describes a machine which is a foundation of modern electronic calculators. In his introduction, Ernest Nagel of Columbia University says, "(Jevons) . . . continues to be of interest as an attempt to articulate the logic of scientific inquiry." Index. liii + 786pp. 5⅜ x 8. S446 Paperbound **$2.98**

*DIALOGUES CONCERNING TWO NEW SCIENCES, Galileo Galilei. A classic of experimental science which has had a profound and enduring influence on the entire history of mechanics and engineering. Galileo based this, his finest work, on 30 years of experimentation. It offers a fascinating and vivid exposition of dynamics, elasticity, sound, ballistics, strength of materials, and the scientific method. Translated by H. Crew and A. de Salvio. 126 diagrams. Index. xxi + 288pp. 5⅜ x 8. S99 Paperbound **$1.75**

DE MAGNETE, William Gilbert. This classic work on magnetism founded a new science. Gilbert was the first to use the word "electricity," to recognize mass as distinct from weight, to discover the effect of heat on magnetic bodies; invented an electroscope, differentiated between static electricity and magnetism, conceived of the earth as a magnet. Written by the first great experimental scientist, this lively work is valuable not only as an historical landmark, but as the delightfully easy-to-follow record of a perpetually searching, ingenious mind. Translated by P. F. Mottelay. 25 page biographical memoir. 90 fix. lix + 368pp. 5⅜ x 8. S470 Paperbound **$2.00**

*OPTICKS, Sir Isaac Newton. An enormous storehouse of insights and discoveries on light, reflection, color, refraction, theories of wave and corpuscular propagation of light, optical apparatus, and mathematical devices which have recently been reevaluated in terms of modern physics and placed in the top-most ranks of Newton's work! Foreword by Albert Einstein. Preface by I. B. Cohen of Harvard U. 7 pages of portraits, facsimile pages, letters, etc. cxvi + 412pp. 5⅜ x 8. S205 Paperbound **$2.25**

A SURVEY OF PHYSICAL THEORY, M. Planck. Lucid essays on modern physics for the general reader by the Nobel Laureate and creator of the quantum revolution. Planck explains how the new concepts came into being; explores the clash between theories of mechanics, electrodynamics, and thermodynamics; and traces the evolution of the concept of light through Newton, Huygens, Maxwell, and his own quantum theory, providing unparalleled insights into his development of this momentous modern concept. Bibliography. Index. vii + 121pp. 5⅜ x 8. S650 Paperbound **$1.15**

A SOURCE BOOK IN MATHEMATICS, D. E. Smith. English translations of the original papers that announced the great discoveries in mathematics from the Renaissance to the end of the 19th century: succinct selections from 125 different treatises and articles, most of them unavailable elsewhere in English—Newton, Leibniz, Pascal, Riemann, Bernoulli, etc. 24 articles trace developments in the field of number, 18 cover algebra, 36 are on geometry, and 13 on calculus. Biographical-historical introductions to each article. Two volume set. Index in each. Total of 115 illustrations. Total of xxviii + 742pp. 5⅜ x 8. S552 Vol I Paperbound **$2.00** S553 Vol II Paperbound **$2.00** The set, boxed **$4.00**

*THE THIRTEEN BOOKS OF EUCLID'S ELEMENTS, edited by T. L. Heath. This is the complete EUCLID — the definitive edition of one of the greatest classics of the western world. Complete English translation of the Heiberg text with spurious Book XIV. Detailed 150-page introduction discusses aspects of Greek and medieval mathematics: Euclid, texts, commentators, etc. Paralleling the text is an elaborate critical exposition analyzing each definition, proposition, postulate, etc., and covering textual matters, mathematical analyses, refutations, extensions, etc. Unabridged reproduction of the Cambridge 2nd edition. 3 volumes. Total of 995 figures, 1426pp. 5⅜ x 8.   S88, 89, 90 — 3 vol. set, Paperbound **$7.50**

*THE GEOMETRY OF RENE DESCARTES. The great work which founded analytic geometry. The renowned Smith-Latham translation faced with the original French text containing all of Descartes' own diagrams! Contains: Problems the Construction of Which Requires Only Straight Lines and Circles; On the Nature of Curved Lines; On the Construction of Solid or Supersolid Problems. Notes. Diagrams. 258pp.   S68 Paperbound **$1.60**

*A PHILOSOPHICAL ESSAY ON PROBABILITIES, P. Laplace. Without recourse to any mathematics above grammar school, Laplace develops a philosophically, mathematically and historically classical exposition of the nature of probability: its functions and limitations, operations in practical affairs, calculations in games of chance, insurance, government, astronomy, and countless other fields. New introduction by E. T. Bell. viii + 196pp.   S166 Paperbound **$1.35**

DE RE METALLICA, Georgius Agricola. Written over 400 years ago, for 200 years the most authoritative first-hand account of the production of metals, translated in 1912 by former President Herbert Hoover and his wife, and today still one of the most beautiful and fascinating volumes ever produced in the history of science! 12 books, exhaustively annotated, give a wonderfully lucid and vivid picture of the history of mining, selection of sites, types of deposits, excavating pits, sinking shafts, ventilating, pumps; crushing machinery, assaying, smelting, refining metals, making salt, alum, nitre, glass, and many other topics. This definitive edition contains all 289 of the 16th century woodcuts which made the original an artistic masterpiece. It makes a superb gift for geologists, engineers, libraries, artists, historians, and everyone interested in science and early illustrative art. Biographical, historical introductions. Bibliography, survey of ancient authors. Indices. 289 illustrations. 672pp. 6¾ x 10¾. Deluxe library edition.   S6 Clothbound **$10.00**

GEOGRAPHICAL ESSAYS, W. M. Davis. Modern geography and geomorphology rest on the fundamental work of this scientist. His new concepts of earth-processes revolutionized science and his broad interpretation of the scope of geography created a deeper understanding of the interrelation of the landscape and the forces that mold it. This first inexpensive unabridged edition covers theory of geography, methods of advanced geographic teaching, descriptions of geographic areas, analyses of land-shaping processes, and much besides. Not only a factual and historical classic, it is still widely read for its reflections of modern scientific thought. Introduction. 130 figures. Index. vi + 777pp. 5⅜ x 8.
                                                                         S383 Paperbound **$3.50**

CHARLES BABBAGE AND HIS CALCULATING ENGINES, edited by P. Morrison and E. Morrison. Friend of Darwin, Humboldt, and Laplace, Babbage was a leading pioneer in large-scale mathematical machines and a prophetic herald of modern operational research—true father of Harvard's relay computer Mark I. His Difference Engine and Analytical Engine were the first successful machines in the field. This volume contains a valuable introduction on his life and work; major excerpts from his fascinating autobiography, revealing his eccentric and unusual personality; and extensive selections from "Babbage's Calculating Engines," a compilation of hard-to-find journal articles, both by Babbage and by such eminent contributors as the Countess of Lovelace, L. F. Menabrea, and Dionysius Lardner. 11 illustrations. Appendix of miscellaneous papers. Index. Bibliography. xxxviii + 400pp. 5⅜ x 8.   T12 Paperbound **$2.25**

*THE WORKS OF ARCHIMEDES WITH THE METHOD OF ARCHIMEDES, edited by T. L. Heath. All the known works of the greatest mathematician of antiquity including the recently discovered METHOD OF ARCHIMEDES. This last is the only work we have which shows exactly how early mathematicians discovered their proofs before setting them down in their final perfection. A 186 page study by the eminent scholar Heath discusses Archimedes and the history of Greek mathematics. Bibliography. 563pp. 5⅜ x 8.   S9 Paperbound **$2.45**

Medicine

CLASSICS OF MEDICINE AND SURGERY, edited by C. N. B. Camac. 12 greatest papers in medical history, 11 in full: Lister's "Antiseptic Principle;" Harvey's "Motion in the Heart and Blood;" Auenbrugger's "Percussion of the Chest;" Laënnec's "Auscultation and the Stethoscope;" Jenner's "Inquiry into Smallpox Vaccine," 2 related papers; Morton's "Administering Sulphuric Ether," letters to Warren, "Physiology of Ether;" Simpson's "A New Anaesthetic Agent;" Holmes' "Puerperal Fever." Biographies, portraits of authors, bibliographies. Formerly "Epoch-making Contributions to Medicine, Surgery, and the Allied Sciences." Introduction. 14 illus. 445pp. 5⅜ x 8. S539 Paperbound **$2.25**

A WAY OF LIFE, Sir William Osler. The complete essay, stating his philosophy of life, as given at Yale University by this great physician and teacher. 30 pages. Copies limited, no more than 1 to a customer. Free.

SOURCE BOOK OF MEDICAL HISTORY, compiled, annotated by Logan Clendening, M.D. Unequalled collection of 139 greatest papers in medical history, by 120 authors, covers almost every area: pathology, asepsis, preventive medicine, bacteriology, physiology, etc. Hippocrates, Gain, Vesalius, Malpighi, Morgagni, Boerhave, Pasteur, Walter Reed, Florence Nightingale, Lavoisier, Claude Bernard, 109 others, give view of medicine unequalled for immediacy. Careful selections give heart of each paper save you reading time. Selections from non-medical literature show lay-views of medicine: Aristophanes, Plato, Arabian Nights, Chaucer, Molière, Dickens, Thackeray, others. "Notable . . . useful to teacher and student alike," Amer. Historical Review. Bibliography. Index. 699pp. 5⅜ x 8. T621 Paperbound **$2.75**

EXPERIMENTS AND OBSERVATIONS ON THE GASTRIC JUICE AND THE PHYSIOLOGY OF DIGESTION, William Beaumont. A gunshot wound which left a man with a 2½ inch hole through his abdomen into his stomach (1822) enabled Beaumont to perform the remarkable experiments set down here. The first comprehensive, thorough study of motions and processes of the stomach, "his work remains a model of patient, persevering investigation. . . . Beaumont is the pioneer physiologist of this country." (Sir William Osler, in his introduction.) 4 illustrations. xi + 280pp. 5⅜ x 8. S527 Paperbound **$1.50**

AN INTRODUCTION TO THE STUDY OF EXPERIMENTAL MEDICINE, Claude Bernard. 90-year-old classic of medical science, only major work of Bernard available in English, records his efforts to transform physiology into exact science. Principles of scientific research illustrated by specific case histories from his work; roles of chance, error, preliminary false conclusions, in leading eventually to scientific truth; use of hypothesis. Much of modern application of mathematics to biology rests on the foundation set down here. New foreword by Professor I. B. Cohen, Harvard Univ. xxv + 266pp. 5⅜ x 8. T400 Paperbound **$1.50**

A WAY OF LIFE, AND OTHER SELECTED WRITINGS, Sir William Osler, Physician and humanist, Osler discourses brilliantly in thought provoking essays and on the history of medicine. He discusses Thomas Browne, Gui Patin, Robert Burton, Michael Servetus, William Beaumont, Laënnec. Includes such favorite writings as the title essay, "The Old Humanities and the New Science," "Creators, Transmitters, and Transmuters," "Books and Men," "The Student Life," and five more of his best discussions of philosophy, religion and literature. 5 photographs. Introduction by G. L. Keynes, M.D., F.R.C.S. Index. xx + 278pp. 5⅜ x 8. T488 Paperbound **$1.50**

THE HISTORY OF SURGICAL ANESTHESIA, Thomas E. Keys. Concise, but thorough and always engrossing account of the long struggle to find effective methods of eliminating pain during surgery, tracing the remarkable story through the centuries to the eventual successes by dedicated researchers, the acceptance of ether, the work of men such as Priestley, Morton, Lundy, and many, many others. Discussions of the developments in local, regional, and spinal anesthesia, etc. "The general reader as well as the medical historian will find material to interest him in this fascinating story," U.S. QUARTERLY BOOKLIST. Revised, enlarged publication of original edition. Introductory essay by C. D. Leake. Concluding chapter by N. A. Gillespie. Appendix by J. F. Fulton. 46 illustrations. New preface by the author. Chronology of events. Extensive bibliographies. Index. xxx + 193pp. 5⅜ x 8½. T1122 Paperbound **$2.00**

A SHORT HISTORY OF ANATOMY AND PHYSIOLOGY FROM THE GREEKS TO HARVEY, Charles Singer. Corrected edition of THE EVOLUTION OF ANATOMY, classic work tracing evolution of anatomy and physiology from prescientific times through Greek & Roman periods, Dark Ages, Renaissance, to age of Harvey and beginning of modern concepts. Centered on individuals, movements, periods that definitely advanced anatomical knowledge: Plato, Diocles, Aristotle, Theophrastus, Herophilus, Erasistratus, the Alexandrians, Galen, Mondino, da Vinci, Linacre, Sylvius, others. Special section on Vesalius; Vesalian atlas of nudes, skeletons, muscle tabulae. Index of names, 20 plates. 270 extremely interesting illustrations of ancient, medieval, Renaissance, Oriental origin. xii + 209pp. 5⅜ x 8. T389 Paperbound **$1.75**

Puzzles, Mathematical Recreations

SYMBOLIC LOGIC and THE GAME OF LOGIC, Lewis Carroll. "Symbolic Logic" is not concerned with modern symbolic logic, but is instead a collection of over 380 problems posed with charm and imagination, using the syllogism, and a fascinating diagrammatic method of drawing conclusions. In "The Game of Logic" Carroll's whimsical imagination devises a logical game played with 2 diagrams and counters (included) to manipulate hundreds of tricky syllogisms. The final section, "Hit or Miss" is a lagniappe of 101 additional puzzles in the delightful Carroll manner. Until this reprint edition, both of these books were rarities costing up to $15 each. Symbolic Logic: Index. xxxi + 199pp. The Game of Logic: 96pp. 2 vols. bound as one. 5⅜ x 8.
T492 Paperbound **$1.75**

PILLOW PROBLEMS and A TANGLED TALE, Lewis Carroll. One of the rarest of all Carroll's works, "Pillow Problems" contains 72 original math puzzles, all typically ingenious. Particularly fascinating are Carroll's answers which remain exactly as he thought them out, reflecting his actual mental process. The problems in "A Tangled Tale" are in story form, originally appearing as a monthly magazine serial. Carroll not only gives the solutions, but uses answers sent in by readers to discuss wrong approaches and misleading paths, and grades them for insight. Both of these books were rarities until this edition, "Pillow Problems" costing up to $25, and "A Tangled Tale" $15. Pillow Problems: Preface and Introduction by Lewis Carroll. xx + 109pp. A Tangled Tale: 6 illustrations. 152pp. Two vols. bound as one. 5⅜ x 8.
T493 Paperbound **$1.50**

AMUSEMENTS IN MATHEMATICS, Henry Ernest Dudeney. The foremost British originator of mathematical puzzles is always intriguing, witty, and paradoxical in this classic, one of the largest collections of mathematical amusements. More than 430 puzzles, problems, and paradoxes. Mazes and games, problems on number manipulation, unicursal and other route problems, puzzles on measuring, weighing, packing, age, kinship, chessboards, joiners', crossing river, plane figure dissection, and many others. Solutions. More than 450 illustrations. vii + 258pp. 5⅜ x 8.
T473 Paperbound **$1.25**

THE CANTERBURY PUZZLES, Henry Dudeney. Chaucer's pilgrims set one another problems in story form. Also Adventures of the Puzzle Club, the Strange Escape of the King's Jester, the Monks of Riddlewell, the Squire's Christmas Puzzle Party, and others. All puzzles are original, based on dissecting plane figures, arithmetic, algebra, elementary calculus and other branches of mathematics, and purely logical ingenuity. "The limit of ingenuity and intricacy," The Observer. Over 110 puzzles. Full Solutions. 150 illustrations. vii + 225pp. 5⅜ x 8.
T474 Paperbound **$1.25**

MATHEMATICAL EXCURSIONS, H. A. Merrill. Even if you hardly remember your high school math, you'll enjoy the 90 stimulating problems contained in this book and you will come to understand a great many mathematical principles with surprisingly little effort. Many useful shortcuts and diversions not generally known are included: division by inspection, Russian peasant multiplication, memory systems for pi, building odd and even magic squares, square roots by geometry, dyadic systems, and many more. Solutions to difficult problems. 50 illustrations. 145pp. 5⅜ x 8.
T350 Paperbound **$1.00**

MAGIC SQUARES AND CUBES, W. S. Andrews. Only book-length treatment in English, a thorough non-technical description and analysis. Here are nasik, overlapping, pandiagonal, serrated squares; magic circles, cubes, spheres, rhombuses. Try your hand at 4-dimensional magical figures! Much unusual folklore and tradition included. High school algebra is sufficient. 754 diagrams and illustrations. viii + 419pp. 5⅜ x 8.
T658 Paperbound **$1.85**

CALIBAN'S PROBLEM BOOK: MATHEMATICAL, INFERENTIAL AND CRYPTOGRAPHIC PUZZLES, H. Phillips (Caliban), S. T. Shovelton, G. S. Marshall. 105 ingenious problems by the greatest living creator of puzzles based on logic and inference. Rigorous, modern, piquant; reflecting their author's unusual personality, these intermediate and advanced puzzles all involve the ability to reason clearly through complex situations; some call for mathematical knowledge, ranging from algebra to number theory. Solutions. xi + 180pp. 5⅜ x 8.
T736 Paperbound **$1.25**

MATHEMATICAL PUZZLES FOR BEGINNERS AND ENTHUSIASTS, G. Mott-Smith. 188 mathematical puzzles based on algebra, dissection of plane figures, permutations, and probability, that will test and improve your powers of inference and interpretation. The Odic Force, The Spider's Cousin, Ellipse Drawing, theory and strategy of card and board games like tit-tat-toe, go moku, salvo, and many others. 100 pages of detailed mathematical explanations. Appendix of primes, square roots, etc. 135 illustrations. 2nd revised edition. 248pp. 5⅜ x 8.
T198 Paperbound **$1.00**

MATHEMAGIC, MAGIC PUZZLES, AND GAMES WITH NUMBERS, R. V. Heath. More than 60 new puzzles and stunts based on the properties of numbers. Easy techniques for multiplying large numbers mentally, revealing hidden numbers magically, finding the date of any day in any year, and dozens more. Over 30 pages devoted to magic squares, triangles, cubes, circles, etc. Edited by J. S. Meyer. 76 illustrations. 128pp. 5⅜ x 8.
T110 Paperbound **$1.00**

MATHEMATICAL RECREATIONS, M. Kraitchik. One of the most thorough compilations of unusual mathematical problems for beginners and advanced mathematicians. Historical problems from Greek, Medieval, Arabic, Hindu sources. 50 pages devoted to pastimes derived from figurate numbers, Mersenne numbers, Fermat numbers, primes and probability. 40 pages of magic, Euler, Latin, panmagic squares. 25 new positional and permutational games of permanent value: fairy chess, latruncles, reversi, jinx, ruma, lasca, tricolor, tetrachrome, etc. Complete rigorous solutions. Revised second edition. 181 illustrations. 333pp. 5⅜ x 8.
T163 Paperbound **$1.75**

MATHEMATICAL PUZZLES OF SAM LOYD, selected and edited by M. Gardner. Choice puzzles by the greatest American puzzle creator and innovator. Selected from his famous collection, "Cyclopedia of Puzzles," they retain the unique style and historical flavor of the originals. There are posers based on arithmetic, algebra, probability, game theory, route tracing, topology, counter, sliding block, operations research, geometrical dissection. Includes the famous "14-15" puzzle which was a national craze, and his "Horse of a Different Color" which sold millions of copies. 117 of his most ingenious puzzles in all, 120 line drawings and diagrams. Solutions. Selected references. xx + 167pp. 5⅜ x 8. T498 Paperbound **$1.00**

MATHEMATICAL PUZZLES OF SAM LOYD, Vol. II, selected and edited by Martin Gardner. The outstanding 2nd selection from the great American innovator's "Cyclopedia of Puzzles": speed and distance problems, clock problems, plane and solid geometry, calculus problems, etc. Analytical table of contents that groups the puzzles according to the type of mathematics necessary to solve them. 166 puzzles, 150 original line drawings and diagrams. Selected references. xiv + 177pp. 5⅜ x 8. T709 Paperbound **$1.00**

ARITHMETICAL EXCURSIONS: AN ENRICHMENT OF ELEMENTARY MATHEMATICS, H. Bowers and J. Bowers. A lively and lighthearted collection of facts and entertainments for anyone who enjoys manipulating numbers or solving arithmetical puzzles: methods of arithmetic never taught in school, little-known facts about the most simple numbers, and clear explanations of more sophisticated topics; mysteries and folklore of numbers, the "Hin-dog-abic" number system, etc. First publication. Index. 529 numbered problems and diversions, all with answers. Bibliography. 60 figures. xiv + 320pp. 5⅜ x 8. T770 Paperbound **$1.65**

CRYPTANALYSIS, H. F. Gaines. Formerly entitled ELEMENTARY CRYPTANALYSIS, this introductory-intermediate level text is the best book in print on cryptograms and their solution. It covers all major techniques of the past, and contains much that is not generally known except to experts. Full details about concealment, substitution, and transposition ciphers; periodic mixed alphabets, multafid, Kasiski and Vigenere methods, Ohaver patterns, Playfair, and scores of other topics. 6 language letter and word frequency appendix. 167 problems, now furnished with solutions. Index. 173 figures. vi + 230pp. 5⅜ x 8.
T97 Paperbound **$2.00**

CRYPTOGRAPHY, L. D. Smith. An excellent introductory work on ciphers and their solution, the history of secret writing, and actual methods and problems in such techniques as transposition and substitution. Appendices describe the enciphering of Japanese, the Baconian biliteral cipher, and contain frequency tables and a bibliography for further study. Over 150 problems with solutions. 160pp. 5⅜ x 8. T247 Paperbound **$1.00**

PUZZLE QUIZ AND STUNT FUN, J. Meyer. The solution to party doldrums. 238 challenging puzzles, stunts and tricks. Mathematical puzzles like The Clever Carpenter, Atom Bomb; mysteries and deductions like The Bridge of Sighs, The Nine Pearls, Dog Logic; observation puzzles like Cigarette Smokers, Telephone Dial; over 200 others including magic squares, tongue twisters, puns, anagrams, and many others. All problems solved fully. 250pp. 5⅜ x 8.
T337 Paperbound **$1.00**

101 PUZZLES IN THOUGHT AND LOGIC, C. R. Wylie, Jr. Brand new problems you need no special knowledge to solve! Take the kinks out of your mental "muscles" and enjoy solving murder problems, the detection of lying fishermen, the logical identification of color by a blindman, and dozens more. Introduction with simplified explanation of general scientific method and puzzle solving. 128pp. 5⅜ x 8. T367 Paperbound **$1.00**

MY BEST PROBLEMS IN MATHEMATICS, Hubert Phillips ("Caliban"). Only elementary mathematics needed to solve these 100 witty, catchy problems by a master problem creator. Problems on the odds in cards and dice, problems in geometry, algebra, permutations, even problems that require no math at all—just a logical mind, clear thinking. Solutions completely worked out. If you enjoy mysteries, alerting your perceptive powers and exercising your detective's eye, you'll find these cryptic puzzles a challenging delight. Original 1961 publication. 100 puzzles, solutions. x + 107pp. 5⅝ x 8. T91 Paperbound **$1.00**

MY BEST PUZZLES IN LOGIC AND REASONING, Hubert Phillips ("Caliban"). A new collection of 100 inferential and logical puzzles chosen from the best that have appeared in England, available for first time in U.S. By the most endlessly resourceful puzzle creator now living. All data presented are both necessary and sufficient to allow a single unambiguous answer. No special knowledge is required for problems ranging from relatively simple to completely original one-of-a-kinds. Guaranteed to please beginners and experts of all ages. Original publication. 100 puzzles, full solutions. x + 107pp. 5⅜ x 8. T119 Paperbound **$1.00**

THE BOOK OF MODERN PUZZLES, G. L. Kaufman. A completely new series of puzzles as fascinating as crossword and deduction puzzles but based upon different principles and techniques. Simple 2-minute teasers, word labyrinths, design and pattern puzzles, logic and observation puzzles — over 150 braincrackers. Answers to all problems. 116 illustrations. 192pp. 5⅜ x 8.
T143 Paperbound **$1.00**

NEW WORD PUZZLES, G. L. Kaufman. 100 ENTIRELY NEW puzzles based on words and their combinations that will delight crossword puzzle, Scrabble and Jotto fans. Chess words, based on the moves of the chess king; design-onyms, symmetrical designs made of synonyms; rhymed double-crostics; syllable sentences; addle letter anagrams; alphagrams; linkograms; and many others all brand new. Full solutions. Space to work problems. 196 figures. vi + 122pp. 5⅜ x 8.
T344 Paperbound **$1.00**

MAZES AND LABYRINTHS: A BOOK OF PUZZLES, W. Shepherd. Mazes, formerly associated with mystery and ritual, are still among the most intriguing of intellectual puzzles. This is a novel and different collection of 50 amusements that embody the principle of the maze: mazes in the classical tradition; 3-dimensional, ribbon, and Möbius-strip mazes; hidden messages; spatial arrangements; etc.—almost all built on amusing story situations. 84 illustrations. Essay on maze psychology. Solutions. xv + 122pp. 5⅜ x 8.
T731 Paperbound **$1.00**

MAGIC TRICKS & CARD TRICKS, W. Jonson. Two books bound as one. 52 tricks with cards, 37 tricks with coins, bills, eggs, smoke, ribbons, slates, etc. Details on presentation, misdirection, and routining will help you master such famous tricks as the Changing Card, Card in the Pocket, Four Aces, Coin Through the Hand, Bill in the Egg, Afghan Bands, and over 75 others. If you follow the lucid exposition and key diagrams carefully, you will finish these two books with an astonishing mastery of magic. 106 figures. 224pp. 5⅜ x 8. T909 Paperbound **$1.00**

PANORAMA OF MAGIC, Milbourne Christopher. A profusely illustrated history of stage magic, a unique selection of prints and engravings from the author's private collection of magic memorabilia, the largest of its kind. Apparatus, stage settings and costumes; ingenious ads distributed by the performers and satiric broadsides passed around in the streets ridiculing pompous showmen; programs; decorative souvenirs. The lively text, by one of America's foremost professional magicians, is full of anecdotes about almost legendary wizards: Dede, the Egyptian; Philadelphia, the wonder-worker; Robert-Houdin, "the father of modern magic;" Harry Houdini; scores more. Altogether a pleasure package for anyone interested in magic, stage setting and design, ethnology, psychology, or simply in unusual people. A Dover original. 295 illustrations; 8 in full color. Index. viii + 216pp. 8⅜ x 11¼.
T774 Paperbound **$2.25**

HOUDINI ON MAGIC, Harry Houdini. One of the greatest magicians of modern times explains his most prized secrets. How locks are picked, with illustrated picks and skeleton keys; how a girl is sawed into twins; how to walk through a brick wall — Houdini's explanations of 44 stage tricks with many diagrams. Also included is a fascinating discussion of great magicians of the past and the story of his fight against fraudulent mediums and spiritualists. Edited by W.B. Gibson and M.N. Young. Bibliography. 155 figures, photos. xv + 280pp. 5⅜ x 8.
T384 Paperbound **$1.35**

MATHEMATICS, MAGIC AND MYSTERY, Martin Gardner. Why do card tricks work? How do magicians perform astonishing mathematical feats? How is stage mind-reading possible? This is the first book length study explaining the application of probability, set theory, theory of numbers, topology, etc., to achieve many startling tricks. Non-technical, accurate, detailed! 115 sections discuss tricks with cards, dice, coins, knots, geometrical vanishing illusions, how a Curry square "demonstrates" that the sum of the parts may be greater than the whole, and dozens of others. No sleight of hand necessary! 135 illustrations. xii + 174pp. 5⅜ x 8.
T335 Paperbound **$1.00**

EASY-TO-DO ENTERTAINMENTS AND DIVERSIONS WITH COINS, CARDS, STRING, PAPER AND MATCHES, R. M. Abraham. Over 300 tricks, games and puzzles will provide young readers with absorbing fun. Sections on card games; paper-folding; tricks with coins, matches and pieces of string; games for the agile; toy-making from common household objects; mathematical recreations; and 50 miscellaneous pastimes. Anyone in charge of groups of youngsters, including hard-pressed parents, and in need of suggestions on how to keep children sensibly amused and quietly content will find this book indispensable. Clear, simple text, copious number of delightful line drawings and illustrative diagrams. Originally titled "Winter Nights Entertainments." Introduction by Lord Baden Powell. 329 illustrations. v + 186pp. 5⅜ x 8½.
T921 Paperbound **$1.00**

STRING FIGURES AND HOW TO MAKE THEM, Caroline Furness Jayne. 107 string figures plus variations selected from the best primitive and modern examples developed by Navajo, Apache, pygmies of Africa, Eskimo, in Europe, Australia, China, etc. The most readily understandable, easy-to-follow book in English on perennially popular recreation. Crystal-clear exposition; step-by-step diagrams. Everyone from kindergarten children to adults looking for unusual diversion will be endlessly amused. Index. Bibliography. Introduction by A. C. Haddon. 17 full-page plates. 960 illustrations. xxiii + 401pp. 5⅜ x 8½.
T152 Paperbound **$2.00**

Chess, Checkers, Games, Go

THE ADVENTURE OF CHESS, Edward Lasker. A lively history of chess, from its ancient beginnings in the Indian 4-handed game of Chaturanga, through to the great players of our day, as told by one of America's finest masters. He introduces such unusual sidelights and amusing oddities as Maelzel's chess-playing automaton that beat Napoleon 3 times. Major discussion of chess-playing machines and personal memories of Nimzovich, Capablanca, etc. 5-page chess primer. 11 illustrations, 53 diagrams. 296pp. 5⅜ x 8. S510 Paperbound **$1.75**

A TREASURY OF CHESS LORE, edited by Fred Reinfeld. A delightful collection of anecdotes, short stories, aphorisms by and about the masters, poems, accounts of games and tournaments, photography. Hundreds of humorous, pithy, satirical, wise, and historical episodes, comments, and word portraits. A fascinating "must" for chess players; revealing and perhaps seductive to those who wonder what their friends see in the game. 48 photographs (14 full page plates) 12 diagrams. xi + 306pp. 5⅜ x 8. T458 Paperbound **$2.00**

HOW DO YOU PLAY CHESS? by Fred Reinfeld. A prominent expert covers every basic rule of chess for the beginner in 86 questions and answers: moves, powers of pieces, rationale behind moves, how to play forcefully, history of chess, and much more. Bibliography of chess publications. 11 board diagrams. 48 pages. **FREE**

THE PLEASURES OF CHESS, Assiac. Internationally known British writer, influential chess columnist, writes wittily about wide variety of chess subjects: Anderssen's "Immortal Game;" only game in which both opponents resigned at once; psychological tactics of Reshevsky, Lasker; varieties played by masters for relaxation, such as "losing chess;" sacrificial orgies; etc. These anecdotes, witty observations will give you fresh appreciation of game. 43 problems. 150 diagrams. 139pp. 5⅜ x 8. T597 Paperbound **$1.25**

WIN AT CHESS, F. Reinfeld. 300 practical chess situations from actual tournament play to sharpen your chess eye and test your skill. Traps, sacrifices, mates, winning combinations, subtle exchanges, show you how to WIN AT CHESS. Short notes and tables of solutions and alternative moves help you evaluate your progress. Learn to think ahead playing the "crucial moments" of historic games. 300 diagrams. Notes and solutions. Formerly titled CHESS QUIZ. vi + 120pp. 5⅜ x 8. T438 Paperbound **$1.00**

THE ART OF CHESS, James Mason. An unabridged reprinting of the latest revised edition of the most famous general study of chess ever written. Also included, a complete supplement by Fred Reinfeld, "How Do You Play Chess?", invaluable to beginners for its lively question and answer method. Mason, an early 20th century master, teaches the beginning and intermediate player more than 90 openings, middle game, end game, how to see more moves ahead, to plan purposefully, attack, sacrifice, defend, exchange, and govern general strategy. Supplement. 448 diagrams. 1947 Reinfeld-Bernstein text. Bibliography. xvi + 340pp. 5⅜ x 8. T463 Paperbound **$2.00**

THE PRINCIPLES OF CHESS, James Mason. This "great chess classic" (N. Y. Times) is a general study covering all aspects of the game: basic forces, resistance, obstruction, opposition, relative values, mating, typical end game situations, combinations, much more. The last section discusses openings, with 50 games illustrating modern master play of Rubinstein, Spielmann, Lasker, Capablanca, etc., selected and annotated by Fred Reinfeld. Will improve the game of any intermediate-skilled player, but is so forceful and lucid that an absolute beginner might use it to become an accomplished player. 1946 Reinfeld edition. 166 diagrams. 378pp. 5⅜ x 8. T646 Paperbound **$2.00**

LASKER'S MANUAL OF CHESS, Dr. Emanuel Lasker. Probably the greatest chess player of modern times, Dr. Emanuel Lasker held the world championship 28 years, independent of passing schools or fashions. This unmatched study of the game, chiefly for intermediate to skilled players, analyzes basic methods, combinations, position play, the aesthetics of chess, dozens of different openings, etc., with constant reference to great modern games. Contains a brilliant exposition of Steinitz's important theories. Introduction by Fred Reinfeld. Tables of Lasker's tournament record. 3 indices. 308 diagrams. 1 photograph. xxx + 349pp. 5⅜ x 8. T640 Paperbound **$2.25**

THE ART OF CHESS COMBINATION, E. Znosko-Borovsky. Proves that combinations, perhaps the most aesthetically satisfying, successful technique in chess, can be an integral part of your game, instead of a haphazard occurrence. Games of Capablanca, Rubinstein, Nimzovich, Bird, etc. grouped according to common features, perceptively analyzed to show that every combination begins in certain simple ideas. Will help you to plan many moves ahead. Technical terms almost completely avoided. "In the teaching of chess he may claim to have no superior," P. W. Sergeant. Introduction. Exercises. Solutions. Index. 223pp. 5⅜ x 8. T583 Paperbound **$1.60**

THE HASTINGS CHESS TOURNAMENT, 1895, edited by Horace F. Cheshire. This is the complete tournament book of the famous Hastings 1895 tournament. One of the most exciting tournaments ever to take place, it evoked the finest play from such players as Dr. Lasker, Steinitz, Tarrasch, Harry Pillsbury, Mason, Tchigorin, Schlecter, and others. It was not only extremely exciting as an event, it also created first-rate chess. This book contains fully annotated all 230 games, full information about the playing events, biographies of the players, and much other material that makes it a chess classic. 22 photos, 174 diagrams. x + 370pp. 5⅝ x 8½.   T288 Paperbound **$2.00**

THE BOOK OF THE NOTTINGHAM INTERNATIONAL CHESS TOURNAMENT, 1936, Annotated by Dr. Alexander Alekhine. The Nottingham 1936 tournament is regarded by many chess enthusiasts as the greatest tournament of recent years. It brought together all the living former world champions, the current world champion, and the future world champion: Dr. Lasker, Capablanca, Alekhine, Euwe, Botvinnik, and Reshevsky, Fine, Flohr, Tartakover, Vidmar, and Bogoljubov. The play was brilliant throughout. This volume contains all 105 of the games played, provided with the remarkable annotations of Alekhine. 1 illustration, 121 diagrams, xx + 291pp. 5⅜ x 8½.   T189 Paperbound **$2.00**

CHESS FOR FUN AND CHESS FOR BLOOD, Edward Lasker. A genial, informative book by one of century's leading masters. Incisive comments on chess as a form of art and recreation, on how a master prepares for and plays a tournament. Best of all is author's move-by-move analysis of his game with Dr. Emanuel Lasker in 1924 World Tournament, a charming and thorough recreation of one of the great games in history: the author's mental processes; how his calculations were upset; how both players blundered; the surprising outcome. Who could not profit from this study-in-depth? For the enthusiast who likes to read about chess as well as play it. Corrected (1942) edition. Preface contains 8 letters to author about the fun of chess. 95 illustrations by Maximilian Mopp. 224pp. 5⅜ x 8½.   T146 Paperbound **$1.25**

HOW NOT TO PLAY CHESS, Eugene A. Znosko-Borovsky. Sticking to a few well-chosen examples and explaining every step along the way, an outstanding chess expositor shows how to avoid playing a hit-or-miss game and instead develop general plans of action based on positional analysis: weak and strong squares, the notion of the controlled square, how to seize control of open lines, weak points in the pawn structure, and so on. Definition and illustration of typical chess mistakes plus 20 problems (from master games) added by Fred Reinfeld for the 1949 edition and a number of good-to-memorize tips make this a lucid book that can teach in a few hours what might otherwise take years to learn. 119pp. 5⅜ x 8.
                                                          T920 Paperbound **$1.00**

THE SOVIET SCHOOL OF CHESS, A. Kotov and M. Yudovich. 128 master games, most unavailable elsewhere, by 51 outstanding players, including Botvinnik, Keres, Smyslov, Tal, against players like Capablanca, Euwe, Reshevsky. All carefully annotated, analyzed. Valuable biographical information about each player, early history of Russian chess, careers and contributions of Chigorin and Alekhine, development of Soviet school from 1920 to present with full over-all study of main features of its games, history of Russian chess literature. The most comprehensive work on Russian chess ever printed, the richest single sourcebook for up-to-date Russian theory and strategy. New introduction. Appendix of Russian Grandmasters, Masters, Master Composers. Two indexes (Players, Games). 30 photographs. 182 diagrams. vi + 390pp. 5⅜ x 8.   T26 Paperbound **$2.00**

THE ART OF THE CHECKMATE, Georges Renaud and Victor Kahn. Two former national chess champions of France examine 127 games, identify 23 kinds of mate, and show the rationale for each. These include Legal's pseudo sacrifice, the double check, the smothered mate, Greco's mate, Morphy's mate, the mate of two bishops, two knights, many, many more. Analysis of ideas, not memorization problems. Review quizzes with answers help readers gauge progress. 80 quiz examples and solutions. 299 diagrams. vi + 208pp.
                                                          T106 Paperbound **$1.50**

HOW TO SOLVE CHESS PROBLEMS, K. S. Howard. Full of practical suggestions for the fan or the beginner—who knows only the moves of the chessmen. Contains preliminary section and 58 two-move, 46 three-move, and 8 four-move problems composed by 27 outstanding American problem creators in the last 30 years. Explanation of all terms and exhaustive index. "Just what is wanted for the student," Brian Harley. 112 problems, solutions. vi +171pp. 5⅜ x 8.
                                                          T748 Paperbound **$1.25**

CHESS STRATEGY, Edward Lasker. Keres, Fine, and other great players have acknowledged their debt to this book, which has taught just about the whole modern school how to play forcefully and intelligently. Covers fundamentals, general strategic principles, middle and end game, objects of attack, etc. Includes 48 dramatic games from master tournaments, all fully analyzed. "Best textbook I know in English," J. R. Capablanca. New introduction by author. Table of openings. Index. 167 illustrations. vii + 282pp. 5⅜ x 8.
                                                          T528 Paperbound **$1.65**

REINFELD ON THE END GAME IN CHESS, F. Reinfeld. Formerly titled PRACTICAL END-GAME PLAY, this book contains clear, simple analyses of 62 end games by such masters as Alekhine, Tarrasch, Marshall, Morphy, Capablanca, and many others. Primary emphasis is on the general principles of transition from middle play to end play. This book is unusual in analyzing weak or incorrect moves to show how error occurs and how to avoid it. Covers king and pawn, minor piece, queen endings, weak squares, centralization, tempo moves, and many other vital factors. 62 diagrams. vi + 177pp. 5⅜ x 8.   T417 Paperbound **$1.25**

THE AMERICAN TWO-MOVE CHESS PROBLEM, Kenneth S. Howard. One of this country's foremost contemporary problem composers selects an interesting, diversified collection of the best two-movers by 58 top American composers. Involving complete blocks, mutates, line openings and closings, other unusual moves, these problems will help almost any player improve his strategic approach. Probably has no equal for all around artistic excellence, surprising keymoves, interesting strategy. Includes 30-page history of development of American two-mover from Loyd, its founder, to the present. Index of composers. vii + 99pp. 5⅜ x 8½.
T997 Paperbound **$1.00**

WIN AT CHECKERS, M. Hopper. (Formerly CHECKERS). The former World's Unrestricted Checker Champion discusses the principles cf the game, expert's shots and traps, problems for the beginner, standard openings, locating your best move, the end game, opening "blitzkrieg" moves, ways to draw when you are behind your opponent, etc. More than 100 detailed questions and answers anticipate your problems. Appendix. 75 problems with solutions and diagrams. Index. 79 figures. xi + 107pp. 5⅜ x 8.
T363 Paperbound **$1.00**

GAMES ANCIENT AND ORIENTAL, AND HOW TO PLAY THEM, E. Falkener. A connoisseur's selection of exciting and different games: Oriental varieties of chess, with unusual pieces and moves (including Japanese shogi); the original pachisi; go; reconstructions of lost Roman and Egyptian games; and many more. Full rules and sample games. Now play at home the games that have entertained millions, not on a fad basis, but for millennia. 345 illustrations and figures. iv + 366pp. 5⅜ x 8.
T739 Paperbound **$2.00**

GO AND GO-MOKU, Edward Lasker. A fascinating Oriental game, Go, is winning new devotees in America daily. Rules that you can learn in a few minutes—a wealth of combinations that makes it more profound than chess! This is an easily followed step-by-step explanation of this 2000-year-old game, beginning with fundamentals. New chapter on advanced strategy in this edition! Also contains rules for Go-Moku, a very easy sister game. 72 diagrams. xix + 215pp. 5⅜ x 8.
T613 Paperbound **$1.50**

HOW TO FORCE CHECKMATE, F. Reinfeld. Formerly titled CHALLENGE TO CHESSPLAYERS, this is an invaluable collection of 300 lightning strokes selected from actual masters' play, which will demonstrate how to smash your opponent's game with strong decisive moves. No board needed — clear, practical diagrams and easy-to-understand solutions. Learn to plan up to three moves ahead and play a superior end game. 300 diagrams. 111pp. 5⅜ x 8.
T439 Paperbound **$1.35**

CHESSBOARD MAGIC! A COLLECTION OF 160 BRILLIANT ENDINGS, I. Chernev. Contains 160 endgame compositions, all illustrating not only ingenuity of composition, but inherent beauty of solution. In one, five Knights are needed to force mate; in another White forces stalemate though Black finishes eight passed pawns ahead; 150 more, all remarkable, all will sharpen your imagination and increase your skill. "Inexhaustible source of entertainment, an endless feast of delight," Reuben Fine, Grandmaster. Introduction. 160 diagrams. Index of composers. vii + 172pp. 5⅜ x 8.
T607 Paperbound **$1.00**

LEARN CHESS FROM THE MASTERS, F. Reinfeld. Formerly titled CHESS BY YOURSELF, this book contains 10 games which you play against such masters as Marshall, Bronstein, Najdorf, and others, and an easy system for grading each move you make against a variety of other possible moves. Detailed annotations reveal the principles of the game through actual play. 91 diagrams. viii + 144pp. 5⅜ x 8.
T362 Paperbound **$1.25**

MORPHY'S GAMES OF CHESS, edited by Philip W. Sergeant. You can put boldness into your game by following the brilliant, forceful moves of the man who has been called the greatest chess player of all time. Here are 300 of Morphy's best games carefully annotated to reveal Morphy's principles. 54 classics against masters like Anderssen, Harrwitz, Bird, Paulsen, and others. 52 games at odds; 54 blindfold games; plus over 100 others. Unabridged reissue of the latest revised edition. Bibliography. New introduction by Fred Reinfeld. Annotations and introduction by Sergeant. Index. 235 diagrams. x + 352pp. 5⅜ x 8. T386 Paperbound **$2.00**

CHESS PRAXIS, Aron Nimzovich. Nimzovich was the stormy petrel of chess in the first decades of this century, and his system, known as hypermodern chess, revolutionized all play since his time. Casting aside the classical chess theory of Steinitz and Tarrasch, he created his own analysis of chess, considering dynamic patterns as they emerge during play. This is the fullest exposition of his ideas, and it is easily one of the dozen greatest books ever written on chess. Nimzovich illustrates each of his principles with at least two games, and shows how he applied his concepts successfully in games against such masters as Alekhine, Tarrasch, Reti, Rubinstein, Capablanca, Spielmann and others. Indispensable to every serious chess player. Translated by J. DuMont. 135 diagrams, 1 photo. xi + 364pp. 5½ x 8⅝.
T296 Paperbound **$2.25**

CHESS AND CHECKERS: THE WAY TO MASTERSHIP, Edward Lasker. Complete, lucid instructions for the beginner—and valuable suggestions for the advanced player! For both games the great master and teacher presents fundamentals, elementary tactics, and steps toward becoming a superior player. He concentrates on general principles rather than a mass of rules, comprehension rather than brute memory. Historical introduction. 118 diagrams. xiv + 167pp. 5⅜ x 8.
T657 Paperbound **$1.15**

Social Sciences

SOCIAL THOUGHT FROM LORE TO SCIENCE, H. E. Barnes and H. Becker. An immense survey of sociological thought and ways of viewing, studying, planning, and reforming society from earliest times to the present. Includes thought on society of preliterate peoples, ancient non-Western cultures, and every great movement in Europe, America, and modern Japan. Analyzes hundreds of great thinkers: Plato, Augustine, Bodin, Vico, Montesquieu, Herder, Comte, Marx, etc. Weighs the contributions of utopians, sophists, fascists and communists; economists, jurists, philosophers, ecclesiastics, and every 19th and 20th century school of scientific sociology, anthropology, and social psychology throughout the world. Combines topical, chronological, and regional approaches, treating the evolution of social thought as a process rather than as a series of mere topics. "Impressive accuracy, competence, and discrimination . . . easily the best single survey," Nation. Thoroughly revised, with new material up to 1960. 2 indexes. Over 2200 bibliographical notes. Three volume set. Total of 1586pp. 5⅜ x 8.

T901 Vol I Paperbound **$2.50**
T902 Vol II Paperbound **$2.50**
T903 Vol III Paperbound **$2.50**
The set **$7.50**

FOLKWAYS, William Graham Sumner. A classic of sociology, a searching and thorough examination of patterns of behaviour from primitive, ancient Greek and Judaic, Medieval Christian, African, Oriental, Melanesian, Australian, Islamic, to modern Western societies. Thousands of illustrations of social, sexual, and religious customs, mores, laws, and institutions. Hundreds of categories: Labor, Wealth, Abortion, Primitive Justice, Life Policy, Slavery, Cannibalism, Uncleanness and the Evil Eye, etc. Will extend the horizon of every reader by showing the relativism of his own culture. Prefatory note by A. G. Keller. Introduction by William Lyon Phelps. Bibliography. Index. xiii + 692pp. 5⅜ x 8. T508 Paperbound **$2.49**

PRIMITIVE RELIGION, P. Radin. A thorough treatment by a noted anthropologist of the nature and origin of man's belief in the supernatural and the influences that have shaped religious expression in primitive societies. Ranging from the Arunta, Ashanti, Aztec, Bushman, Crow, Fijian, etc., of Africa, Australia, Pacific Islands, the Arctic, North and South America, Prof. Radin integrates modern psychology, comparative religion, and economic thought with first-hand accounts gathered by himself and other scholars of primitive initiations, training of the shaman, and other fascinating topics. "Excellent," NATURE (London). Unabridged reissue of 1st edition. New author's preface. Bibliographic notes. Index. x + 322pp. 5⅜ x 8.
T393 Paperbound **$2.00**

PRIMITIVE MAN AS PHILOSOPHER, P. Radin. A standard anthropological work covering primitive thought on such topics as the purpose of life, marital relations, freedom of thought, symbolism, death, resignation, the nature of reality, personality, gods, and many others. Drawn from factual material gathered from the Winnebago, Oglala Sioux, Maori, Baganda, Batak, Zuni, among others, it does not distort ideas by removing them from context but interprets strictly within the original framework. Extensive selections of original primitive documents. Bibliography. Index. xviii + 402pp. 5⅜ x 8. T392 Paperbound **$2.25**

A TREATISE ON SOCIOLOGY, THE MIND AND SOCIETY, Vilfredo Pareto. This treatise on human society is one of the great classics of modern sociology. First published in 1916, its careful catalogue of the innumerable manifestations of non-logical human conduct (Book One); the theory of "residues," leading to the premise that sentiment not logic determines human behavior (Book Two), and of "derivations," beliefs derived from desires (Book Three); and the general description of society made up of non-elite and elite, consisting of "foxes" who live by cunning and "lions" who live by force, stirred great controversy. But Pareto's passion for isolation and classification of elements and factors, and his allegiance to scientific method as the key tool for scrutinizing the human situation made his a truly twentieth-century mind and his work a catalytic influence on certain later social commentators. These four volumes (bound as two) require no special training to be appreciated and any reader who wishes to gain a complete understanding of modern sociological theory, regardless of special field of interest, will find them a must. Reprint of revised (corrected) printing of original edition. Translated by Andrew Bongiorno and Arthur Livingston. Index. Bibliography. Appendix containing index-summary of theorems. 48 diagrams. Four volumes bound as two. Total of 2063pp. 5⅜ x 8½. The set Clothbound **$15.00**

THE POLISH PEASANT IN EUROPE AND AMERICA, William I. Thomas, Florian Znaniecki. A seminal sociological study of peasant primary groups (family and community) and the disruptions produced by a new industrial system and immigration to America. The peasant's family, class system, religious and aesthetic attitudes, and economic life are minutely examined and analyzed in hundreds of pages of primary documentation, particularly letters between family members. The disorientation caused by new environments is scrutinized in detail (a 312-page autobiography of an immigrant is especially valuable and revealing) in an attempt to find common experiences and reactions. The famous "Methodological Note" sets forth the principles which guided the authors. When out of print this set has sold for as much as $50. 2nd revised edition. 2 vols. Vol. 1: xv + 1115pp. Vol. 2: 1135pp. Index. 6 x 9.
T478 Clothbound 2 vol. set **$12.50**

Dover Classical Records

Now available directly to the public exclusively from Dover: top-quality recordings of fine classical music for only $2 per record! Originally released by a major company (except for the previously unreleased Gimpel recording of Bach) to sell for $5 and $6, these records were issued under our imprint only after they had passed a severe critical test. We insisted upon:

First-rate music that is enjoyable, musically important and culturally significant.

First-rate performances, where the artists have carried out the composer's intentions, in which the music is alive, vigorous, played with understanding and sympathy.

First-rate sound—clear, sonorous, fully balanced, crackle-free, whir-free.

Have in your home music by major composers, performed by such gifted musicians as Elsner, Gitlis, Wührer, the Barchet Quartet, Gimpel. Enthusiastically received when first released, many of these performances are definitive. The records are not seconds or remainders, but brand new pressings made on pure vinyl from carefully chosen master tapes. "All purpose" 12" monaural 33⅓ rpm records, they play equally well on hi-fi and stereo equipment. Fine music for discriminating music lovers, superlatively played, flawlessly recorded: there is no better way to build your library of recorded classical music at remarkable savings. There are no strings; this is not a come-on, not a club, forcing you to buy records you may not want in order to get a few at a lower price. Buy whatever records you want in any quantity, and never pay more than $2 each. Your obligation ends with your first purchase. And that's when ours begins. Dover's money-back guarantee allows you to return any record for any reason, even if you don't like the music, for a full, immediate refund, no questions asked.

MOZART: STRING QUARTET IN A MAJOR (K.464); STRING QUARTET IN C MAJOR ("DISSONANT", K.465), Barchet Quartet. The final two of the famed Haydn Quartets, high-points in the history of music. The A Major was accepted with delight by Mozart's contemporaries, but the C Major, with its dissonant opening, aroused strong protest. Today, of course, the remarkable resolutions of the dissonances are recognized as major musical achievements. "Beautiful warm playing," MUSICAL AMERICA. "Two of Mozart's loveliest quartets in a distinguished performance," REV. OF RECORDED MUSIC. (Playing time 58 mins.) HCR 5200 **$2.00**

MOZART: QUARTETS IN G MAJOR (K.80); D MAJOR (K.155); G MAJOR (K.156); C MAJOR (K157), Barchet Quartet. The early chamber music of Mozart receives unfortunately little attention. First-rate music of the Italian school, it contains all the lightness and charm that belongs only to the youthful Mozart. This is currently the only separate source for the composer's work of this time period. "Excellent," HIGH FIDELITY. "Filled with sunshine and youthful joy; played with verve, recorded sound live and brilliant," CHRISTIAN SCI. MONITOR. (Playing time 51 mins.) HCR 5201 **$2.00**

MOZART: SERENADE #9 IN D MAJOR ("POSTHORN", K.320); SERENADE #6 IN D MAJOR ("SERENATA NOTTURNA", K.239), Pro Musica Orch. of Stuttgart, under Edouard van Remoortel. For Mozart, the serenade was a highly effective form, since he could bring to it the immediacy and intimacy of chamber music as well as the fine fantasy of larger group music. Both these serenades are distinguished by a playful, mischievous quality, a spirit perfectly captured in this fine performance. "A triumph, polished playing from the orchestra," HI FI MUSIC AT HOME. "Sound is rich and resonant, fidelity is wonderful," REV. OF RECORDED MUSIC. (Playing time 51 mins.) HCR 5202 **$2.00**

MOZART: DIVERTIMENTO IN E FLAT MAJOR FOR STRING TRIO (K.563); ADAGIO AND FUGUE IN F MINOR FOR STRING TRIO (K.404a), Kehr Trio. The Divertimento is one of Mozart's most beloved pieces, called by Einstein "the finest, most perfect trio ever heard." It is difficult to imagine a music lover who will not be delighted by it. This is the only recording of the lesser known Adagio and Fugue, written in 1782 and influenced by Bach's Well-Tempered Clavichord. "Extremely beautiful recording, strongly recommended," THE OBSERVER. "Superior to rival editions," HIGH FIDELITY. (Playing time 51 mins.) HCR 5203 **$2.00**

SCHUMANN: KREISLERIANA (OP.16); FANTASY IN C MAJOR ("FANTASIE," OP.17), Vlado Perlemuter, Piano. The vigorous Romantic imagination and the remarkable emotional qualities of Schumann's piano music raise it to special eminence in 19th century creativity. Both these pieces are rooted to the composer's tortuous romance with his future wife, Clara, and both receive brilliant treatment at the hands of Vlado Perlemuter, Paris Conservatory, proclaimed by Alfred Cortot "not only a great virtuoso but also a great musician." "The best Kreisleriana to date," BILLBOARD. (Playing time 55 mins.) HCR 5204 **$2.00**

SCHUMANN: TRIO #1, D MINOR; TRIO #3, G MINOR, Trio di Bolzano. The fiery, romantic, melodic Trio #1, and the dramatic, seldom heard Trio #3 are both movingly played by a fine chamber ensemble. No one personified Romanticism to the general public of the 1840's more than did Robert Schumann, and among his most romantic works are these trios for cello, violin and piano. "Ensemble and overall interpretation leave little to be desired," HIGH FIDELITY. "An especially understanding performance," REV. OF RECORDED MUSIC. (Playing time 54 mins.) HCR 5205 **$2.00**

SCHUMANN: TRIOS #1 IN D MINOR (OPUS 63) AND #3 IN G MINOR (OPUS 110), Trio di Bolzano. The fiery, romantic, melodic Trio #1 and the dramatic, seldom heard Trio #3 are both movingly played by a fine chamber ensemble. No one personified Romanticism to the general public of the 1840's more than did Robert Schumann, and among his most romantic works are these trios for cello, violin and piano. "Ensemble and overall interpretation leave little to be desired," HIGH FIDELITY. "An especially understanding performance," REV. OF RECORDED MUSIC. (Playing time 54 mins.) HCR 5205 **$2.00**

SCHUBERT: QUINTET IN A ("TROUT") (OPUS 114), AND NOCTURNE IN E FLAT (OPUS 148), Friedrich Wührer, Piano and Barchet Quartet. If there is a single piece of chamber music that is a universal favorite, it is probably Schubert's "Trout" Quintet. Delightful melody, harmonic resources, musical exuberance are its characteristics. The Nocturne (played by Wührer, Barchet, and Reimann) is an exquisite piece with a deceptively simple theme and harmony. "The best Trout on the market—Wührer is a fine Viennese-style Schubertian, and his spirit infects the Barchets," ATLANTIC MONTHLY. "Exquisitely recorded," ETUDE. (Playing time 44 mins.) HCR 5206 **$2.00**

SCHUBERT: PIANO SONATAS IN C MINOR AND B (OPUS 147), Friedrich Wührer. Schubert's sonatas retain the structure of the classical form, but delight listeners with romantic freedom and a special melodic richness. The C Minor, one of the Three Grand Sonatas, is a product of the composer's maturity. The B Major was not published until 15 years after his death. "Remarkable interpretation, reproduction of the first rank," DISQUES. "A superb pianist for music like this, musicianship, sweep, power, and an ability to integrate Schubert's measures such as few pianists have had since Schnabel," Harold Schonberg. (Playing time 49 mins.) HCR 5207 **$2.00**

STRAVINSKY: VIOLIN CONCERTO IN D, Ivry Gitlis, Cologne Orchestra; DUO CONCERTANTE, Ivry Gitlis, Violin, Charlotte Zelka, Piano, Cologne Orchestra; JEU DE CARTES, Bamberg Symphony, under Hollreiser. Igor Stravinsky is probably the most important composer of this century, and these three works are among the most significant of his neoclassical period of the 30's. The Violin Concerto is one of the few modern classics. Jeu de Cartes, a ballet score, bubbles with gaiety, color and melodiousness. "Imaginatively played and beautifully recorded," E. T. Canby, HARPERS MAGAZINE. "Gitlis is excellent, Hollreiser beautifully worked out," HIGH FIDELITY. (Playing time 55 mins.) HCR 5208 **$2.00**

GEMINIANI: SIX CONCERTI GROSSI, OPUS 3, Helma Elsner, Harpsichord, Barchet Quartet, Pro Musica Orch. of Stuttgart, under Reinhardt. Francesco Geminiani (1687-1762) has been rediscovered in the same musical exploration that revealed Scarlatti, Vivaldi, and Corelli. In form he is more sophisticated than the earlier Italians, but his music delights modern listeners with its combination of contrapuntal techniques and the full harmonies and rich melodies charcteristic of Italian music. This is the only recording of the six 1733 concerti: D Major, B Flat Minor, E Minor, G Minor, E Minor (bis), and D Minor. "I warmly recommend it, spacious, magnificent, I enjoyed every bar," C. Cudworth, RECORD NEWS. "Works of real charm, recorded with understanding and style," ETUDE. (Playing time 52 mins.) HCR 5209 **$2.00**

MODERN PIANO SONATAS: BARTOK: SONATA FOR PIANO; BLOCH: SONATA FOR PIANO (1935); PROKOFIEV, PIANO SONATA #7 IN B FLAT ("STALINGRAD"); STRAVINSKY: PIANO SONATA (1924), István Nádas, Piano. Shows some of the major forces and directions in modern piano music: Stravinsky's crisp austerity; Bartok's fusion of Hungarian folk motives; incisive diverse rhythms, and driving power; Bloch's distinctive emotional vigor; Prokofiev's brilliance and melodic beauty couched in pre-Romantic forms. "A most interesting documentation of the contemporary piano sonata. Nadas is a very good pianist." HIGH FIDELITY. (Playing time 59 mins.) HCR 5215 **$2.00**

VIVALDI: CONCERTI FOR FLUTE, VIOLIN, BASSOON, AND HARPSICHORD: #8 IN G MINOR, #21 IN F, #27 IN D, #7 IN D; SONATA #1 IN A MINOR, Gastone Tassinari, Renato Giangrandi, Giorgio Semprini, Arlette Eggmann. More than any other Baroque composer, Vivaldi moved the concerto grosso closer to the solo concert we deem standard today. In these concerti he wrote virtuosi music for the solo instruments, allowing each to introduce new material or expand on musical ideas, creating tone colors unusual even for Vivaldi. As a result, this record displays a new area of his genius, offering some of his most brilliant music. Performed by a top-rank European group. (Playing time 45 mins.) HCR 5216 **$2.00**

LÜBECK: CANTATAS: HILF DEINEM VOLK; GOTT, WIE DEIN NAME, Stuttgart Choral Society, Swabian Symphony Orch.; PRELUDES AND FUGUES IN C MINOR AND IN E, Eva Hölderlin, Organ. Vincent Lübeck (1654-1740), contemporary of Bach and Buxtehude, was one of the great figures of the 18th-century North German school. These examples of Lübeck's few surviving works indicate his power and brilliance. Voice and instrument lines in the cantatas are strongly reminiscent of the organ: the preludes and fugues show the influence of Bach and Buxtehude. This is the only recording of the superb cantatas. Text and translation included. "Outstanding record," E. T. Canby, SAT. REVIEW. "Hölderlin's playing is exceptional," AM. RECORD REVIEW. "Will make [Lübeck] many new friends," Philip Miller. (Playing time 37 mins.) HCR 5217 **$2.00**

DONIZETTI: BETLY (LA CAPANNA SVIZZERA), Soloists of Compagnia del Teatro dell'Opera Comica di Roma, Societa del Quartetto, Rome, Chorus and Orch. Betly, a delightful one-act opera written in 1836, is similar in style and story to one of Donizetti's better-known operas, L'Elisir. Betly is lighthearted and farcical, with bright melodies and a freshness characteristic of the best of Donizetti. Libretto (English and Italian) included. "The chief honors go to Angela Tuccari who sings the title role, and the record is worth having for her alone," M. Rayment, GRAMOPHONE REC. REVIEW. "The interpretation . . . is excellent . . . This is a charming record which we recommend to lovers of little-known works," DISQUES.
HCR 5218 **$2.00**

ROSSINI: L'OCCASIONE FA IL LADRO (IL CAMBIO DELLA VALIGIA), Soloists of Compagnia del Teatro dell'Opera Comica di Roma, Societa del Quartetto, Rome, Chorus and Orch. A charming one-act opera buffa, this is one of the first works of Rossini's maturity, and it is filled with the wit, gaiety and sparkle that make his comic operas second only to Mozart's. Like other Rossini works, L'Occasione makes use of the theme of impersonation and attendant amusing confusions. This is the only recording of this important buffa. Full libretto (English and Italian) included. "A major rebirth, a stylish performance . . . the Roman recording engineers have outdone themselves," H. Weinstock, SAT. REVIEW. (Playing time 53 mins.)
HCR 5219 **$2.00**

DOWLAND: "FIRST BOOKE OF AYRES," Pro Musica Antiqua of Brussels, Safford Cape, Director. This is the first recording to include all 22 of the songs of this great collection, written by John Dowland, one of the most important writers of songs of 16th and 17th century England. The participation of the Brussels Pro Musica under Safford Cape insures scholarly accuracy and musical artistry. "Powerfully expressive and very beautiful," B. Haggin. "The musicianly singers . . . never fall below an impressive standard," Philip Miller. Text included. (Playing time 51 mins.)
HCR 5220 **$2.00**

FRENCH CHANSONS AND DANCES OF THE 16TH CENTURY, Pro Musica Antiqua of Brussels, Safford Cape, Director. A remarkable selection of 26 three- or four-part chansons and delightful dances from the French Golden Age—by such composers as Orlando Lasso, Crecquillon, Claude Gervaise, etc. Text and translation included. "Delightful, well-varied with respect to mood and to vocal and instrumental color," HIGH FIDELITY. "Performed with . . . discrimination and musical taste, full of melodic distinction and harmonic resource," Irving Kolodin. (Playing time 39 mins.)
HCR 5221 **$2.00**

GALUPPI: CONCERTI A QUATRO: #1 IN G MINOR, #2 IN G, #3 IN D, #4 IN C MINOR, #5 IN E FLAT, AND #6 IN B FLAT, Biffoli Quartet. During Baldassare Galuppi's lifetime, his instrumental music was widely renowned, and his contemporaries Mozart and Haydn thought highly of his work. These 6 concerti reflect his great ability; and they are among the most interesting compositions of the period. They are remarkable for their unusual combinations of timbres and for emotional elements that were only then beginning to be introduced into music. Performed by the well-known Biffoli Quartet, this is the only record devoted exclusively to Galuppi. (Playing time 47 mins.)
HCR 5222 **$2.00**

HAYDN: DIVERTIMENTI FOR WIND BAND, IN C; IN F; DIVERTIMENTO A NOVE STROMENTI IN C FOR STRINGS AND WIND INSTRUMENTS, reconstructed by H. C. Robbins Landon, performed by members of Vienna State Opera Orch.; MOZART DIVERTIMENTI IN C, III (K. 187) AND IV (K. 188), Salzburg Wind Ensemble. Robbins Landon discovered Haydn manuscripts in a Benedictine monastery in Lower Austria, edited them and restored their original instrumentation The result is this magnificent record. Two little-known divertimenti by Mozart—of great charm and appeal—are also included. None of this music is available elsewhere (Playing time 58 mins.)
HCR 5223 **$2.00**

PURCELL: TRIO SONATAS FROM "SONATAS OF FOUR PARTS" (1697): #9 IN F ("GOLDEN"), #7 IN C, #1 IN B MINOR, #10 IN D, #4 IN D MINOR, #2 IN E FLAT, AND #8 IN G MINOR, Giorgio Ciompi, and Werner Torkanowsky, Violins, Geo. Koutzen, Cello, and Herman Chessid, Harpsichord. These posthumously-published sonatas show Purcell at his most advanced and mature. They are certainly among the finest musical examples of pre-modern chamber music. Those not familiar with his instrumental music are well-advised to hear these outstanding pieces. "Performance sounds excellent," Harold Schonberg. "Some of the most noble and touching music known to anyone," AMERICAN RECORD GUIDE. (Playing time 58 mins.)
HCR 5224 **$2.00**

BARTOK: VIOLIN CONCERTO; SONATA FOR UNACCOMPANIED VIOLIN, Ivry Gitlis, Pro Musica of Vienna, under Hornstein. Both these works are outstanding examples of Bartok's final period, and they show his powers at their fullest. The Violin Concerto is, in the opinion of many authorities, Bartok's finest work, and the Sonata, his last work, is "a masterpiece" (F. Sackville West). "Wonderful, finest performance of both Bartok works I have ever heard," GRAMOPHONE. "Gitlis makes such potent and musical sense out of these works that I suspect many general music lovers (not otherwise in sympathy with modern music) will discover to their amazement that they like it. Exceptionally good sound," AUDITOR. (Playing time 54 mins.)
HCR 5211 **$2.00**

J. S. BACH: PARTITAS FOR UNACCOMPANIED VIOLIN: #2 in D Minor and #3 in E, Bronislav Gimpel. Bach's works for unaccompanied violin fall within the same area that produced the Brandenburg Concerti, the Orchestral Suites, and the first part of the Well-Tempered Clavichord. The D Minor is considered one of Bach's masterpieces; the E Major is a buoyant work with exceptionally interesting bariolage effects. This is the first release of a truly memorable recording by Bronislav Gimpel, "as a violinist, the equal of the greatest" (P. Leron, in OPERA, Paris). (Playing time 53 mins.) **HCR 5212 $2.00**

ROSSINI: QUARTETS FOR WOODWINDS: #1 IN F, #4 IN B FLAT, #5 IN D, AND #6 IN F, N. Y. Woodwind Quartet Members: S. Baron, Flute, J. Barrows, French Horn; B. Garfield, Bassoon; D. Glazer, Clarinet. Rossini's great genius was centered in the opera, but he also wrote a small amount of first-rate non-vocal music. Among these instrumental works, first place is usually given to the very interesting quartets. Of the three different surviving arrangements, this wind group version is the original, and this is the first recording of these works. "Each member of the group displays wonderful virtuosity when the music calls for it, at other times blending sensitively into the ensemble," HIGH FIDELITY. "Sheer delight," Philip Miller. (Playing time 45 mins.) **HCR 5214 $2.00**

TELEMANN: THE GERMAN FANTASIAS FOR HARPSICHORD (#1-12), Helma Elsner. Until recently, Georg Philip Telemann (1681-1767) was one of the mysteriously neglected great men of music. Recently he has received the attention he deserved. He created music that delights modern listeners with its freshness and originality. These fantasias are free in form and reveal the intricacy of thorough bass music, the harmonic wealth of the "new music," and a distinctive melodic beauty. "This is another blessing of the contemporary LP output. Miss Elsner plays with considerable sensitivity and a great deal of understanding," REV. OF RECORDED MUSIC. "Fine recorded sound," Harold Schonberg. "Recommended warmly, very high quality," DISQUES. (Playing time 50 mins.) **HCR 5210 $2.00**

Nova Recordings

In addition to our reprints of outstanding out-of-print records and American releases of first-rate foreign recordings, we have established our own new records. In order to keep every phase of their production under our own control, we have engaged musicians of world renown to play important music (for the most part unavailable elsewhere), have made use of the finest recording studios in New York, and have produced tapes equal to anything on the market, we believe. The first of these entirely new records are now available.

RAVEL: GASPARD DE LA NUIT, LE TOMBEAU DE COUPERIN, JEUX D'EAU, Beveridge Webster, Piano. Webster studied under Ravel and played his works in European recitals, often with Ravel's personal participation in the program. This record offers examples of the three major periods of Ravel's pianistic work, and is a must for any serious collector or music lover. (Playing time about 50 minutes). Monaural HCR 5213 **$2.00**
Stereo HCR ST 7000 **$2.00**

EIGHTEENTH CENTURY FRENCH FLUTE MUSIC, Jean-Pierre Rampal, Flute, and Robert Veyron-Lacroix, Harpsichord. Contains Concerts Royaux #7 for Flute and Harpsichord in G Minor, Francois Couperin; Sonata dite l'Inconnue in G for Flute and Harpsichord, Michel de la Barre; Sonata #6 in A Minor, Michel Blavet; and Sonata in D Minor, Anne Danican-Philidor. In the opinion of many Rampal is the world's premier flutist. (Playing time about 45 minutes) Monaural HCR 5238 **$2.00**
Stereo HCR ST 7001 **$2.00**

SCHUMANN: NOVELLETTEN (Opus 21), Beveridge Webster, Piano. Brilliantly played in this original recording by one of America's foremost keyboard performers. Connected Romantic pieces. Long a piano favorite. (Playing time about 45 minutes) Monaural HCR 5239 **$2.00**
Stereo HCR ST 7002 **$2.00**

Music

A GENERAL HISTORY OF MUSIC, Charles Burney. A detailed coverage of music from the Greeks up to 1789, with full information on all types of music: sacred and secular, vocal and instrumental, operatic and symphonic. Theory, notation, forms, instruments, innovators, composers, performers, typical and important works, and much more in an easy, entertaining style. Burney covered much of Europe and spoke with hundreds of authorities and composers so that this work is more than a compilation of records . . . it is a living work of careful and first-hand scholarship. Its account of thoroughbass (18th century) Italian music is probably still the best introduction on the subject. A recent NEW YORK TIMES review said, "Surprisingly few of Burney's statements have been invalidated by modern research . . . still of great value." Edited and corrected by Frank Mercer. 35 figures. Indices. 1915pp. 5⅜ x 8. 2 volumes. T36 The Set, Clothbound **$12.50**

A DICTIONARY OF HYMNOLOGY, John Julian. This exhaustive and scholarly work has become known as an invaluable source of hundreds of thousands of important and often difficult to obtain facts on the history and use of hymns in the western world. Everyone interested in hymns will be fascinated by the accounts of famous hymns and hymn writers and amazed by the amount of practical information he will find. More than 30,000 entries on individual hymns, giving authorship, date and circumstances of composition, publication, textual variations, translations, denominational and ritual usage, etc. Biographies of more than 9,000 hymn writers, and essays on important topics such as Christmas carols and children's hymns, and much other unusual and valuable information. A 200 page double-columned index of first lines — the largest in print. Total of 1786 pages in two reinforced clothbound volumes. 6¼ x 9¼. The set, T333 Clothbound **$17.50**

MUSIC IN MEDIEVAL BRITAIN, F. Ll. Harrison. The most thorough, up-to-date, and accurate treatment of the subject ever published, beautifully illustrated. Complete account of institutions and choirs; carols, masses, and motets; liturgy and plainsong; and polyphonic music from the Norman Conquest to the Reformation. Discusses the various schools of music and their reciprocal influences; the origin and development of new ritual forms; development and use of instruments; and new evidence on many problems of the period. Reproductions of scores, over 200 excerpts from medieval melodies. Rules of harmony and dissonance; influence of Continental styles; great composers (Dunstable, Cornysh, Fairfax, etc.); and much more. Register and index of more than 400 musicians. Index of titles. General Index. 225-item bibliography. 6 Appendices. xix + 491pp. 5⅝ x 8¾. T705 Clothbound **$10.00**

THE MUSIC OF SPAIN, Gilbert Chase. Only book in English to give concise, comprehensive account of Iberian music; new Chapter covers music since 1941. Victoria, Albéniz, Cabezón, Pedrell, Turina, hundreds of other composers; popular and folk music; the Gypsies; the guitar; dance, theatre, opera, with only extensive discussion in English of the Zarzuela; virtuosi such as Casals; much more. "Distinguished . . . readable," Saturday Review. 400-item bibliography. Index. 27 photos. 383pp. 5⅜ x 8. T549 Paperbound **$2.25**

ON STUDYING SINGING, Sergius Kagen. An intelligent method of voice-training, which leads you around pitfalls that waste your time, money, and effort. Exposes rigid, mechanical systems, baseless theories, deleterious exercises. "Logical, clear, convincing . . . dead right," Virgil Thomson, N.Y. Herald Tribune. "I recommend this volume highly," Maggie Teyte, Saturday Review. 119pp. 5⅜ x 8. T622 Paperbound **$1.35**

WILLIAM LAWES, M. Lefkowitz. This is the definitive work on Lawes, the versatile, prolific, and highly original "King's musician" of 17th century England. His life is reconstructed from original documents, and nearly every piece he ever wrote is examined and evaluated: his fantasias, pavans, violin "sonatas," lyra viol and bass viol suites, and music for harp and theorbo; and his songs, masques, and theater music to words by Herrick ("Gather Ye Rosebuds"), Jonson, Suckling, Shirley, and others. The author shows the innovations of dissonance, augmented triad, and other Italian influences Lawes helped introduce to England. List of Lawes' complete works and several complete scores by this major precursor of Purcell and the 18th century developments. Index. 5 Appendices. 52 musical excerpts, many never before in print. Bibliography. x + 320pp. 5⅜ x 8. T706 Clothbound **$10.00**

THE FUGUE IN BEETHOVEN'S PIANO MUSIC, J. V. Cockshoot. The first study of a neglected aspect of Beethoven's genius: his ability as a writer of fugues. Analyses of early studies and published works demonstrate his original and powerful contributions to composition. 34 works are examined, with 143 musical excerpts. For all pianists, teachers, students, and music-minded readers with a serious interest in Beethoven. Index. 93-item bibliography. Illustration of original score for "Fugue in C." xv + 212pp. 5⅝ x 8⅜. T704 Clothbound **$6.00**

JOHANN SEBASTIAN BACH, Philipp Spitta. The complete and unabridged text of the definitive study of Bach. Written some 70 years ago, it is still unsurpassed for its coverage of nearly all aspects of Bach's life and work. There could hardly be a finer non-technical introduction to Bach's music than the detailed, lucid analyses which Spitta provides for hundreds of individual pieces. 26 solid pages are devoted to the B minor mass, for example, and 30 pages to the glorious St. Matthew Passion. This monumental set also includes a major analysis of the music of the 18th century: Buxtehude, Pachelbel, etc. "Unchallenged as the last word on one of the supreme geniuses of music," John Barkham, SATURDAY REVIEW SYNDICATE. Total of 1819pp. 2 volumes. Heavy cloth binding. 5⅜ x 8. T252 The set, Clothbound **$13.50**

THE LIFE OF MOZART, O. Jahn. Probably the largest amount of material on Mozart's life and works ever gathered together in one book! Its 1350 authoritative and readable pages cover every event in his life, and contain a full critique of almost every piece he ever wrote, including sketches and intimate works. There is a full historical-cultural background, and vast research into musical and literary history, sources of librettos, prior treatments of Don Juan legend, etc. This is the complete and unaltered text of the definitive Townsend translation, with foreword by Grove. 5 engraved portraits from Salzburg archives. 4 facsimiles in Mozart's hand. 226 musical examples. 4 Appendixes, including complete list of Mozart's compositions, with Köchel numbers (fragmentary works included). Total of xxviii + 1352pp. Three volume set. 5⅜ x 8.
T85 Vol. I Clothbound **$5.00**
T86 Vol. II Clothbound **$5.00**
The set **$10.00**

BEETHOVEN'S QUARTETS, J. de Marliave. The most complete and authoritative study ever written, enjoyable for scholar and layman alike. The 16 quartets and Grand Fugue are all analyzed bar by bar and theme by theme, not over-technically, but concentrating on mood and effects. Complete background material for each composition: influences, first reviews, etc. Preface by Gabriel Fauré. Introduction and notes by J. Escarra. Translated by Hilda Andrews. 321 musical examples. xxiii + 379pp. 5⅜ x 8. T694 Paperbound **$2.00**

STRUCTURAL HEARING: TONAL COHERENCE IN MUSIC, Felix Salzer. Written by a pupil of the late Heinrich Schenker, this is not only the most thorough exposition in English of the Schenker method but also extends the Schenker approach to include modern music, the middle ages, and renaissance music. It explores the phenomenon of tonal organization by means of a detailed analysis and discussion of more than 500 musical pieces. It casts new light for the reader acquainted with harmony upon the understanding of musical compositions, problems of musical coherence, and connection between theory and composition. "Has been the foundation on which all teaching in music theory has been based at this college," Leopold Mannes, President of The Mannes College of Music. 2 volumes. Total of 658pp. 6½ x 9¼. The set, T418 Clothbound **$8.00**

ANTONIO STRADIVARI: HIS LIFE AND WORK (1644-1737), W. Henry Hill, Arthur F. Hill, and Alfred E. Hill. Still the only book that really delves into life and art of the incomparable Italian craftsman, maker of the finest musical instruments in the world today. The authors, expert violin-makers themselves, discuss Stradivari's ancestry, his construction and finishing techniques, distinguished characteristics of many of his instruments and their locations. Included, too, is story of introduction of his instruments into France, England, first revelation of their supreme merit, and information on his labels, number of instruments made, prices, mystery of ingredients of his varnish, tone of pre-1684 Stradivari violin and changes between 1684 and 1690. An extremely interesting, informative account for all music lovers, from craftsman to concert-goer. Republication of original (1902) edition. New introduction by Sydney Beck, Head of Rare Book and Manuscript Collections, Music Division, New York Public Library. Analytical index by Rembert Wurlitzer. Appendixes. 68 illustrations. 30 full-page plates. 4 in color. xxvi + 315pp. 5⅜ x 8½. T425 Paperbound **$2.25**

THREE CLASSICS IN THE AESTHETIC OF MUSIC, Claude Debussy, Ferrucio Busoni, and Charles Ives. Three very different points of view by three top-ranking modern composers. "M. Croche, the Dilettante-Hater" consists of twenty-five brief articles written by Debussy between the years 1901 and 1905, a sparkling collection of personal commentary on a wide range of topics. Busoni's "Toward a New Aesthetic of Music" considers the nature of absolute music in an attempt to suggest answers to the question, What are the aims of music?, and discusses modern systems of tonality and harmony, the concept of unity of keys, etc. Ives's "Essays Before a Sonata," a literary complement to the movements of the author's "Concord, 1845" piano sonata, contains his most mature analysis of his art. Stimulating reading for musicians, music lovers, and philosophers of the arts. iv + 188pp. 5⅜ x 8½. T320 Paperbound **$1.50**

Art, History of Art, Antiques, Graphic Arts, Handcrafts

ART STUDENTS' ANATOMY, E. J. Farris. Outstanding art anatomy that uses chiefly living objects for its illustrations. 71 photos of undraped men, women, children are accompanied by carefully labeled matching sketches to illustrate the skeletal system, articulations and movements, bony landmarks, the muscular system, skin, fasciae, fat, etc. 9 x-ray photos show movement of joints. Undraped models are shown in such actions as serving in tennis, drawing a bow in archery, playing football, dancing, preparing to spring and to dive. Also discussed and illustrated are proportions, age and sex differences, the anatomy of the smile, etc. 8 plates by the great early 18th century anatomic illustrator Siegfried Albinus are also included. Glossary. 158 figures, 7 in color. x + 159pp. 5⅝ x 8⅜.   T744 Paperbound **$1.50**

AN ATLAS OF ANATOMY FOR ARTISTS, F Schider. A new 3rd edition of this standard text enlarged by 52 new illustrations of hands, anatomical studies by Cloquet, and expressive life studies of the body by Barcsay. 189 clear, detailed plates offer you precise information of impeccable accuracy. 29 plates show all aspects of the skeleton, with closeups of special areas, while 54 full-page plates, mostly in two colors, give human musculature as seen from four different points of view, with cutaways for important portions of the body. 14 full-page plates provide photographs of hand forms, eyelids, female breasts, and indicate the location of muscles upon models. 59 additional plates show how great artists of the past utilized human anatomy. They reproduce sketches and finished work by such artists as Michelangelo, Leonardo da Vinci, Goya, and 15 others. This is a lifetime reference work which will be one of the most important books in any artist's library. "The standard reference tool," AMERICAN LIBRARY ASSOCIATION. "Excellent," AMERICAN ARTIST. Third enlarged edition. 189 plates, 647 illustrations. xxvi + 192pp. 7⅞ x 10⅝.   T241 Clothbound **$6.00**

AN ATLAS OF ANIMAL ANATOMY FOR ARTISTS, W. Ellenberger, H. Baum, H. Dittrich. The largest, richest animal anatomy for artists available in English. 99 detailed anatomical plates of such animals as the horse, dog, cat, lion, deer, seal, kangaroo, flying squirrel, cow, bull, goat, monkey, hare, and bat. Surface features are clearly indicated, while progressive beneath-the-skin pictures show musculature, tendons, and bone structure. Rest and action are exhibited in terms of musculature and skeletal structure and detailed cross-sections are given for heads and important features. The animals chosen are representative of specific families so that a study of these anatomies will provide knowledge of hundreds of related species. "Highly recommended as one of the very few books on the subject worthy of being used as an authoritative guide," DESIGN. "Gives a fundamental knowledge," AMERICAN ARTIST. Second revised, enlarged edition with new plates from Cuvier, Stubbs, etc. 288 illustrations. 153pp. 11⅜ x 9.   T82 Clothbound **$6.00**

THE HUMAN FIGURE IN MOTION, Eadweard Muybridge. The largest selection in print of Muybridge's famous high-speed action photos of the human figure in motion. 4789 photographs illustrate 162 different actions: men, women, children—mostly undraped—are shown walking, running, carrying various objects, sitting, lying down, climbing, throwing, arising, and performing over 150 other actions. Some actions are shown in as many as 150 photographs each. All in all there are more than 500 action strips in this enormous volume, series shots taken at shutter speeds of as high as 1/6000th of a second! These are not posed shots, but true stopped motion. They show bone and muscle in situations that the human eye is not fast enough to capture. Earlier, smaller editions of these prints have brought $40 and more on the out-of-print market. "A must for artists," ART IN FOCUS. "An unparalleled dictionary of action for all artists," AMERICAN ARTIST. 390 full-page plates, with 4789 photographs. Printed on heavy glossy stock. Reinforced binding with headbands. xxi + 390pp. 7⅞ x 10⅝.
T204 Clothbound **$10.00**

ANIMALS IN MOTION, Eadweard Muybridge. This is the largest collection of animal action photos in print. 34 different animals (horses, mules, oxen, goats, camels, pigs, cats, guanacos, lions, gnus, deer, monkeys, eagles—and 21 others) in 132 characteristic actions. The horse alone is shown in more than 40 different actions. All 3919 photographs are taken in series at speeds up to 1/6000th of a second. The secrets of leg motion, spinal patterns, head movements, strains and contortions shown nowhere else are captured. You will see exactly how a lion sets his foot down; how an elephant's knees are like a human's—and how they differ; the position of a kangaroo's legs in mid-leap; how an ostrich's head bobs; details of the flight of birds—and thousands of facets of motion only the fastest cameras can catch. Photographed from domestic animals and animals in the Philadelphia zoo, it contains neither semiposed artificial shots nor distorted telephoto shots taken under adverse conditions. Artists, biologists, decorators, cartoonists, will find this book indispensable for understanding animals in motion. "A really marvelous series of plates," NATURE (London). "The dry plate's most spectacular early use was by Eadweard Muybridge," LIFE. 3919 photographs; 380 full pages of plates. 440pp. Printed on heavy glossy paper. Deluxe binding with headbands. 7⅞ x 10⅝.   T203 Clothbound **$10.00**

ART ANATOMY, William Rimmer, M.D. Often called one of America's foremost contributions to art instruction, a work of art in its own right. More than 700 line drawings by the author, first-rate anatomist and dissector as well as artist, with a non-technical anatomical text. Impeccably accurate drawings of muscles, skeletal structure, surface features, other aspects of males and females, children, adults and aged persons show not only form, size, insertion and articulation but personality and emotion as reflected by physical features usually ignored in modern anatomical works. Complete unabridged reproduction of 1876 edition slightly rearranged. Introduction by Robert Hutchinson. 722 illustrations. xiii + 153pp. 7¾ x 10¾.
T908 Paperbound **$2.00**

ANIMAL DRAWING: ANATOMY AND ACTION FOR ARTISTS, C. R. Knight. The author and illustrator of this work was "the most distinguished painter of animal life." This extensive course in animal drawing discusses musculature, bone structure, animal psychology, movements, habits, habitats. Innumerable tips on proportions, light and shadow play, coloring, hair formation, feather arrangement, scales, how animals lie down, animal expressions, etc., from great apes to birds. Pointers on avoiding gracelessness in horses, deer; on introducing proper power and bulk to heavier animals; on giving proper grace and subtle expression to members of the cat family. Originally titled "Animal Anatomy and Psychology for the Artist and Layman." Over 123 illustrations. 149pp. 8¼ x 10½. T426 Paperbound **$2.00**

DESIGN FOR ARTISTS AND CRAFTSMEN, L. Wolchonok. The most thorough course ever prepared on the creation of art motifs and designs. It teaches you to create your own designs out of things around you — from geometric patterns, plants, birds, animals, humans, landscapes, and man-made objects. It leads you step by step through the creation of more than 1300 designs, and shows you how to create design that is fresh, well-founded, and original. Mr. Wolchonok, whose text is used by scores of art schools, shows you how the same idea can be developed into many different forms, ranging from near representationalism to the most advanced forms of abstraction. The material in this book is entirely new, and combines full awareness of traditional design with the work of such men as Miro, Léger, Picasso, Moore, and others. 113 detailed exercises, with instruction hints, diagrams, and details to enable you to apply Wolchonok's methods to your own work. "A great contribution to the field of design and crafts," N. Y. SOCIETY OF CRAFTSMEN. More than 1300 illustrations. xv + 207pp. 7⅞ x 10¾. T274 Clothbound **$4.95**

HAWTHORNE ON PAINTING. A vivid recreation, from students' notes, of instruction by Charles W. Hawthorne, given for over 31 years at his famous Cape Cod School of Art. Divided into sections on the outdoor model, still life, landscape, the indoor model, and water color, each section begins with a concise essay, followed by epigrammatic comments on color, form, seeing, etc. Not a formal course, but comments of a great teacher-painter on specific student works, which will solve problems in your own painting and understanding of art. "An excellent introduction for laymen and students alike," Time. Introduction. 100pp. 5⅜ x 8.
T653 Paperbound **$1.00**

THE ENJOYMENT AND USE OF COLOR, Walter Sargent. This book explains fascinating relations among colors, between colors in nature and art; describes experiments that you can perform to understand these relations more thoroughly; points out hundreds of little known facts about color values, intensities, effects of high and low illumination, complementary colors, color harmonies. Practical hints for painters, references to techniques of masters, questions at chapter ends for self-testing all make this a valuable book for artists, professional and amateur, and for general readers interested in world of color. Republication of 1923 edition. 35 illustrations, 6 full-page plates. New color frontispiece. Index. xii + 274pp. 5⅜ x 8. T944 Paperbound **$2.25**

DECORATIVE ALPHABETS AND INITIALS, ed. by Alexander Nesbitt. No payment, no permission needed to reproduce any one of these 3924 different letters, covering 1000 years. Crisp, clear letters all in line, from Anglo-Saxon mss., Luebeck Cathedral, 15th century Augsburg; the work of Dürer, Holbein, Cresci, Beardsley, Rossing Wadsworth, John Moylin, etc. Every imaginable style. 91 complete alphabets. 123 full-page plates. 192pp. 7¾ x 10¾.
T544 Paperbound **$2.25**

THREE CLASSICS OF ITALIAN CALLIGRAPHY, edited by Oscar Ogg. Here, combined in a single volume, are complete reproductions of three famous calligraphic works written by the greatest writing masters of the Renaissance: Arrighi's OPERINA and IL MODO, Tagliente's LO PRESENTE LIBRO, and Palatino's LIBRO NUOVO. These books present more than 200 complete alphabets and thousands of lettered specimens. The basic hand is Papal Chancery, but scores of other alphabets are also given: European and Asiatic local alphabets, foliated and art alphabets, scrolls, cartouches, borders, etc. Text is in Italian. Introduction. 245 plates. x + 272pp. 6⅛ x 9¼. T212 Paperbound **$2.75**

CALLIGRAPHY, J. G. Schwandner. One of the legendary books in the graphic arts, copies of which brought $500 each on the rare book market, now reprinted for the first time in over 200 years. A beautiful plate book of graceful calligraphy, and an inexhaustible source of first-rate material copyright-free, for artists, and directors, craftsmen, commercial artists, etc. More than 300 ornamental initials forming 12 complete alphabets, over 150 ornate frames and panels, over 200 flourishes, over 75 calligraphic pictures including a temple, cherubs, cocks, dodos, stags, chamois, foliated lions, greyhounds, etc. Thousand of calligraphic elements to be used for suggestions of quality, sophistication, antiquity, and sheer beauty. Historical introduction. 158 full-page plates. 368pp. 9 x 13.
T475 Clothbound **$10.00**

THE HISTORY AND TECHNIQUE OF LETTERING, A. Nesbitt. The only thorough inexpensive history of letter forms from the point of view of the artist. Mr. Nesbitt covers every major development in lettering from the ancient Egyptians to the present and illustrates each development with a complete alphabet. Such masters as Baskerville, Bell, Bodoni, Caslon, Koch, Kilian, Morris, Garamont, Jenson, and dozens of others are analyzed in terms of artistry and historical development. The author also presents a 65-page practical course in lettering, besides the full historical text. 89 complete alphabets; 165 additional lettered specimens. xvii + 300pp. 5⅜ x 8. T427 Paperbound **$2.00**

FOOT-HIGH LETTERS: A GUIDE TO LETTERING (A PRACTICAL SYLLABUS FOR TEACHERS), M. Price. A complete alphabet of Classic Roman letters, each a foot high, each on a separate 16 x 22 plate—perfect for use in lettering classes. In addition to an accompanying description, each plate also contains 9 two-inch-high forms of letter in various type faces, such as "Caslon," "Empire," "Onyx," and "Neuland," illustrating the many possible derivations from the standard classical forms. One plate contains 21 additional forms of the letter A. The fully illustrated 16-page syllabus by Mr. Price, formerly of the Pratt Institute and the Rhode Island School of Design, contains dozens of useful suggestions for student and teacher alike. An indispensable teaching aid. Extensively revised. 16-page syllabus and 30 plates in slip cover, 16 x 22. T239 Clothbound **$6.00**

THE STYLES OF ORNAMENT, Alexander Speltz. Largest collection of ornaments in print— 3765 illustrations of prehistoric, Lombard, Gothic, Frank, Romanesque, Mohammedan, Renaissance, Polish, Swiss, Rococo, Sheraton, Empire, U. S. Colonial, etc., ornament. Gargoyles, dragons, columns, necklaces, urns, friezes, furniture, buildings, tapestries, fantastic animals, armor, religious objects, much more, all in line. Reproduce any one free. Index. Bibliography. 400 plates. 656pp. 5⅝ x 8⅜. T557 Paperbound **$3.00**

HANDBOOK OF DESIGNS AND DEVICES, C. P. Hornung. This unique book is indispensable to the designer, commercial artist, and hobbyist. It is not a textbook but a working collection of 1836 basic designs and variations, carefully reproduced, which may be used without permission. Variations of circle, line, band, triangle, square, cross, diamond, swastika, pentagon, octagon, hexagon, star, scroll, interlacement, shields, etc. Supplementary notes on the background and symbolism of the figures. "A necessity to every designer who would be original without having to labor heavily," ARTIST AND ADVERTISER. 204 plates. 240pp. 5⅜ x 8. T125 Paperbound **$2.00**

THE UNIVERSAL PENMAN, George Bickham. This beautiful book, which first appeared in 1743, is the largest collection of calligraphic specimens, flourishes, alphabets, and calligraphic illustrations ever published. 212 full-page plates are drawn from the work of such 18th century masters of English roundhand as Dove, Champion, Bland, and 20 others. They contain 22 complete alphabets, over 2,000 flourishes, and 122 illustrations, each drawn with a stylistic grace impossible to describe. This book is invaluable to anyone interested in the beauties of calligraphy, or to any artist, hobbyist, or craftsman who wishes to use the very best ornamental handwriting and flourishes for decorative purposes. Commercial artists, advertising artists, have found it unexcelled as a source of material suggesting quality. "An essential part of any art library, and a book of permanent value," AMERICAN ARTIST. 212 plates. 224pp. 9 x 13¾. T20 Clothbound **$10.00**

1800 WOODCUTS BY THOMAS BEWICK AND HIS SCHOOL. Prepared by Dover's editorial staff, this is the largest collection of woodcuts by Bewick and his school ever compiled. Contains the complete engravings from all his major works and a wide range of illustrations from lesser-known collections, all photographed from clear copies of the original books and reproduced in line. Carefully and conveniently organized into sections on Nature (animals and birds, scenery and landscapes, plants, insects, etc.), People (love and courtship, social life, school and domestic scenes, misfortunes, costumes, etc.), Business and Trade, and illustrations from primers, fairytales, spelling books, frontispieces, borders, fables and allegories, etc. In addition to technical proficiency and simple beauty, Bewick's work is remarkable as a mode of pictorial symbolism, reflecting rustic tranquility, an atmosphere of rest, simplicity, idyllic contentment. A delight for the eye, an inexhaustible source of illustrative material for art studios, commercial artists, advertising agencies. Individual illustrations (up to 10 for any one use) are copyright free. Classified index. Bibliography and sources. Introduction by Robert Hutchinson. 1800 woodcuts. xiv + 247pp. 9 x 12. T766 Clothbound **$10.00**

A HANDBOOK OF EARLY ADVERTISING ART, C. P. Hornung. The largest collection of copyright-free early advertising art ever compiled. Vol. I contains some 2,000 illustrations of agricultural devices, animals, old automobiles, birds, buildings, Christmas decorations (with 7 Santa Clauses by Nast), allegorical figures, fire engines, horses and vehicles, Indians, portraits, sailing ships, trains, sports, trade cuts — and 30 other categories! Vol. II, devoted to typography, has over 4000 specimens: 600 different Roman, Gothic, Barnum, Old English faces; 630 ornamental type faces; 1115 initials, hundreds of scrolls, flourishes, etc. This third edition is enlarged by 78 additional plates containing all new material. "A remarkable collection," PRINTERS' INK. "A rich contribution to the history of American design," GRAPHIS. Volume I, Pictorial. Over 2000 illustrations. xiv + 242pp. 9 x 12. T122 Clothbound **$10.00** Volume II, Typographical. Over 4000 specimens. vii + 312pp. 9 x 12. T123 Clothbound **$10.00** Two volume set, T121 Clothbound, only **$18.50**

THE 100 GREATEST ADVERTISEMENTS, WHO WROTE THEM AND WHAT THEY DID, J. L. Watkins. 100 (plus 13 added for this edition) of most successful ads ever to appear. "Do You Make These Mistakes in English," "They laughed when I sat down," "A Hog Can Cross the Country," "The Man in the Hathaway Shirt," over 100 more ads that changed habits of a nation, gave new expressions to the language, built reputations. Also salient facts behind ads, often in words of their creators. "Useful . . . valuable . . . enlightening," Printers' Ink. 2nd revised edition. Introduction. Foreword by Raymond Rubicam. Index. 130 illustrations. 252pp. 7¾ x 10¾. T540 Paperbound **$2.50**

THE DIDEROT PICTORIAL ENCYCLOPEDIA OF TRADES AND INDUSTRY, MANUFACTURING AND THE TECHNICAL ARTS IN PLATES SELECTED FROM "L'ENCYCLOPEDIE OU DICTIONNAIRE RAISONNE DES SCIENCES, DES ARTS, ET DES METIERS" OF DENIS DIDEROT, edited with text by C. Gillispie. The first modern selection of plates from the high point of 18th century French engraving, Diderot's famous Encyclopedia. Over 2000 illustrations on 485 full-page plates, most of them original size, illustrating the trades and industries of one of the most fascinating periods of modern history, 18th century France. These magnificent engravings provide an invaluable source of fresh, copyright-free material to artists and illustrators, a lively and accurate social document to students of cultures, an outstanding find to the lover of fine engravings. The plates teem with life, with men, women, and children performing all of the thousands of operations necessary to the trades before and during the early stages of the industrial revolution. Plates are in sequence, and show general operations, closeups of difficult operations, and details of complex machinery. Such important and interesting trades and industries are illustrated as sowing, harvesting, beekeeping, cheesemaking, operating windmills, milling flour, charcoal burning, tobacco processing, indigo, fishing, arts of war, salt extraction, mining, smelting iron, casting iron steel, extracting mercury, zinc, sulphur, copper, etc., slating, tinning, silverplating, gilding, making gunpowder, cannons, bells, shoeing horses, tanning, papermaking, printing, dying, and more than 40 other categories. Besides being a work of remarkable beauty and skill, this is also one of the largest collections of working figures in print. 920pp. 9 x 12. Heavy library cloth. T421 Two volume set **$18.50**

THE HANDBOOK OF PLANT AND FLORAL ORNAMENT, R. G. Hatton. One of the truly great collections of plant drawings for reproduction: 1200 different figures of flowering or fruiting plants—line drawings that will reproduce excellently. Selected from superb woodcuts and copperplate engravings appearing mostly in 16th and 17th century herbals including the fabulously rare "Kreuter Büch" (Bock) "Cruijde Boeck" (Dodoens), etc. Plants classified according to botanical groups. Also excellent reading for anyone interested in home gardening or any phase of horticulture. Formerly "The Craftsman's Plant-Book: or Figures of Plants." Introductions. Over 1200 illustrations. Index. 548pp. 6⅛ x 9¼. T649 Paperbound **$3.00**

HANDBOOK OF ORNAMENT, F. S. Meyer. One of the largest collections of copyright-free traditional art in print. It contains over 3300 line cuts from Greek, Roman, Medieval, Islamic, Renaissance, Baroque, 18th and 19th century sources. 180 plates illustrate elements of design with networks, Gothic tracery, geometric elements, flower and animal motifs, etc., while 100 plates illustrate decorative objects: chairs, thrones, daises, cabinets, crowns, weapons, utensils, vases, jewelry, armor, heraldry, bottles, altars, and scores of other objects. Indispensable for artists, illustrators, designers, handicrafters, etc. Full text. 3300 illustrations. xiv + 548pp. 5⅜ x 8. T302 Paperbound **$2.50**

COSTUMES OF THE GREEKS AND ROMANS, Thomas Hope. Authentic costumes from all walks of life in Roman, Greek civilizations, including Phrygia, Egypt, Persia, Parthia, Etruria, in finely drawn, detailed engravings by Thomas Hope (1770-1831). Scores of additional engravings of ancient musical instruments, furniture, jewelry, sarcophagi, other adjuncts to ancient life. All carefully copied from ancient vases and statuary. Textual introduction by author. Art and advertising personnel, costume and stage designers, students of fashion design will find these copyright-free engravings a source of ideas and inspiration and a valuable reference. Republication of 1st (1812) edition. 300 full-page plates, over 700 illustrations. xliv + 300pp. 5⅝ x 8⅜. T21 Paperbound **$2.00**

PRINCIPLES OF ART HISTORY, H. Wölfflin. Analyzing such terms as "baroque," "classic," "neoclassic," "primitive," "picturesque," and 164 different works by artists like Botticelli, van Cleve, Dürer, Hobbema, Holbein, Hals, Rembrandt, Titian, Brueghel, Vermeer, and many others, the author establishes the classifications of art history and style on a firm, concrete basis. This classic of art criticism shows what really occurred between the 14th century primitives and the sophistication of the 18th century in terms of basic attitudes and philosophies. "A remarkable lesson in the art of seeing," SAT. REV. OF LITERATURE. Translated from the 7th German edition. 150 illustrations. 254pp. 6⅛ x 9¼. T276 Paperbound **$2.00**

AFRICAN SCULPTURE, Ladislas Segy. First publication of a new book by the author of critically acclaimed AFRICAN SCULPTURE SPEAKS. It contains 163 full-page plates illustrating masks, fertility figures, ceremonial objects, etc., representing the culture of 50 tribes of West and Central Africa. Over 85% of these works of art have never been illustrated before, and each is an authentic and fascinating tribal artifact. A 34-page introduction explains the anthropological, psychological, and artistic values of African sculpture. "Mr. Segy is one of its top authorities," NEW YORKER. 164 full-page photographic plates. Bibliography. 244pp. 6 x 9. T396 Paperbound **$2.00**

Fiction

FLATLAND, E. A. Abbott. A science-fiction classic of life in a 2-dimensional world that is also a first-rate introduction to such aspects of modern science as relativity and hyperspace. Political, moral, satirical, and humorous overtones have made FLATLAND fascinating reading for thousands. 7th edition. New introduction by Banesh Hoffmann. 16 illustrations. 128pp. 5⅜ x 8.   T1 Paperbound **$1.00**

THE WONDERFUL WIZARD OF OZ, L. F. Baum. Only edition in print with all the original W. W. Denslow illustrations in full color—as much a part of "The Wizard" as Tenniel's drawings are of "Alice in Wonderland." "The Wizard" is still America's best-loved fairy tale, in which, as the author expresses it, "The wonderment and joy are retained and the heartaches and nightmares left out." Now today's young readers can enjoy every word and wonderful picture of the original book. New introduction by Martin Gardner. A Baum bibliography. 23 full-page color plates. viii + 268pp. 5⅜ x 8.   T691 Paperbound **$1.50**

THE MARVELOUS LAND OF OZ, L. F. Baum. This is the equally enchanting sequel to the "Wizard," continuing the adventures of the Scarecrow and the Tin Woodman. The hero this time is a little boy named Tip, and all the delightful Oz magic is still present. This is the Oz book with the Animated Saw-Horse, the Woggle-Bug, and Jack Pumpkinhead. All the original John R. Neill illustrations, 10 in full color. 287 pp. 5⅜ x 8.   T692 Paperbound **$1.50**

28 SCIENCE FICTION STORIES OF H. G. WELLS. Two full unabridged novels, MEN LIKE GODS and STAR BEGOTTEN, plus 26 short stories by the master science-fiction writer of all time! Stories of space, time, invention, exploration, future adventure—an indispensable part of the library of everyone interested in science and adventure. PARTIAL CONTENTS: Men Like Gods, The Country of the Blind, In the Abyss, The Crystal Egg, The Man Who Could Work Miracles, A Story of the Days to Come, The Valley of Spiders, and 21 more! 928pp. 5⅜ x 8.
T265 Clothbound **$4.50**

THREE MARTIAN NOVELS, Edgar Rice Burroughs. Contains: Thuvia, Maid of Mars; The Chessmen of Mars; and The Master Mind of Mars. High adventure set in an imaginative and intricate conception of the Red Planet. Mars is peopled with an intelligent, heroic human race which lives in densely populated cities and with fierce barbarians who inhabit dead sea bottoms. Other exciting creatures abound amidst an inventive framework of Martian history and geography. Complete unabridged reprintings of the first edition. 16 illustrations by J. Allen St. John. vi + 499pp. 5⅜ x 8½.   T39 Paperbound **$1.85**

SEVEN SCIENCE FICTION NOVELS, H. G. Wells. Full unabridged texts of 7 science-fiction novels of the master. Ranging from biology, physics, chemistry, astronomy to sociology and other studies, Mr. Wells extrapolates whole worlds of strange and intriguing character. "One will have to go far to match this for entertainment, excitement, and sheer pleasure . . . ," NEW YORK TIMES. Contents: The Time Machine, The Island of Dr. Moreau, First Men in the Moon, The Invisible Man, The War of the Worlds, The Food of the Gods, In the Days of the Comet. 1015pp. 5⅜ x 8.   T264 Clothbound **$4.50**

THE LAND THAT TIME FORGOT and THE MOON MAID, Edgar Rice Burroughs. In the opinion of many, Burroughs' best work. The first concerns a strange island where evolution is individual rather than phylogenetic. Speechless anthropoids develop into intelligent human beings within a single generation. The second projects the reader far into the future and describes the first voyage to the Moon (in the year 2025), the conquest of the Earth by the Moon, and years of violence and adventure as the enslaved Earthmen try to regain possession of their planet. "An imaginative tour de force that keeps the reader keyed up and expectant," NEW YORK TIMES. Complete, unabridged text of the original two novels (three parts in each). 5 illustrations by J. Allen St. John. vi + 552pp. 5⅜ x 8½.
T1020 Clothbound **$3.75**
T358 Paperbound **$2.00**

3 ADVENTURE NOVELS by H. Rider Haggard. Complete texts of "She," "King Solomon's Mines," "Allan Quatermain." Qualities of discovery; desire for immortality; search for primitive, for what is unadorned by civilization, have kept these novels of African adventure exciting, alive to readers from R. L. Stevenson to George Orwell. 636pp. 5⅜ x 8.
T584 Paperbound **$2.00**

A PRINCESS OF MARS and A FIGHTING MAN OF MARS: TWO MARTIAN NOVELS BY EDGAR RICE BURROUGHS. "Princess of Mars" is the very first of the great Martian novels written by Burroughs, and it is probably the best of them all; it set the pattern for all of his later fantasy novels and contains a thrilling cast of strange peoples and creatures and the formula of Olympian heroism amidst ever-fluctuating fortunes which Burroughs carries off so successfully. "Fighting Man" returns to the same scenes and cities—many years later. A mad scientist, a degenerate dictator, and an indomitable defender of the right clash—with the fate of the Red Planet at stake! Complete, unabridged reprinting of original editions. Illustrations by F. E. Schoonover and Hugh Hutton. v + 356pp. 5⅜ x 8½.
T1140 Paperbound **$1.75**

THE PIRATES OF VENUS and LOST ON VENUS: TWO VENUS NOVELS BY EDGAR RICE BURROUGHS.
Two related novels, complete and unabridged. Exciting adventure on the planet Venus with
Earthman Carson Napier broken-field running through one dangerous episode after another.
All lovers of swashbuckling science fiction will enjoy these two stories set in a world of
fascinating societies, fierce beasts, 5000-ft. trees, lush vegetation, and wide seas. Illustra-
tions by Fortunino Matania. Total of vi + 340pp. 5⅜ x 8½.   T1053 Paperbound **$1.75**

RURITANIA COMPLETE: THE PRISONER OF ZENDA and RUPERT OF HENTZAU, Anthony Hope.
The first edition to include in one volume both the continually-popular "Prisoner of Zenda"
and its equally-absorbing sequel. Hope's mythical country of Ruritania has become a household word and the activities of its inhabitants almost a common heritage. Unabridged
reprinting. 14 illustrations by Charles Dana Gibson. vi + 414pp. 5⅜ x 8.
T69 Paperbound **$1.35**

GHOST AND HORROR STORIES OF AMBROSE BIERCE, Selected and introduced by E. F. Bleiler.
24 morbid, eerie tales—the cream of Bierce's fiction output. Contains such memorable
pieces as "The Moonlit Road," "The Damned Thing," "An Inhabitant of Carcosa," "The Eyes
of the Panther," "The Famous Gilson Bequest," "The Middle Toe of the Right Foot," and
other chilling stories, plus the essay, "Visions of the Night" in which Bierce gives us a
kind of rationale for his aesthetic of horror. New collection (1964). xxii + 199pp. 5⅜ x
8⅜.   T767 Paperbound **$1.00**

BEST GHOST STORIES OF J. S. LE FANU, Selected and introduced by E. F. Bleiler. LeFanu is
deemed the greatest name in Victorian supernatural fiction. Here are 16 of his best horror
stories, including 2 nouvelles: "Carmilla," a classic vampire tale couched in a perverse
eroticism, and "The Haunted Baronet." Also: "Sir Toby's Will," "Green Tea," "Schalken the
Painter," "Ultor de Lacy," "The Familiar," etc. The first American publication of about half
of this material: a long-overdue opportunity to get a choice sampling of LeFanu's work. New
selection (1964). 8 illustrations. 5⅜ x 8⅜.   T415 Paperbound **$1.85**

FIVE GREAT DOG NOVELS, edited by Blanche Cirker. The complete original texts of five classic
dog novels that have delighted and thrilled millions of children and adults throughout the
world with stories of loyalty, adventure, and courage. Full texts of Jack London's "The Call
of the Wild"; John Brown's "Rab and His Friends"; Alfred Ollivant's "Bob, Son of Battle";
Marshall Saunders' "Beautiful Joe"; and Ouida's "A Dog of Flanders." 21 illustrations from
the original editions. 495pp. 5⅜ x 8.   T777 Paperbound **$1.75**

THE CASTING AWAY OF MRS. LECKS AND MRS. ALESHINE, F. R. Stockton. A charming light
novel by Frank Stockton, one of America's finest humorists (and author of "The Lady, or the
Tiger?"). This book has made millions of Americans laugh at the reflection of themselves in
two middle-aged American women involved in some of the strangest adventures on record.
You will laugh, too, as they endure shipwreck, desert island, and blizzard with maddening
tranquility. Also contains complete text of "The Dusantes," sequel to "The Casting Away."
49 original illustrations by F. D. Steele. vii + 142pp. 5⅜ x 8.   T743 Paperbound **$1.00**

**AT THE EARTH'S CORE, PELLUCIDAR, TANAR OF PELLUCIDAR: THREE SCIENCE FICTION NOVELS
BY EDGAR RICE BURROUGHS.** Complete, unabridged texts of the first three Pellucidar novels.
Tales of derring-do by the famous master of science fiction. The locale for these three
related stories is the inner surface of the hollow Earth where we discover the world of
Pellucidar, complete with all types of bizarre, menacing creatures, strange peoples, and
alluring maidens—guaranteed to delight all Burroughs fans and a wide circle of adventure
lovers. Illustrated by J. Allen St. John and P. F. Berdanier. vi + 433pp. 5⅜ x 8½.
T1051 Paperbound **$2.00**

**THE WAR IN THE AIR, IN THE DAYS OF THE COMET, THE FOOD OF THE GODS: THREE SCIENCE
FICTION NOVELS BY H. G. WELLS.** Three exciting Wells offerings bearing on vital social and
philosophical issues of his and our own day. Here are tales of air power, strategic bomb-
ing, East vs. West, the potential miracles of science, the potential disasters from outer
space, the relationship between scientific advancement and moral progress, etc. First
reprinting of "War in the Air" in almost 50 years. An excellent sampling of Wells at his
storytelling best. Complete, unabridged reprintings. 16 illustrations. 645pp. 5⅜ x 8½.
T1135 Paperbound **$2.00**

DAVID HARUM, E. N. Westcott. This novel of one of the most lovable, humorous characters
in American literature is a prime example of regional humor. It connotes to delight people
who like their humor dry, their characters quaint, and their plots ingenuous. First book
edition to contain complete novel plus chapter found after author's death. Illustrations from
first illustrated edition. 192pp. 5⅜ x 8.   T580 Paperbound **$1.15**

TO THE SUN? and OFF ON A COMET!, Jules Verne. Complete texts of two of the most imaginative flights into fancy in world literature display the high adventure that have kept Verne's
novels read for nearly a century. Only unabridged edition of the best translation, by Edward
Roth. Large, easily readable type. 50 illustrations selected from first editions. 462pp.
5⅜ x 8.   T634 Paperbound **$1.75**

FROM THE EARTH TO THE MOON and ALL AROUND THE MOON, Jules Verne. Complete editions of two of Verne's most successful novels, in finest Edward Roth translations, now available after many years out of print. Verne's visions of submarines, airplanes, television, rockets, interplanetary travel; of scientific and not-so-scientific beliefs; of peculiarities of Americans; all delight and engross us today as much as when they first appeared. Large, easily readable type. 42 illus. from first French edition. 476pp. 5⅜ x 8. T633 Paperbound **$1.75**

THREE PROPHETIC NOVELS BY H. G. WELLS, edited by E. F. Bleiler. Complete texts of "When the Sleeper Wakes" (1st book printing in 50 years), "A Story of the Days to Come," "The Time Machine" (1st complete printing in book form). Exciting adventures in the future are as enjoyable today as 50 years ago when first printed. Predict TV, movies, intercontinental airplanes, prefabricated houses, air-conditioned cities, etc. First important author to foresee problems of mind control, technological dictatorships. "Absolute best of imaginative fiction," N. Y. Times. Introduction. 335pp. 5⅜ x 8. T605 Paperbound **$1.50**

GESTA ROMANORUM, trans. by Charles Swan, ed. by Wynnard Hooper. 181 tales of Greeks, Romans, Britons, Biblical characters, comprise one of greatest medieval story collections, source of plots for writers including Shakespeare, Chaucer, Gower, etc. Imaginative tales of wars, incest, thwarted love, magic, fantasy, allegory, humor, tell about kings, prostitutes, philosophers, fair damsels, knights, Noah, pirates, all walks, stations of life. Introduction. Notes. 500pp. 5⅜ x 8. T535 Paperbound **$1.85**

Prices subject to change without notice.

Dover publishes books on art, music, philosophy, literature, languages, history, social sciences, psychology, handcrafts, orientalia, puzzles and entertainments, chess, pets and gardens, books explaining science, intermediate and higher mathematics, mathematical physics, engineering, biological sciences, earth sciences, classics of science, etc. Write to:

Dept. catrr.
Dover Publications, Inc.
180 Varick Street, N.Y. 14, N.Y.